RECLAIMING
THE GREAT
TRADITION

EVANGELICALS, CATHOLICS
& ORTHODOX IN DIALOGUE

Edited by James S. Cutsinger

InterVarsity Press
Downers Grove, Illinois

InterVarsity Press® is the book-publishing division of InterVarsity Christian Fellowship®, a student movement active on campus at hundreds of universities, colleges and schools of nursing in the United States of America, and a member movement of the International Fellowship of Evangelical Students. For information about local and regional activities, write Public Relations Dept., InterVarsity Christian Fellowship, 6400 Schroeder Rd., P.O. Box 7895, Madison, WI 53707-7895.

Cover illustration: Scala/Art Resource, NY. Theopan the Greek, Transfiguration. Russian icon. Tretyakov Gallery, Moscow.

ISBN 0-8308-1889-8

Printed in the United States of America

Library of Congress Cataloging-in-Publication Data

Reclaiming the great tradition: Evangelicals, Catholics & Orthodox in
  dialogue/James S. Cutsinger, ed.
     p.   cm.
  Collection of papers presented at an ecumenical conference for
traditional Christians held at Rose Hill College and other sites,
Aiken, South Carolina, May 16-20, 1995.
  Includes bibliographical references.
  ISBN 0-8308-1889-8 (alk. paper)
  1. Evangelicalism—Relations—Catholic Church.   2. Catholic
Church—Relations—Evangelicalism.   3. Evangelicalism—Relations—
Orthodox Eastern Church.   4. Orthodox Eastern Church—Relations—
Evangelicalism.   I. Cutsinger, James S., 1953- .
BR1641.C37R43   1997
280'.042—dc21
                                          96-39119
                                            CIP

22 21 20 19 18 17 16 15 14 13 12 11 10 9 8 7 6 5 4 3 2 1

15 14 13 12 11 10 09 08 07 06 05 04 03 02 01 00 99 98 97

INTRODUCTION
Finding the Center

James S. Cutsinger

*E*arly in the spring of 1994, representatives of Rose Hill College and the Fellowship of Saint James considered the possibility of sponsoring an ecumenical conference for traditional Christians. It seemed an excellent marriage. Rose Hill is a new Christian college where the classical pursuit of liberal education, based on the study of great books, is closely tied to the liturgical worship and patristic worldview of the Orthodox tradition. The Fellowship of Saint James, publisher of *Touchstone: A Journal of Ecumenical Orthodoxy,* is an association of Christians from a variety of traditions who are dedicated to upholding the faith and practice of the historic church.

Gathering on the campus of Rose Hill College and at other sites in the beautiful town of Aiken, South Carolina, invited speakers and respondents joined nearly two hundred pastors and laity from every part of the country for five days of discussion and prayer (May 16-20, 1995). The papers collected in this volume include the six plenary addresses and six of the responses presented in small group discussions.

The aim was to do something new. Ecumenical gatherings are hardly unique in our day, but they too often have been excuses for dismantling the faith, as if tolerance and moral platitudes were more important than truth. Conferences of conservative Christians are certainly common too, though these have usually been along denominational lines or for the sake of addressing specific ethical issues.

Here the plan was to try something different: to test whether an ecumenical orthodoxy, solidly based on the classic Christian faith as expressed in the Scriptures and ecumenical councils, could become the foundation for a unified and transformative witness to the present age. Is it possible, we asked ourselves, for those who are deeply committed to differing theological perspectives to help each other in defending and communicating their common faith? And if so, then how? How can Protestants, Roman Catholics and Eastern Orthodox Christians talk to each other so as together to speak with Christ's mind to the modern world? This is a problem for every generation of Christians, for every world is a "modern" world, with the spirit of each parading itself as the end of all wisdom. And yet there seems to be a growing consensus that some larger, perhaps more definitive, crisis is at hand, and that it is therefore time for serious Christians to join forces for a common task.

When we first conceived of this gathering, our hope was to attract the interest of serious Christian scholars who, precisely because of the tenacity with which they hold to their differing views, would ordinarily be diffident about attending such meetings. The words *ecumenical* and *traditional* were to be seen in a certain sense as in tension, concern for the former having so often gone hand in hand with a neglect of the latter. In fact someone suggested early in the planning that our slogan should be "Let all the antiecumenical forces of the Christian world unite!" A few such forces, not surprisingly, turned down our invitation to participate.

We had what might seem a rather odd idea: if only each of us could be brought to confess with utter candor why precisely he is Orthodox and not Catholic or Protestant, or Protestant and not Catholic or Orthodox, or Catholic and not Orthodox or Protestant, these outwardly divergent confessions, far better than any list of agreements drafted by a task force or a committee, might together point to the very heart of our faith. Father Richard John Neuhaus captured the spirit of our thinking in the opening address when he observed that in many cases "our unity in the truth is more evident in our quarreling about the truth than in our settling for something less than the truth."

The recipe for what we had in mind was well put in the 1940s by a man who put many things well, a writer to whom several of the conferees readily admitted their debt. In describing "an agreed, or common, or central, or 'mere' Christianity," C. S. Lewis, in the preface to his book by that name, puts forward a most important ecumenical principle. Lewis writes, "It is at her center, where her truest children dwell, that each communion is really closest to every other in spirit, if not in doctrine. And this suggests," he continues, "that at the center of each there is something, or a Someone, who against all divergences of belief, all differences of temperament, all memories of mutual persecution, speaks with the same voice."[1] As usual Lewis's words are deceptively simple—so simple that one may not see at first how profound and perhaps controversial they are. What he suggests is something running against the grain of what might otherwise have been expected: that the truest Christian ecumenism is most likely to come from those who on the surface most strongly disagree.

The great mistake of the many liberal varieties of ecumenical dialogue has been to think that we come closest to each other along our edges. If this were true, it would follow that at those points where friction occurs the solution is to smooth over the rough places in our relationships with other believers by ignoring or forgoing what leads to conflict. Peace is the treasured goal of such dialogue—not, however, "the peace of God, which passeth all understanding" (Phil 4:7), but the contrived and artificial peace that we have been warned "the world giveth" (Jn 14:27). Traditional Christians are only too familiar with this sort of thinking, and they know how far it can go in blithely abandoning even the most essential of Christian truths. English theologian John Hick provides a well-known and especially egregious example. Since Muslims and Jews are inevitably scandalized by the traditional claim that Christ is God, Christians (as Hick sees it) are obliged out of charity to reject that claim themselves, admitting to the world that it was a misunderstanding and a myth.

Such an approach is worlds apart from the ecumenism we meant to stress at the conference. A traditionalist ecumenism must at the very least refuse to compromise the integrity of the Christian tradition, even if this refusal means paradoxically that our unity will be "more evident in our quarrelling about the truth than in our settling for something less than the truth." But how are we to understand this unity? How is the traditional Christian to make sense of Lewis's claim that we are closest to each other at our centers?

Suppose we picture the Protestant, Roman Catholic and Orthodox traditions as three distinct geometrical figures. Several configurations would be possible. Some will prefer to envision these figures as lying in three parallel and therefore never-intersecting planes, and as having assorted sizes and shapes representing various degrees of perfection and comprehensiveness. One's own tradition would doubtless be seen as the largest figure, perhaps circular in shape, with competing communions being more or less irregular departures from that norm. Other Christians, more optimistic about the prospects of ecumenical unity, may imagine the three figures as existing instead on a single plane, where real contact becomes possible. Certain of these hopeful ecumenists may picture the shapes as divided by distances of varying sizes, while others may see them as already contiguous or perhaps even overlapping.

The problem with all these representations, however, is that they end up depicting the relationships between our several traditions in a strictly superficial or peripheral way, as if the possibility of union were a function solely of external proximity and contact, whether between planes or between discrete figures in the same plane. But this is to repeat the common liberal error. It is to understand ecumenism in merely political and planimetric categories.

Lewis, I believe, is suggesting a different model. He is saying that our ecumenism must be both three-dimensional and centripetal. Orthodoxy, Roman Catholicism and Protestantism are to be envisioned as three figures, but with each of them equally circular. (You are still free to make them different sizes if you wish!) Furthermore, all of these circles are understood as inscribed inside a single sphere where, to take account of their differences, they are deployed at right angles to each other. Some Christians may choose to say that the sphere symbolizes the invisible church. But if calling it the church is going too far, as it will be for those who believe theirs is the only true Christian communion, then let us say that the sphere is Lewis's "mere Christianity," a common body of doctrine and morals. It is what J. I. Packer calls in his paper (as in the title of the present volume) the "great tradition." More important than the precise meaning of the sphere as such, however, this alternative way of picturing things provides a clear indication of where we ought to be headed in search of real unity. Though existing on three distinct planes, each with its own well-known attitudes and emphases, our differing traditions (if Lewis is right) nevertheless share a common center, which is Christ himself.

Not everyone will be pleased with this model. While it is obvious that a desire for unity should animate all who call themselves Christians, and that we should all be happy for anything that might help to encourage its pursuit, it is hard not to feel a certain measure of sympathy for those traditionalists who out of prayerful choice did not join us at the conference. Father Neuhaus pointed out that Protestant "evangelicalism has tended to approach all things bearing the name 'ecumenical' with an attitude ranging from robust skepticism to impassioned hostility," and there are numerous examples of Roman Catholics and Eastern Orthodox with the same reservations.

These reservations must be fully respected. I sympathize with those of my own church who believe that ecumenism, at least in its usual forms, comes into "screaming conflict with Orthodox Tradition and Orthodox Consciousness."[2] And yet it seems to me that Lewis's insight can still be a most valuable one for us all, including even the most exclusive and antiecumenical of Christian traditionalists. If "it is at her center, where her truest children dwell, that each communion is really closest to every other," then there cannot fail to be gaps between our several peripheries, and it is only natural that we should find differences, even hostilities and mutual anathematizations, between serious Christians whenever and wherever they encounter each other along their outlying frontiers. The person who is struggling to love God with his entire heart, soul and mind, who is intent on following the shortest path to the center, simply does not have the time (whatever the other issues might be) to consider other paths than his own. And when he is forced to, when the presence of other paths can no longer be ignored, often the only way to keep them from interfering with his focus on Christ is to reject them as errors. As Peter Kreeft points out, the only alternative in such a case is indifference, and indifference means spiritual death.

It is with good reason that we put blinders on a horse if we mean for it to plow a straight row. Geometrical models may be nice in theory, but in practice each of us is obliged for salvation's sake to follow a specific path, and this means sticking to a given plane. Ecumenical conferees have the leisure to ponder which of the Christian circles is biggest, or at precisely how many degrees their respective planes may diverge from each other, or whether it might be possible to rotate these several circles around the axes of their diameters until their circumferences coincide. But it is important to realize, even as we embark upon these ecumenical reflections, that when it comes to the actual spiritual life, global thinking can be dangerous. Practically speaking we must all be flat-earthers, and we need to be careful that our busyness around the *oikoumenē*—the ecumenical household—does not distract us, like Martha, from the "one thing . . . needful" (Lk 10:42).

This does not mean that we have to give up hoping for and looking for unity. I do not wish to conclude this introduction on a skeptical note or to take anything away from the contributions that follow. If Lewis is right, however, it does mean that, like Mary, we should be constantly mindful of the One in whom alone, if at all, we ourselves can be one. Bishop Kallistos Ware has occasion to refer to the prayer of our Lord "that they all may be one; as thou, Father, art in me, and I in thee, that they also may be one in us" (Jn 17:21). Taking just that little preposition *in* on its own is quite enough to confirm Lewis's point and my own earlier critique of the liberals. Where should we expect to find unity? Certainly not on the surface or along the edges, but at the heart. On the inside, not the outside—an inside, moreover, of a very particular kind. Christ makes it clear that the interiority of real Christian union is not the same as the inwardness of pious feeling or tolerant sentiment. True unity will come instead only in the interior of God himself and to the measure that we are drawn into his trinitarian life.

Not in the rewording of doctrines, nor in the modification of devotional styles, nor in the reports of committees, nor even in the pages of this book should we expect to find unanimity between our several communions. Our desire for true unity, if it is sincere, will instead be expressed in our daily prayers and ascetic disciplines, in our continuing life in the sacraments and in our weak attempts to grow up to the full stature of Christ. For it is by these means alone that we may be drawn by grace ever more inward toward the center: a center that, God willing, will turn out to be at once our own and our neighbor's.

I wish to thank all those who contributed to the conference and to the present volume: the participants themselves, both plenary speakers and respondents; James Kushiner and his colleagues at *Touchstone;* Rodney Clapp of InterVarsity Press; and the staff and many friends of Rose Hill College, without whose help the conference would not have been possible. A special word of gratitude is owed to Owen and Julie Jones and the Rose Hill Foundation for their generous support.

1

ECUMENICAL JIHAD

Peter Kreeft

*P*icture to yourself the scene. You are Augustine, and you have just heard the news: the unthinkable has happened. Rome, the Eternal City, the heart of the world's first and only unified global civilization, has fallen. The brink of a long Dark Age is opening up before your feet. What do you do?

You do one of the most radical things a man can do: you write a book, the world's first philosophy of history, *The City of God,* a book that would be a lantern for millions through the darkly twisting roads of history—a book that demands to be dusted off and reread almost sixteen centuries later, now that another and far more formidable dark age looms, not the age of the barbarians but the age of the antichrist.

As Augustine lay dying in North Africa, he could see the fires of his burning city, an echo of Rome's fall. When the queen bee falls, the other bees in the hive cannot survive. Rome was the queen bee then; America is the queen bee today. Our empire is cultural, not military, but most of the world, with the notable exception of Islamic nations, is becoming increasingly Americanized. What happens here happens everywhere.

The Problem: "Today" = "Decay"

What we see happening is that spiritual war between the City of God and the City of the World that Augustine detected as the fundamental plot of human history. In America, for the first time in the nation's history the term "culture war" is now becoming familiar and accepted, especially since the election of Bill Clinton as the president of the United States.

The war is very old, of course—as old as Eden. What is new is the global strategy of the City of the World. The battle lines are becoming clearer. The war on earth is more closely resembling the war in heaven. Time is more closely mirroring eternity, as if Platonic archetypes were incarnating themselves, inhabiting their earthly instances, like ghosts haunting houses.

At Armageddon there will be no more uncertainty, no neutral corners. Armageddon may be a million years away, or a dozen, but it is approaching, like a wave from the invisible other side of the world. If you listen, you can almost hear the sound of millions of troops being moved like cosmic chess pieces, jostling for position, spirit-wings opening and closing.

This is not fantasy or mythology. The spiritual war is literal. It is fully as real as any physical war. It has real casualties: eternal souls. It also has physical casualties that already surpass in numbers those of any war in history. In America alone the blood of thirty million unborn babies has been spilled into the thirsty maw of Moloch.

A modern Rip van Winkle falling asleep in 1955 and waking up in the United States in 1995 would not believe his ears when he heard the statistics of our decay. What moralist, complaining of the 10 percent divorce rate then, foresaw the 50 percent divorce rate now? Who foresaw a 5,000 percent increase in teenage violent crimes? When black society was being declared beyond repair because of a 30 percent illegitimacy rate, who thought that by 1995 white society would nearly equal it, while the rate climbed to 68 percent among blacks? Who would have thought even ten years ago that Russian public schools would be showing films about Jesus and American schools would be banned from showing them?

If the next forty years continue the movement of the last forty, does anyone have the slightest hope for the survival of anything resembling civilization? What would another 5,000 percent increase in teenage violent crimes mean? Or another significant increase in the illegitimacy rate? Or another administration that would be to Clinton what Clinton was to Eisenhower? Extend the line, follow the road, and you will see the cliff.

Many of our citizens have not heard the statistics, though they live them; and most of those who know the symptoms of decay do not know the disease that is causing them. They wonder what is the source of the massive destruction of morality, honesty, safety, families, marriages, trust, the sanctity of life, sex, and even belief in objective truth and goodness—all these things at once.

The root cause of all these poisonous fruits is invisible. It is spiritual, not political or economic or military or criminological. No such partial cause can account for such a massive darkness descending over everything at once, like the night sky, like an eclipse of the sun, or an eclipse of the Son of God.

As the City of the World increasingly oozes its decay, what of the City of God? What is the city set on a hill doing about the fact that all the septic tanks on the hill are backing up? It is riddled with division and dissent: division between Eastern and Western religions, division in the West among Jew, Christian and Muslim, division within Christendom among Protestant, Catholic and Orthodox, and division within Protestantism among some twenty thousand Protestant denominations. The enemy's battle strategy has been the oldest and most obvious in military science: divide and conquer. Wherever he has been able to divide God's people, he has been able to conquer them. Wherever he has succeeded in fomenting civil wars among God's people, he has conquered them.

And not only wars between churches but also within them. Within the Roman Catholic Church in America, "dissenters" (they used to be called heretics) control nearly all the theology departments of major universities, ensuring that the majority of freshmen who enter with a robust faith will graduate with a wimpy one or none at all. A generation ago Fulton Sheen was telling Catholic parents, "The best way I know to ensure that your children will lose their faith is to send them to Catholic colleges."

What is this dissent about? Are the Nestorian or Docetic or Apollonarian or Monophysite heresies being revived? No, the dissent is almost always moral, not theological. And within moral theology, do the dissenters defend theft, or rape, or oppression, or nuclear war or social injustice? No. Within the moral area the dissent is almost always about one thing: sex. Every one of the specific issues dissenters dissent from concerns traditional sexual morality versus the sexual revolution, which the church stubbornly refuses to bless. Abortion, contraception, fornication, adultery, divorce, homosexual acts, priestesses, even "inclusive language"—all are sexual issues.

Even theological issues like the dating of the Gospels and the facticity of the resurrection are driven by sexual questions. For if Jesus did not really rise, he is not really God; and if the Gospels were not written by eyewitnesses and do not tell us the words of God incarnate but only the words of a man or (as the favorite code phrase goes) "the early Christian community," then their authority and that of the church they say Christ founded is undermined. Authority over what? The biblical modernist's strategy is driven by the demand to break one of the links of the iron chain that binds our gonads to our God.

There used to be a silly saying that "the way to a man's heart is through his stomach." Satan has used sounder psychology: the way to a man's heart is through his hormones. He has learned from the sign on Chuck Colson's desk, when he was working for Nixon instead of for God: "When you got them by their balls, their hearts and minds will follow."

Here is Satan's Spectacularly Successful Seven-Step Sexual Strategy:

1. The summum bonum, the end, is to win souls.

2. A powerful means to this end is the corruption of society. This works especially well in a society of conformists, of other-directed people. After all, a good society is one that makes it easy to be good, as Peter Maurin has said. The satanic opposite is also true: a bad society makes it easy to be bad. Has there ever been a time when we have had more and easier opportunities to be bad?

3. The most powerful means to destroy society is to destroy its one fundamental building block, the family, the only institution in which most of us learn life's most important lesson, unselfish love.

4. The family is destroyed by destroying its foundation, stable marriage.

5. Marriage is destroyed by loosening its glue, sexual fidelity.

6. Fidelity is destroyed by the sexual revolution.

7. The sexual revolution is propagated mainly by the media, which are now quite securely in enemy hands.

The sexual revolution will possibly prove to be the most destructive revolution in history, far more than any political or military revolution, because it touches not just lives but the wellsprings of life. It is still in its infancy. We do not yet see many of its consequences. At present other areas of morality are relatively unchanged. This can only be temporary. Once Satan's soldiers secure this part of the battlefield, they will begin to attack the next one. Already

Holland and Oregon say it is okay to kill people to save them from pain. The same un-Socratic principle fuels the euthanasia movement as fuels the sexual revolution: "the unpleasant life is not worth living."

If there is any one principle of morality that one may think so obvious that it could never be eradicated from the human heart, it is surely "Thou shalt not murder" (that is, kill innocent human beings). Yet the sexual revolution has already conquered conscience's surprisingly vulnerable hold on this principle; for abortion means the willingness to murder for the sake of the willingness to copulate. Prochoicers are repeatedly asserting that the abortion battle is not over babies but over sex. If abortion had nothing to do with sex, it would never have been legalized. Why does anyone want an abortion? Abortion is demanded as a form of birth control, backup birth control. And why is birth control demanded? Birth control is the demand to have sex without having babies. If storks brought babies, Wade would have defeated Roe.

We are even willing to murder to preserve our so-called sexual freedom. We will murder the most innocent among us, the only innocent among us, the most defenseless of all. And in the teeth of the strongest instinct: motherhood. It is a miracle of black magic, a stunning success, explainable only by supernatural power and defeatable only by supernatural power. Argument is insufficient. America needs exorcism.

The Solution to the Crisis
There are not a number of possible solutions to this problem. There is only one. It has two parts.

Unless two principles are as certain in our minds as they are in fact, we will continue to treat this cancer with aspirin and our society will die, as Rome did, whether with a bang or with a whimper. First, the main foundation of social order is morality. Second, the main foundation of morality is religion.

No society has ever succeeded without morality. As everyone knows, moral practice in America and elsewhere is declining at an alarmingly rapid rate. But not everyone knows that the decline of moral theory, or belief, is even more radical and destructive. For a nation that does not practice its principles can at least still have principles and can therefore be recalled to them. If the road maps are still there, we can find our way back to the road. But to disbelieve in principles is to burn the maps; and how likely is it then that we will find our way back?

Here is just a tiny sample of evidence that the map-burning is in a very advanced state, two typical facts out of thousands:

1. Not one nonreligious law school in America teaches or even tolerates the theory of a real, moral natural law.

2. In a nationwide U.S. poll a few years ago only 11 percent of future teachers in schools of education said that, among the options they could in good conscience present to their students as alternative moral theories for the students to consider and choose from, one such teachable moral theory was the belief that there is a real, objective, absolute morality. Eighty-nine percent of our children's future teachers said this idea was not one of the ones they could even tolerate presenting as an option in their teaching.

But objective morality, or the natural law, is not one among many moral options; it is the very definition of morality. "Subjective morality" is an oxymoron; it is no morality at all; it is a mere game. If I (or we) make the rules, I (or we) can change them. If I tie myself up, I am not really bound. And a nonbinding morality is not morality, only some good ideas. It has no laws, only values: soft, squooshy things that somehow feel like teddy bears.

C. S. Lewis wrote that moral subjectivism "will certainly end our species and damn our souls." Please remember that Englishmen are not given to exaggeration. Lewis calls this "the abolition of Man." It is fatal. It is like not paying attention to the doctor's diagnosis of your cancer. It is like turning off the lights in the operating room and playing fantasy hospital. And this is precisely the orthodoxy of our three major mind-molding establishments: education, from day-care centers to graduate schools; entertainment, that is, informal education; and journalism.

The second principle is that morality in turn depends on religion for the vast majority of all people in all times, places and cultures. Only an elite few, like Plato and Aristotle, can believe an absolute morality without an absolute Being. Our current attempt at a purely rational, secular morality is a leftover hangnail from the Enlightenment (which is the Orwellian name for the Endarkenment). The vast majority of people agree with Dostoyevsky that "if there is no God, everything is permissible." No one has ever given an adequate answer to the simple question, Why not? Why not do any evil I passionately and sincerely and "authentically" want to do, if there is no superhuman lawmaker and no superhuman law? Only because I might get caught, because crime doesn't pay? But crime often does pay: it is estimated that well over half of all crimes are never detected or punished. And if the only deterrent is cops, not conscience, what of the conscience of the cops? Who will guard the guards? And how many guards must we have to police a society of immoralists? A state full of moral subjectivists must become a police state.

Cops and conscience are the only two effective deterrents to crime. Secular, sociological, "reasonable" answers to the fatal *why not?* question—like "utility to the community"—will not deter us from strongly desired evil. For why ought I to care about the community? If all oughts are in question, then that one will not stand any more than the others.

We are beginning more and more to ask this fatal question, Why not? It is parallel in the moral order to Nietzsche's fatal question about truth: Why truth? Why not rather untruth? Suppose I do not like the truth? Why not tell and even believe lies? There is no answer to this unless truth is absolute. The death of God, Nietzsche saw with blinding, prophetic accuracy, was also the death of objective truth. For truth is simply "God without a face." "How can there be eternal truth if there is no eternal mind to think it?" asks Sartre, that pale, professorial copy of Nietzsche.

What happens when society becomes secularized? What happens when God dies? When God dies, his image dies too. The abolition of God entails the abolition of man, the abolition of the specifically human faculty of conscience, God's prophet in the soul. The authority of conscience, like that of any prophet, depends on the authority of God. Why should we revere the king's messenger when we have killed the king?

When a person leaves a room, his or her image disappears from the mirror. We are living in that split second between the disappearance of God and the disappearance of his image in the mirror. That image is the life of our souls, our consciences. That is what our present culture war is about. It is not merely about getting our rights in the naked public square; it is about the salvation of the soul. It is very probably about the continued biological survival of our species and our civilization on this planet in the next millennium, for the death within will necessarily spill out into a visible death without, like oozing pus. It is certainly about eternal life or eternal death, for without repentance there can be no salvation, and without a real moral law there can be no repentance, and the culture war's Pearl Harbor is the attack on the moral law.

The Obstacles to the Only Possible Solution

So: without religion, no morality, and without morality, no salvation of society.

But there are two structural obstacles to this solution, this only possible solution. One is the separation between American society and religion and the other the separation and split within and among the religions.

I will mention the first only very briefly, because I have no bright ideas about it at all, and Father Neuhaus does. So you should ask him about it, not me.

Even though most Americans probably misunderstand what our founding fathers would have meant by the phrase "separation of church and state," the basic point seems desirable to most Americans; something desirable for church as well as state. Unlike traditional civilizations, we are religiously pluralistic and our government is religiously neutral.

Our founding fathers conceived this neutrality as specific: no one specific church will be the state church. But our present legal establishment conceives religious neutrality as generic: the state will not favor religion as such.

Now suppose this is reformed. Suppose we turn back the clock (a reasonable and possible thing to do when the clock is keeping very bad time). Suppose the state supports generic religion again. That is certainly better than the state opposing religion or trying to be neutral (is that always possible?). But it would still be a religiously weaker thing than the older, pre-American system, which was a close linking of the state with one particular religion. Generic religion is like generic love: it lacks the passion and power of specificity. It appeals less to ordinary people than to scholars, for whom abstractions are important.

So we have the following trilemma for the state: either it must support a specific religion, which is not going to happen in a religiously plural society and is probably unjust as well; or it supports generic religion, which is weak; or it supports no religion, which is fatal.

No one in our time has done more than Father Neuhaus to address this problem and to define and defend what seems to be the only possible solution, the generic one. And his prescriptions for saving America within America's own parameters may even be adequate—though I think I am a bit more pessimistic than he is, probably because I live much closer to Fenway Park. I know of no better solutions, short of massive religious revival and conversion.

But the second problem is that religion speaks with a divided and therefore weakened voice. Christianity itself speaks with a tongue forked by the divisions of 1054 and 1517 and by the swords and fires of fratricidal wars. In our half-century there has been a remarkable upsurge and outcry of the longing for unity. Yet no one can say how to achieve it.

The problem is simple and obvious: religions contradict each other. And contradictories cannot both be true. And unity between the true and the false is false unity.

Sometimes religions complement each other; "truth is symphonic" indeed. But sometimes religions contradict each other. Either God has a will or not. Either he created the world or not. Either he gave Muhammad the Qur'an or not. Either he chose the Jews or he did not. Either he became incarnate in Christ or not. Either he founded the Roman Catholic Church or not. And whichever side is wrong about any of these things is very dreadfully wrong about a dreadfully important thing.

When religions contradict each other, the only logically possible way to unity seems to be either for one or both sides in each religious dispute to compromise and betray some of its convictions or for one side to convert the other, to convince the other side of its errors. The first—compromise—is the dream of the liberal and the nightmare of the conservative. The second—conversion—is the dream of the conservative and the nightmare of the liberal. But both seem impossible dreams. True believers are not going to compromise or convert.

So in confronting the disease of the moral decay of modern society with the prescription of religion, we run up against the problem of the plurality of doctors, each with a preferred medicine: the so-called problem of comparative religion, a problem over which tens of thousands of theologians, philosophers, historians, Scripture scholars and other assorted experts have spilled millions of tons of ink without making a single map to the promised land.

The only map the optimists have come up with has been the old picture of many roads up the same mountain. There are two major problems with this. First, it ignores real contradictions between religions or denies the law of noncontradiction itself (thus presupposing it, by the way, for in contradicting noncontradiction and preferring contradiction, it assumes a contradiction between noncontradiction and contradiction). Second, it appeals to no one but weak believers in each religion, for the picture of religions as many roads up the mountain assumes that religions are man-made yogas, not God-made revelations; useful, not true; therapy, not prophecy. But all three Western religions claim to be God's definitive road down, not one of humanity's many nondefinitive roads up.

A Hindu can easily "accept" Christianity as another *bhakti yoga,* but how can a Christian accept Hinduism as another way of salvation? No guru ever claimed that no one could come to the Father except through him. A Catholic accepts the Protestant principle of the infallibility of Scripture, but how can he add *sola* to *scriptura* without betraying the church? A Protestant can accept a Catholic's faith in Christ, but how can he accept or respect an error so egregious and idolatrous as bowing to bread, worshiping a wafer that the church insists is God incarnate? And how can a Jew or a Muslim accept the essence of Christianity, Christ himself as God, and thus the Trinity, without betraying his own religion? Clearly these things are not possible. Each religion must believe that the others are making dreadful errors about the things that matter most of all; or else they must cease to believe that and become indifferent, reducing religion to a kind of transcendental pop psychology.

What can we do to solve this problem? If we are honest, the answer is nothing. Nothing that we can see.

How God Solves the Unsolvable

We turn now from what we can do to what God is doing.

God has a way of changing the very parameters of our problems. Often within those parameters there is no solution. For instance, the Pharisees ask Jesus, Should we withhold tax money from Caesar the tyrant or not? If he says yes, he violates Roman law; if he says no, he offends Jewish law. Should we stone the adulteress or not? If he says yes, he offends mercy; if he says no, he offends justice. Also, if he says yes he violates Roman law, which did not grant the Jews the right of capital punishment; but if he says no he violates Mosaic law, which commanded capital punishment for this crime. And if he says nothing, he wimps out. Within the terms of the problem there is no possible answer.

The stunning style of Jesus' answers is well known.

What is their common source? That God is not confined to the terms of any human problem; that no cage can contain Christ the tiger.

Take the man beside the pool of Bethesda (Jn 5). He needs the healing that only the angel-troubled water of the pool can give him because he is crippled; but he can't get into the pool to the healing because he is crippled. Catch-22. No possible solution within the logical parameters of the problem. Jesus cuts through those parameters like the sword through the Gordian knot and heals the man instantly.

What is impossible for man is possible for God. It is impossible for us to solve the tangled problem of comparative religions. It is also impossible, it seems, to win the war against secularization and moral decadence that has been the main story of Western civilization since the end of the Middle Ages, especially since the Enlightenment, more especially in this, the devil's century (according to Leo XIII's vision), and most especially of all since the sexual revolution of the 1960s. And so God, I suggest, is working right now to deal with both problems with the same stroke, which I will call "ecumenical jihad." The age of religious wars is ending; the age of religious war is beginning: a war of all religious against none. The first world war of religion is upon us.

The battle lines are obviously changing. No longer are Protestants and Catholics anathematizing each other. Relations with Jews and even Muslims are beginning to show signs of understanding and respect never seen before in history. Our hearts, if not our heads, are in fact being brought closer together, and it seems that our divine commander's strategy is to do this by confronting us with the increasingly clear and present danger of the common enemy, the new tower of Babel. Nothing unites like a common enemy and a common emergency. A blizzard makes neighbors into friends. War can make even enemies into friends. Some of the Irish volunteered to risk their lives in the trenches of two world wars side by side with their hated British overlords and enemies because compared with the global threat of German barbarism their local civil war appeared an unaffordable luxury. Feuding brothers stop feuding when a maniac invades their house.

God let the maniac Satan loose, or rather slackened his hold on his leash, as he did with Job, for a definite purpose. Ever since Judas betrayed Christ and thus made our salvation possible, God has been using Satan to undo Satan. He has now allowed Satan to let loose on the world a worldwide spiritual war, which by attacking not one religion but all religions is uniting God-loving Catholics, Orthodox, Anglicans and Protestants (and even Jews and Muslims) more powerfully than anything else in history has ever done.

The delicious irony of it all is that the very brilliance of Satan's strategy is destined to defeat Satan, now as it did then with Judas. Satan's strategy was to divide and conquer. And because he has divided, he is conquering. And because he is conquering, we are uniting to defeat him. So because he has divided us, he is uniting us.

Of course, even if this invisible scenario for the cosmic jihad is accurate, it does not solve a single one of the classic theoretical and theological problems of comparative religion. It does not make it possible for a Catholic to accept *sola scriptura* or for a Lutheran to accept papal infallibility. All it does is make them love each other and fight side by side to the death for the love of the same Christ. Is that a lesser achievement or a greater one? What theological and ecclesiastical solutions will emerge from this new situation and this new alliance no one can tell, because the alliance is still in the early stages of formation—a formation that is in a clearer and more advanced stage in front of abortuaries and in inner-city drug centers than it is in the churches or seminaries or universities.

I have no idea what new theological understanding might emerge from this new practical moral alliance, but I think that will happen. I think love causes knowledge. I think orthopraxy leads to orthodoxy, as well as vice versa. I think that unity in action opens new eyes to understanding unity in thought. It is the principle taught by Dostoyevsky in *The Brothers Karamazov* when he has his wise old *starets* Father Zosima hear the confession of Madame Hohlokov, "a lady of little faith," who has lost her faith through an Enlightenment education, thinks everything can be explained by science and matter, and is terrified that when she dies there will be "only the burdocks on my grave." She asks how she can get her faith back. And Father Zossima tells her in effect that orthopraxy will lead to orthodoxy. Just as faith can lead to good works, to charity, so charity can lead to faith. "Love your neighbor indefatigably, and you will come to see the immortality of his soul. This has been tried. This is certain." But it has to be real and costly love, charity, not just spontaneous human feeling, compassion. "I am sorry I can tell you nothing more comforting. For love in action is a harsh and dreadful thing compared with love in dreams."

Apparently the woman fails the test, for she is one of those who has grand schemes for the salvation of humanity but cannot stand her next-door neighbor, especially when he gets too close. We, however, need not fail the test. If we will work and fight and love in action side by side with our Protestant and Catholic and Orthodox and Jewish and Muslim neighbors, we will come to perceive something we did not understand before. What will it be? We do not know yet. We will be able to perceive it only by working the works of love and war, not by speculating.

Some Specific Clues: Pearls on the Thread of God's Strategy
Here are some more specific pieces of evidence for my basic contention that
divine providence is introducing us into this new age of ecumenical jihad. Any
of the following sixteen events should be cause for rejoicing and for thinking
that there is a radical change of battle lines. All of them together, when
connected under this theme, make an overwhelming case—sixteen fingerprints
of the same divine finger.

1. Let's begin with the remarkable fact that in the last three years perhaps
half the people in America have finally waked up to the simple, crucial
realization that we are at war. Before the 1992 presidential election, the only
ones who thought we were in a spiritual war, or even a culture war, were a
small minority whom the media effectively dismissed as extremists. But today
awareness of the culture war is common. The fog—Satan's most powerful
weapon—is lifting. Light is dawning. The truth-tumor is rapidly metastasizing.

2. Specifically and locally Americans only have to look at the 1994 elections:
not a single prolife candidate lost to a prochoice candidate, whether in the
Senate or the House or a gubernatorial election. The so-called social issues,
scorned by the experts, clearly rank first in the minds of the people. The next
few years will test whether we have a government of the experts, by the experts
and for the experts, or a government of the people, by the people and for the
people.

3. What the media calls "the rise of the Religious Right" is a formidable
phenomenon, one no one expected twenty years ago. And it is not going away.

4. Within the Roman Catholic Church we have a pope who knows where
the battles are and who fights like a great, gentle bear—a new Gregory the
Great. He has surely done more than anyone in the twentieth century to save
the world from communism and from nuclear war. He fights with a formidable
array of weapons: holiness, willpower, intelligence, preaching, philosophizing,
writing, politicking and prophetic foresight. He is a spiritual Robert E. Lee, a
winner of unwinnable battles.

5. Cairo. Who could have predicted it? Who did? The firmly in-place UN
secular establishment's plans were defeated by a coalition of the Vatican and
Islamic countries. Has such a coalition ever taken place before? What could
have done it? Only awareness of a common supernatural war against a common
supernatural enemy who hates the sanctity of life, wants to destroy unborn
babies, femininity, masculinity, families and chastity. I would call Cairo a

greater victory with Islam than Lepanto was against it.

6. Within the Roman Catholic Church, Satan's new strategy has been to fill the ranks, especially the ranks of middle management, with spies who are no longer heretics but dissenters, cafeteria Catholics. A whole generation of catechumens has been lost. Most have never even been taught how to get to heaven, much less the meaning of the Trinity or the Incarnation. But the satanic strategy is now beginning to backfire, for the church is an organism, and the organism is producing antibodies. Nearly all the interesting new Catholic writers are orthodox; nearly all the orthodox seminaries are bursting full while the liberal ones are drearily empty; dozens of new Catholic magazines are appearing, all robustly orthodox; and truly orthodox Catholic colleges are springing up, schools that are clearly the wave of the future: Steubenville, St. Thomas Aquinas, Dallas, St. Thomas More, Christendom—soon even an ecumenical evangelical and Catholic Great Books School, C. S. Lewis College.

7. Lewis himself is a phenomenon. Without the slightest compromise or watering down of the claims of any church or denomination, he showed to millions of readers that "mere Christianity" is a real and solid center, not a lowest-common-denominator abstraction, and that it is far more attractive and defensible and interesting than anything else in the world. His appeal increases every year.

It is hard for us to realize how far we have come to clearly see that; hard for us to realize that as recently as forty years ago most Catholics and most Protestants would have been surprised, confused or even scandalized to hear what all now see as obvious: that whether Christ really rose is more important than whether he authorized popes; that whether there is one Savior or many is more important than whether there are two sacraments or seven; and that consequently an orthodox Baptist has more in common with the pope than with a modernist Baptist, that Cardinal O'Connor is closer to Jerry Falwell than to Richard McBrien. In dividing each church, the modernists have begun to unite all churches.

8. From the beginning of his pontificate John Paul looked East: both to his enemy, communism, and his friend, Orthodoxy. Long ago he said he wanted to accomplish three great tasks: defeating communism and the threat of nuclear war, reunion with Orthodoxy and reforming the church in America. The first was relatively easy; the third may prove impossible. But the second, I think, is closest to his heart. How can the church breathe with only one of

her two lungs? he has often asked. No pope has ever been as adamant about that before.

9. I was amazed to be told, at a recent Luther-Aquinas conference, that most Lutherans seriously hope for reunion with Rome. The major obstacle, the uncompromisable thing that justified Luther in his own mind in the terrible act of tearing apart the visible fabric of Christ's body, was of course the doctrine of justification by faith, close to the very heart of the gospel. The joint statement by the Vatican and the German Lutheran bishops about ten years ago announced in effect that that problem is solved, that both churches agree, though in different terminology. It took us four and a half centuries and many bloody wars to see it, but there it is.

When Tom Howard became a Catholic, Gordon College fired him because all faculty had to believe and sign its statement of faith, which included the tenet of justification by faith. I had been teaching there part time too, and they told Tom and me that though we both signed the statement we could not teach there because we could not really believe it, since we were Catholics. When we both protested that we did indeed believe this—how could we not? it's in our data, Scripture!—they could not understand this. So they gave us a friendly little lecture on what Catholics believed.

There are fewer and fewer Protestants each year, and fewer Catholics, who are misled by that old misunderstanding. It is becoming clear to both sides that we are saved only by Christ, by grace; that faith is our acceptance of that grace, so we are saved by faith; and that good works, the works of love, necessarily follow that faith if it is real and saving faith, so we cannot be saved by a faith that is without good works. Both sides agree with this, because both sides accept the scriptural data and the solution is right there in the data. Unity always comes about by return to the sources, to the data.

There are still many who do not know the data, the gospel. Most of my Catholic students at Boston College have never heard it. They do not even know how to get to heaven. When I ask them what they would say to God if they died tonight and God asked them why he should take them into heaven, nine out of ten do not even mention Jesus Christ. Most of them say they have been good or kind or sincere or did their best. So I seriously doubt God will undo the Reformation until he sees to it that Luther's reminder of Paul's gospel has been heard throughout the church.

11. "Evangelicals and Catholics Together," while solving no theological

problems, was also a major new step, a great air-cleanser and fog-dispeller and proper-perspective-restorer.

12. The Vatican has also taken the Reformed tradition more seriously than ever before, especially in dialoguing with it continually in the catechism that came out about ten years ago. Cardinal Ratzinger and Walter Kasper were its major authors, I think.

13. Protestant fundamentalists who formerly fulminated fire from the mouth at the church as the whore of Babylon have been seen marching and praying side by side with Catholics before abortion clinics and going with them to jail. Sharing a prison cell unites you much more powerfully than sharing a conference table.

14. Representatives from all the major religions of the world met and prayed together for peace at Assisi. A small step, perhaps, but this never happened before in the history of the world.

15. Catholic-Jewish relations have become notably closer, especially since *Nostra Aestate* told Catholics it was wrong to single out the Jews to blame for the crucifixion, and since the Vatican's recognition of the state of Israel. This relationship is crucial, since it is between the only two visible religious entities we know will last till the end of time: a visible Israel and the visible church. Israel is a central channel or conduit of divine providence in world history.

16. Islam, our ancient foe, is beginning to become our friend. If we did not balk at having Stalin's followers as our allies against Hitler, we should not balk at having Muhammad's followers as our allies against Satan. The new alliance emerged most notably at Cairo, but there were troublesome little hints before that. For instance, when the British Broadcasting Corporation ran a blasphemous skit about Christ, the Muslims demanded and got an apology when Christians wimped out. A telling example from my own experience: It took a Muslim student in my class at Boston College to berate the Catholics for taking down their crucifixes. "We don't have images of that man, as you do," he said. "But if we did, we would never take them down, even if we were forced to. We revere that man and we would die for his honor. But you are so ashamed of him that you take him down from your walls. You are more afraid of what his enemies might think if you kept them up than of what he might think if you took them down. So I think we are better Christians than you are."

How dare we be worse Christians than Muslims are! Why is Islam expanding so spectacularly? Sociologists and psychologists and historians and economists and demographers and politicians are quick to explain this with worldly wisdom from each of their specialties; but to any Christian familiar with the Bible, the answer is obvious: because God keeps his promises and blesses those who obey his laws and fear him, and punishes those who do not. Much too simple for scholars to see. Compare the amounts of abortion, adultery, fornication and sodomy among Muslims and among Christians. Then compare the amounts of prayer.

An Objection: Too Warlike?

A typical Christian, reading this essay thus far, is likely to criticize me for sounding more like a Muslim than a Christian. My response is, Do you mean by "Christian" "harmless wimp"? Granted that most Muslims fail to understand the Christian paradox that suffering love is the most powerful of all weapons in spiritual warfare, is it not equally true, alas, that most Christians in America today also fail to understand the Christian paradox that suffering love is the most powerful of all weapons in spiritual warfare? Are Muslims the only ones left who smell the smoke of battle or the only ones who are still eager to enlist in God's army?

Let us consider some specific forms of the objection that my position is too polemical that are likely to come from mainline American Christians today.

Objection 1: If you emphasize spiritual war, it inevitably turns into literal, physical war. Look at the Muslims with their jihads.

Reply: Only a small minority of Muslims worldwide identify jihad with physical violence, and our media gleefully swoop on the opportunity to tar them all with this fundamentalist brush—the same glee with which they swoop on Jim and Tammy Bakker and priestly pedophiles.

But the substantive answer to the objection is simple: *abusus non tollit usus* (the abuse does not take away the [proper] use). There is nothing distinctive here about the doctrine of spiritual warfare: every Christian doctrine is dangerous and destructive when abused. That is why we need the church: to tame this herd of wild tigers (to use Chesterton's image).

Two opposite errors are always possible. For "there is one angle at which to stand upright, but many angles at which to fall." (That's another quote from Chesterton. He is like potato chips: you can't eat just one.) Our typically modern error is insensitivity to the hard virtues: courage, self-discipline, self-denial, chastity, passionate honesty. Our ancestors' typical error was insensitivity to the soft virtues: compassion, sensitivity to the weak and handicapped, kindness. They would be as shocked at our self-indulgence as we are at their cruelty. Let us avoid errors instead of falling into the devil's trap of arguing which one is worse, thus half-justifying the other.

Objection 2: Talk about war fills you with hate. Christians are supposed to be filled with love, not with hateful talk about war and enemies.

Reply: If Christianity means what Christ taught, then Christians are supposed to love their enemies. How can you love your enemies if you have no enemies?

The key principle, which avoids both the soft and the hard errors, is to love the sinner but hate the sin. That principle used to be well known. Many have never heard it today. Many reject it today. Many sinners explicitly argue that if you hate their sin, you hate them.

For some reason I have never heard this argument about anything except sexual sin, usually sodomy. I do not understand why it is only certain homosexuals who so identify their whole selves with their chosen sin that they refuse even to distinguish their very selves from their sins. It is a terrifying identification, no matter what the sin, for that is almost exactly the definition of hell.

Of course the more you love the sinner the more you hate and make war on the sin, just as the more you love the person the more you hate and kill the cancer cells that are killing the person. Compassion to cancer cells does not come from compassion to persons; it comes precisely from lack of compassion to persons.

Objection 3: This is rhetoric rather than responsible, objective, scholarly analysis. Furthermore, it is polemical rhetoric and therefore dangerous. It could inflame another John Salvi.

Reply: It is rhetoric rather than scholarly analysis; an alarm bell rather than a sonata; an imitation of Demosthenes rather than Cicero. (When Cicero addressed the Senate, everyone said, "How beautifully he speaks"—but remained seated. When Demosthenes addressed his troops, they all stood and said, "Let us march!") When we are at war and in danger of dying, we need marchers, and speechmakers to motivate marchers.

As for the danger of motivating more potential Salvis, I doubt there are any reading this book. And is not the far commoner danger indifference and ignorance and sloth? There is a time for a Henry Clay, and there is a time for a Paul Revere. Is there any doubt what time it is today?

Objection 4: Spiritual warfare is not central or essential to Christianity. Charity is.

Reply: In a sin-filled world, charity is an act of spiritual warfare. When divine love incarnates itself east of Eden, it forms a cross. At the center of Christianity is the cross. The cross is indeed a symbol of charity—stunning, shattering charity. It is also clearly a symbol of spiritual warfare. It is like a sword held at the hilt by the hand of heaven and stuck into the earth, not to draw blood but to give it.

Objection 5: But Christ came to bring peace. We should work for peace.

Reply: He also said he came to bring a sword. He did not come to bring us the peace that the world gives. He explicitly said that. He clearly distinguished his peace from the world's peace, just as he clearly distinguished his love from the world's love, saying that by this all people would know and recognize and distinguish his disciples, by the new kind of love they had for each other. The peace that the world gives is saying yes to the world, the flesh and the devil. The peace Christ gives is saying yes to poverty, chastity and obedience, and thus no to the world, the flesh and the devil. The peace Christ brought, the peace the world cannot give, is a peace with neighbor, with self and with God. This peace means making war on greed and lust and pride, which are the enemies of peace with neighbor, self and God. The two forms of peace are exact opposites. They are at war with each other. All the saints knew and lived this. If we do not, that is why we are not saints.

Let me quote a letter to a Catholic journal from an ordinary Catholic woman:

> We're always being told to pray for peace. I wonder: aren't we allowed to pray for *victory* any more? We're supposed to be "the Church Militant," fighting against the powers of darkness. Since there's no shortage of darkness, I think we should be allowed to pray for victory.

Yes, we are supposed to be the Church Militant. And we sound more like the Church Mumbling.

Objection 6: The only Christlike form of spiritual warfare is service, not aggression. God emptied himself and became a slave, not a warrior.

Reply: That is exactly right. But a slave first of all to the Father, not to the *Zeitgeist*. A slave obeys his master. Our divine master commands us to do what Christ did: to aggress on sin, though not on sinners. And first of all our own sins. If we are not racists but we are fornicators, it does us no good to make war on racism. Or vice versa. It is easy to be warlike against unfashionable evils, especially when they are far away. It is less easy to be warlike against fashionable evils, or ones close to home.

Christ the slave is Christ the warrior. The prototypical Christian act is martyrdom, and martyrs are warriors as well as slaves. Joan Andrews is a warrior. If one hundred bishops went to jail with Joan Andrews, abortion would be conquered. Yes, our weapon is not power but suffering love. And it is the most powerful weapon in the world. It saved the world from hell. It can certainly save it from the American Civil Liberties Union.

Objection 7: Doesn't this talk of war instead of peace contradict Vatican II? Aren't you proposing a return to a Trentlike model of polemics?

Reply: No, just the opposite. I am suggesting that the Holy Spirit in the church is orchestrating an even more radical revision of Tridentine strategy than we think. Let me try to explain this suggestion.

Most of us thought at the time that Vatican II was a kind of loosening. I think we can now see that it was also a kind of tightening, a tightening of our belts for battle, a girding up of loins. We thought it made the faith less polemical than Trent since it did not anathematize heretics. But in fact it was preparing us for a greater polemic than Trent: not against Protestants, our separated brethren, but against the City of the World; not the civil war but the world war. Why did divine providence lead John XXIII to call Vatican II, and Vatican II to write *Lumen gentium,* and *Lumen gentium* to call for a new openness to non-Catholic religions? I think at least partly for this strategical, global, polemical reason. God, who knew the future, was preparing for battle. He saw that the enemy was so formidable and so global that this was the providential time to turn our energy away from our local, in-house battles and gather our allies against the devil's axis.

Objection 8: Aren't you overdoing it a bit, exaggerating for the sake of drama?

Reply: How can you overdo the survival of the human race? That is what is at stake. How can it survive if the whole world becomes as increasingly Americanized in the next fifty years as it has been in the last fifty, and as long as "Americanized" continues to mean "adulterated, sodomized, contracepted and aborted"? Do we really expect God to allow a civilization that enshrines Moloch-worship by the deliberate murder of millions of God's beloved babies in the womb to be permitted to go on indefinitely? God is patient, but God is not wimpy. The cup of divine wrath must be drunk somehow, somewhere, sometime. Or, to put the same point in other, less scriptural and less offensive terms, the necessary laws of human nature that all civilizations before except ours knew—natural law, Tao, Rta, Dike, karma, "the will of heaven"—make it impossible to get away with murder. Our most complete channel of knowledge of what God feels and thinks, sweet Jesus, had some terrifying words about those who led his little children astray—something about millstones. I think it is not a very safe bet that he has changed since then, become more tolerant toward those who collaborate in murdering his little children.

Objection 9: By your polemics you are being divisive and exclusionary rather than reconciling, atoning, uniting. The latter is the divine direction.

Reply: To attain this unity we must defeat its opponent, Satan. To do this today, God is raising an army, forging a new alliance of all who hate evil. This new alliance may prove to be more inclusive, more unifying, than anything else in the history of religions. Perhaps all the world's religions will eventually be united in this cause; but so far in the West we can see this army being made up of five religious groups, all of which are consistently vilified and libeled in the Establishment media because they are the only five identifiable groups in Western society that have not bought into the sexual revolution and its child, abortion: orthodox Catholics, evangelical and fundamentalist Protestants, Muslims, religious Jews and Eastern Orthodox (the latter not quite as socially prominent and well known and thus not quite as threatening to the media, but just as adamant and unprogressive). Perhaps these five kings of orthodoxy are the five good kings of the battle of Armageddon.

The longing for religious unity has echoed down four decades of dreamy optimism. Perhaps it will be forged only in the heat of hellish battle. What could not be accomplished irenically may be accomplished polemically.

Objection 10: You are demonizing your opponents.

Reply: You cannot demonize a demon, any more than you can personalize a person. Our enemies are demons. We have been clearly told that in Scripture. The theme of supernatural spiritual warfare runs from Genesis through Revelation. It is on every page.

Flesh and blood are not our enemies but our patients. We are God's nurses.

Our enemies are the invisible viruses that are killing our flesh-and-blood patients.

Objection 11: You are being aggressive. Just wars are defensive, not aggressive.

Reply: Against flesh and blood, yes. Against evil, no. We must be more, not less, aggressive against evil.

And defense can be as passionate as aggression: look at any mother in the animal kingdom.

Objection 12: Your model sounds more like Archie Bunker than like Christ.

Reply: Models are important. The fear of being passionate and polemical often stems from the fear of becoming like those abusive fathers who play God and push around their wives and children like poker chips or swat them like insect pests. But true polemics would be to fight against just that. Just war is in the service of peace.

Jesus, our model, said, "I am the good shepherd." The good shepherd fights the wolves because he loves the sheep. Not to fight the wolves is not to love the sheep.

Objection 13: You major in minors. You emphasize courage, the military virtue, more than charity.

Reply: I emphasize courage because we have forgotten we need it. We have not forgotten we need charity. We hear that every other sermon, and rightly so. But when do we hear the need for courage? If there is one virtue conspicuous by its absence from modern life in that protected bubble, that self-indulgent consumerist paradise that is America, it must be courage.

This was what the prophet Aleksandr Solzhenitsyn said when he came to Harvard in 1978—that the West had lost its courage. And if you doubt the decadence of Western civilization, I ask you to read the *New York Times's* whining and sniveling reactions to that magisterial speech the following day.

One wins even physical wars with spiritual weapons, with courage more than with arms. That eminently practical wisdom is in our Scriptures too, remember—all that stuff in the Psalms about how useless physical weapons like horses and chariots are without spiritual weapons like faith and courage and resolution. It works! Our faith and courage and resolution defeated Hitler and the greatest military machine in history, and our lack of faith and resolution then lost to Ho Chi Minh.

Courage is not only the specifically military virtue. It is also a virtue you need for any other virtue, for all virtues take effort and sacrifice. Especially charity. Charity without courage is like faith without works.

Objection 14: We have not heard much from you about compassion.

Reply: That is because most people are confused about it, as they are about love. They confuse both love and compassion with feelings. But feelings are not virtues. Even feelings of sympathy and compassion, though good, are not virtues. The compassion that is a virtue is the compassion God has and commands us to have. Feelings cannot be commanded. Choices and deeds can.

Feelings are often substitutes for virtue. Walker Percy wrote the astonishing line that "compassion led to the [Nazi] death camps." He meant, I think, that the substitution of the feeling of compassion and the "compassionate" quality-of-life ethic for the hard, courageous sanctity-of-life ethic among German intellectuals had already paved the way for Hitler. Compassion for what was called "life unworthy of life" had led to euthanasia, and that was the "quality-of-life" camel's nose under the tent. After the nose followed the more rearward, smelly parts of the camel. It is a one-piece camel. First it was the hopelessly ill who were eliminated, then the suffering, then the severely retarded, then the "inferior" races and the politically incorrect.

"Compassion" for mothers is the reason most often given for butchering babies before birth. Hard reason asks, Why not after? Have we no compassion for mothers of unwanted babies outside the womb, who are even more bothersome to their parents? No reason but sentiment holds back the inevitable extension of abortion to infanticide. And where is the dividing line between unwanted infant and unwanted child or unwanted teenager? Surely teenagers make parents suffer as much as babies do. So do old folks. Why not be compassionate to those who are suffering because of unwanted teenagers or unwanted parents? Might the Menendez brothers' case be the harbinger of the future?

The thought of slaughtering born people is still shocking to most people. But the thought of slaughtering unborn babies was equally shocking to most people only a short time ago. How long will it take for the rest of the camel to enter the tent? Eventually the "compassionate" demand for a world without suffering will necessitate the most ruthless extermination of anyone or anything that causes or reminds us of suffering.

Prescription and Prognosis

My prescription is a conscious and deliberate alliance against our common enemy, an alliance that will channel our energies away from our civil wars against each other and into this common world war. But is this legitimate? Is it not to ignore real and important civil-war issues?

The alliance is tactical, not theoretical. It is not a religious syncretism or indifference. It is an alliance. Allies put their disputes on hold for tactical, practical reasons. Such tactical moves are matters of prudential wisdom.

When Cardinal Law suggested an indefinite but temporary moratorium on prolife demonstrations outside abortion clinics in Boston, he made it clear that he was not implying that these honorable and legal protests had been at all responsible for Salvi's killing spree. It was a tactical move—perhaps wise, perhaps not, but certainly legitimate. Perhaps soon we should effect a similar moratorium on our polemics against each other and our attempts to convert each other to what each of us believes is the fullest and truest and most Christian room in the earthly "house with many mansions"—not because these attempts are not honest and honorable activities, but because the heat of battle may soon require us to spend all our energies against our common enemy, for the sake of the salvation of millions of souls and of global human society.

To call for such a halt to criticisms of each other is not to call for indifferentism. Nor is it a hidden plan to create a single one-world religion, or to convert all people to one. Nor is it a way to solve any of our real and important theological and ecclesial problems. It is none of these things not because it is something weaker and thus less threatening, but because it is even more powerful and important. It is a matter of life or death, heaven or hell for millions of souls, humanity's conquest of Satan or Satan's conquest of humanity.

Our common commander has issued a common command to all of us, and a common promise: obedience brings victory. The essential prescription for victory is the simplest possible, both in religion and in war: obey your commanding officer. Bow the whole heart and head and knee to God. Without the slightest doubt or compromise of your particular faith—Protestant, Orthodox, Catholic, Jewish—practice "islam": total and absolute submission and surrender to God's will. Offer yourself for whatever role he will have you play in his battle plan, even if it turns out to be none. Make out a blank check to

God. Each of these faiths at its very center commands us to do just that. So all I am proposing we do is a more resolute and clear-minded doing of what we already admit we should above all do.

This does not sound at all new or clever, because it is not. But what will happen if we do it? What prognosis follows this prescription?

I am sure only of one thing: that if we let God have his way, he will surprise us. He will do something we will not have predicted, something wonderful, something Godlike, something eye has not seen, something ear has not heard, something that has not entered into the heart of man, something that would make the hairs on our neck stand up and our ears tremble.

His style is always to outguess us, to do something more wonderful than we could ever have imagined.

If we were pure spirits, would we have ever come up with the idea of creating matter?

And how did Omnipotence ever invent the idea of creating beings with free will who could defy him?

And who would ever have thought he would choose the Jews and violate every known law of history with them?

Above all, who ever predicted the Incarnation, the most incredible, astonishing, impossible event in all time, "the absolute paradox"? How could anyone ever have understood that the God whose unchangeable essence is to be eternal and not to have a cause or a beginning in time or a body, should have a cause and a beginning in time and body through a creature, the Virgin Mary? How could any theist ever have thought of calling a woman "the mother of God"?

And how could the deathless God die? How could *hagios athanatos* give up the ghost?

And his saints, who reproduce the life of Christ, are just as unpredictable. And his church—he will heal it as strangely and unpredictably as he founded it. We do not know how. Whatever he will do, it will be far better and wiser and more wonderful than the best any of us can imagine.

Will it solve the problem of comparative religions? Will it give us the unity we long for? Yes, in time. Perhaps this is the beginning of that time, or perhaps this is not yet that time, or perhaps that time will not come until heaven. But in time the practice of total submission to God's will will necessarily solve the problem of comparative religions, will necessarily create among us the unity we know we lack and need, whatever form that unity will take. Why "necessarily"? It's a simple syllogism:

The practice of this submission means letting God's will be done.
God has told us that his will for us is unity (e.g., Jn 17).
Therefore submission to his will will lead to unity.

The way to make music, harmonious music, unified music, is for all the players in the orchestra to obey the conductor's baton.

If and when we do, what music will he make? Let him do it, and you will see.

Reasserting Boundaries: A Response to Peter Kreeft

Theodore Pulcini

*I*n "Ecumenical Jihad" Professor Kreeft presents a vivid description and intriguing analysis of the dynamics of the moral decline that seems to be gathering momentum daily in our world. He depicts the mechanisms by which the world stage is being set for the "age of antichrist," for a "culture war" in which the City of God is pitted against the City of the World, an earthly war reflecting the spiritual "war in heaven," in which souls are the fatalities. Even though this scenario is described in terms a bit too apocalyptic and mystical for my tastes, I nonetheless accept his fundamental point: that something is amiss in the moral order of the modern world, that we are experiencing a serious decline in individual and communal standards of behavior.

This decline, Professor Kreeft maintains, can be checked only by a restoration of moral standards, which in turn depends on a restoration of religion to the social fabric. However, this restoration is hindered by two obstacles: the wedge that has been driven between religion and society and the division that bedevils the world's religions, seriously impairing the effectiveness of their witness in the secular order. How can these divergences of belief be overcome so that religion's hand can be strengthened and morality restored? In human terms, Professor Kreeft admits, the situation seems hopeless, the problem unsolvable. But he sees divine providence at work in recent developments. Tradition-minded adherents of the major monotheistic religions, he observes, are coming together in a remarkable new kind of struggle (a jihad) against the forces of evil afoot in the world. This struggle may lead to a convergence of faith; ecumenical orthopraxy will perhaps be the means by which an ecumenical orthodoxy will emerge, thus fulfilling God's plan for solving the seemingly unsolvable dilemma of mutually contradictory doctrinal systems.

I would like to question Professor Kreeft's diagnosis of the causes of the current moral crisis and his understanding of what is actually occurring in the ecumenical jihad that is emerging in response to that crisis.

A Misdiagnosis?

A workable system of morality, in order to be effective and enduring, must rest on a religious foundation; on this matter I agree wholeheartedly with Professor Kreeft. I would take exception to the other prong of his two-pronged diagnosis of moral decline, namely, that religion must be interwoven into the mainstream social fabric in order to have its desired effect. This is a weak link in the chain of Professor Kreeft's argumentation. Even he appears to recognize it as so.

To explain further: Professor Kreeft longs for religion to have impact in the public forum, and so he concludes somewhat reluctantly that at least a generic religion should be operative in society. His reluctance stems from recognition of the fact that "generic religion is like generic love; it lacks the passion and power of specificity." But what else can we do? he asks. In a pluralistic society a state cannot support a particular religion over others. The alternative is for the state totally to withdraw support for religion, an option that he considers to be "fatal." Generic religion is therefore not the best alternative in theory, but "short of massive religious revival and conversion," it is the best that we can hope for in practice.

I question this conclusion. If I were to see divine providence at work in the current moral crisis, I would see it specifically in this ever-increasing distinction between mainstream society and religious life, in the progressive estrangement between civil culture and religious culture. In my opinion, it is precisely the bland mixture of mainstream culture and religion that has so blunted the effectiveness of the latter. In order to be restored to its proper strength, religion must detach itself from "societal domestication."

Please do not misunderstand this. I am not calling for a sectarian, world-fleeing form of religion cut off from interaction with the larger society in which it finds itself. The role of religion—real religion, not a generic version of it—is not to reject society. Neither is its role to subject society to its demands through appropriation of political power. Such high-handedness only breeds an unfortunate kind of antireligious reaction. I believe we are now suffering from no small amount of this because nonreligious members of the society are reducing religion to just another competing force at work in the dynamics of the secular political system. By insisting that religion not be deprived of its role within that system, religion has actually empowered that system to reject its influence on an ever-increasing scale. Those who see the need to "take back this nation one school district at a time" are locking themselves into a political battle they can never win.

I therefore do not share Professor Kreeft's lament. I am not so disturbed by the marginalization of religion in the political machinations of the public sphere. Only by stepping outside that sphere can religion become what it is meant to be in a pluralistic society and world: a means of providing an alternative to what the world offers. It should project into the world a different vision and a different strategy. It should truly be in the world but not of it. When the God-rejecting system of the world collapses (as it inevitably will), then religion can bear witness to another way. If religion is woven into the fabric of that world, it will undoubtedly fall with the world.

I am therefore suspicious of any call for a generic, mainstream form of religion. I would insist, rather, that our energies be devoted to building up a religious subculture, or a whole set of religious subcultures, in our society. These subcultures would be open-ended, that is, not so sectlike that people would find it too difficult to get in and not so cultlike that they would find it difficult to get out. Nevertheless, they would be subcultures, not concerned in the least with sacralization of the mainstream culture. Society is best served when such a wedge exists between itself and religion. The same wedge best serves religion as well.

Is it not the case that the sort of dynamic I have just described has already shaped the United States in innumerable ways? Before its being "main-streamed" into American culture in the 1950s and 1960s, the Roman Catholic Church was a massive, powerful, creative subculture that by its very existence and coherence had a massive impact on the fabric of American society. Now that it has been mainstreamed, is its impact as great, even though its involvement in the internal workings of the American system has increased dramatically? An interesting question to ask. By deemphasizing its subcultural identity and mainstreaming, American Catholicism has gained much, to be sure; but I believe that it has lost more.

And how can one account for the enormous impact that such a tiny group as the Society of Friends has had in American culture except by recognizing that its subcultural identity has given it a strength all out of proportion to its numbers? (I would suggest that many of the weaknesses experienced by Orthodoxy in America today are the result of the impulse to blend into the cultural mainstream rather than to assert subcultural identity. My hunch is that Orthodoxy's witness to and impact on American society would have been greatly enhanced if Orthodox had opted for subculturation rather than mainstreaming.)

I can certainly understand Professor Kreeft's desire to see religious influence restored to the human experience in the United States and throughout the world. I agree with him that such a restoration is necessary before any moral renascence can occur. I question the mechanism he suggests, however; weaving some sort of generic religion into the social fabric will undercut religion's influence once and for all. The wedge between society and religion, I believe, is an opportunity for us to seek to affect society by withdrawing from its inner circles. It is a call for us to cultivate (or recultivate) religious subcultures that can provide viable alternatives to the systems in moral decay all around us.

The Real Dynamics of Ecumenical Jihad

As we saw, Professor Kreeft believes that "God is raising an army, forging a new alliance of all who hate evil." A common enemy, the evil running rampant in the modern world, is bringing together orthodox Catholics, evangelical and fundamentalist Christians, religious Jews, Muslims and Eastern Orthodox (who, he suggests, may be none other than the "five good kings of the battle of Armageddon") in an unprecedented way. They are together headed for a hellish battle, in the heat of which, perhaps, the religious unity for which people have so long hoped will be forged. In other words, common praxis will lead to common belief.

I believe that Professor Kreeft is quite correct in asserting that hitherto unknown alliances among traditional adherents of the major monotheistic religions are emerging. James Davison Hunter has made a similar observation.[1] But I believe he may have misinterpreted the dynamics characterizing this new alliance. I would maintain that the common ground that religious now share on a practical level will not lead to a greater unity of faith among them but rather to sharper boundaries between them. The sociological theory of globalization, especially as it applies to contemporary religious phenomena, can help explain why I believe that this, rather than Professor Kreeft's interpretation, is the case.

Roland Robertson of the University of Pittsburgh is the major proponent of the theory of globalization. He argues that the world has shrunk; it is becoming increasingly difficult and unproductive to think of cultures in isolation. It has become imperative that we "think globally," that is, think in terms of a planetwide interaction of cultural expressions. Moreover, it is becoming more and more common for specific places on the planet to become "world spaces," spaces in which the world is "compressed," where a vast spectrum of cultures come together to form a world in microcosm.

This globalization leads to "relativization" of both societies and persons, "a process involving the placing of sociocultural or psychic entities in larger categorical contexts, such that the relativized entities are constrained to be more self-reflexive relative to other entities in the larger context."[2] In other words, globalization involves a certain cultural homogenization, the emergence of a "global humanity." This is precisely what one would expect.

However, Robertson also points to another aspect of globalization that we might not at first anticipate: the opposite of this relativization and homogenization, "the absolutizing of the perspectives of selves, ethnic groups, and national societies,"[3] and the affirmation of particular over against the universal. Globalization holds two dynamics in tension: relativization and homogenization on the one hand and absolutization and particularization on the other.

Specifically with regard to religious phenomena on the global scene, Robertson applies this insight as follows:

The process of globalization does not occur without strains or discontents occurring within societies; or, if you will, reaction—indeed resistance— from within societal contexts. As globalization proceeds, pressures are exerted on societies and individuals-in-societies to define the identity of particular societies—a matter which analysts used to think was the special problem of new national societies, but which is now clearly of ubiquitous significance. At the collective-societal level there is thus a thrust in a quasi-religious direction as some take it upon themselves to define in politcoreligious terms what "their" society "ultimately stands for" and what is sacred about it.[4]

This, I believe, is happening in the new alliance of world religions to which Professor Kreeft refers. In reaction to the homogenization that has led to a blurring of the boundaries of identity, traditionalists in Judaism, Christianity and Islam are all moving to reassert their distinctiveness, to reaffirm their particularity, to reabsolutize what they feel the trends of secular society have relativized to their detriment. They are all attempting to regalvanize their respective identities. On the surface it looks as if this process might lead to a convergence of belief among them; this is a development for which Professor Kreeft hopes.

But this hope, I would maintain, is unfounded. Those traditional Christians, Jews and Muslims who appear to be converging are really in the process of distinguishing themselves ever more sharply, at least on a theological level, from one another. In attempting to restore well-defined identity to their communities, they are returning to traditional religious forms, ones that emphasize distinctiveness and difference, not shared beliefs and perspectives. Then why do they appear to be converging? Simply because of their common reemphasis of traditional religious forms and categories. Traditionalists across theological boundaries look much more alike than do traditionalists and modernists within the boundaries of the same theological tradition; thus Professor Kreeft observes—correctly, I would say—that "an orthodox Baptist has more in common with the pope than with a modernist Baptist, . . . Cardinal O'Connor is closer to Jerry Falwell than to Richard McBrien." Nevertheless, for the traditional adherents of Christianity, Judaism and Islam, the boundaries that separate their particular religious tradition from others is of utmost importance; blurring of the boundaries is steadfastly repudiated. Division is of the essence in affirming one's distinctive identity.

Professor Kreeft laments this division, seeing it as leading inevitably to a weakening of the religious witness in the modern world. I am not sure I agree. If this division is the necessary concomitant of newly sharpened identity, then I think it is highly desirable. Only when believers can speak from a conviction born of firm identity will religion again be taken seriously as a cultural force.

A homogenized, generic religion lacks the self-assuredness that is the necessary precondition of strength.

But are we, in the midst of this renewed absolutization of particularity, condemned to repeat the age-old animosities and antagonisms that have separated us in the past? Not necessarily. The convergence of praxis among Jews, Christians and Muslims working side by side to reaffirm traditional values—even if in an attempt to reassert their particular identities in contradistinction to one another on a theological level—does have a salutary effect. Their engagement in common cause has enabled them to know and to understand and to respect one another in an unprecedented way. And it is much harder to demonize someone whom one knows and understands and respects.

The mutual contact so typical of our globalized world can and should enhance mutual tolerance. Thus even though traditionalist Muslims are more Muslim than ever, and traditionalist Jews are more Jewish than ever, and traditionalist Orthodox are more Orthodox than ever, and traditional Catholics are more Catholic than ever, and traditionalist Protestants are more Protestant than ever, they all can respect and understand, and therefore tolerate, "the other" more than ever. I do not believe we can hope for a convergence of faith among these traditionalists, but we can realistically hope for a convergence of tolerance among them. The important and constructive impact of such a development cannot be overestimated.

Conclusion

I fully agree with Professor Kreeft that we are experiencing a decline in morality that has resulted from the decline in religious influence in society. But I disagree with him on the way in which religion can again become influential in the civil realm. Advocating a place for generic religion in secular political mechanisms is not the answer. The more religion manages to extricate itself from those mechanisms the better. Religion is not to reject the world; but neither is it to try to subject it by using the political strategies of the world. It is rather to project into the world, from without, an alternative way of seeing the world and living in it.

I also bring some questions to Professor Kreeft's interpretation of what he perceives to be a growing convergence among traditional adherents of the various world religions; as noted earlier, he sees this convergence as leading to a theological unity. I think that indeed there is a convergence developing, but it is a convergence based on a return to traditional forms within the conservative circles of each of these religions, a return that signals a reaffirmation of particularist identity, not a compromise of traditional (and therefore mutually divisive) theological stances.

Nevertheless, like Professor Kreeft, I hope that the convergence of praxis among these traditionalists can lead to good. It can lead to greater mutual tolerance (even as each tradition reasserts its individual identity) and a reassertion of religious influence in the public sphere (even as boundaries between traditions are emphasized). Like Professor Kreeft, I am uncomfortable with the theological differences that separate the various religious traditions. (After all, how can such divisions be tolerated if one believes that truth is one?) Yet I am confident that honest striving after God on the part of all committed religious men and women, of whatever tradition, can somehow accomplish God's will, even across sharply defined religious boundaries. Renewed identity within religious groups and renewed tolerance among them can create a force in the world than can be truly redemptive. It can provide the religious underpinnings for a renewed morality—something that I, like Professor Kreeft, long to see.

2

A NEW THING
Ecumenism at the Threshold
of the Third Millennium

■

Richard John Neuhaus

*T*he very title of this gathering—"An Ecumenical Conference of Traditional Christians"—helpfully puts a number of the most important questions on the table. As I understand it, the title implicitly assumes that one question is definitively answered, namely, the question of whether we encounter one another as Christians, whether we recognize one another as brothers and sisters in Christ. This should not be assumed casually; it represents a great change, a great achievement and most importantly a great gift. In the two-thousand-year history of the one church of which we are all part, however confusedly and imperfectly, a gathering such as this bears the intimation of something new, something filled with high promise and something freighted with a sobering sense of responsibility. In view of the millennia-long breach between East and West, the breach of almost five hundred years between Rome and the Reformation, and the subsequent divisions among those who claim the Reformation heritage—in view of all that we must attend to the words of the prophet Isaiah, "Behold, I am doing a new thing; now it springs forth, do you not perceive it?" (Is 43:19).

If our title assumes that we recognize one another as Christians, it also poses questions on which we no doubt have differences, and they are differences that make a very important difference. Of course I have in mind two words in the title, *ecumenical* and *traditional*. In the course of this paper I will address the meaning of ecumenism and accountability to tradition. In acknowledging one another as Christians, we have already taken a very major ecumenical step. That is, we understand ourselves to be living in the same *oikoumenē*, the same world of faith. "So then you are no longer strangers and sojourners, but you are fellow citizens with the saints and members of the household of God, built upon the foundation of the apostles and prophets, Christ Jesus himself being the cornerstone" (Eph 2:19-20).

Although we are members of the one *oikoumenē,* of the world inhabited by faith, within the household there are important differences in our relationship to what has been called ecumenism in the twentieth century. The modern ecumenical movement dating from the 1910 World Missionary Conference in Edinburgh was launched as a very Protestant affair. Among Protestants it would soon be perceived as a project of that sector of Protestantism described as liberal or mainline or oldline; a sector of Protestantism more recently and not always charitably described as sideline. Out of that project would come institutions such as the World Council of Churches and the National Council of Churches, institutions that are today but a pale reflection of what they were even thirty years ago.

In these same decades a vibrantly resurgent, albeit maddeningly diverse, evangelical Protestantism has asserted its presence in world Christianity. For complicated reasons with which most of us are familiar, evangelicalism has tended to approach all things bearing the name *ecumenical* with an attitude ranging from robust skepticism to impassioned hostility. The ecumenical establishment was and to a large extent still is composed of those who consigned evangelicalism to the outer darkness of that category of presumably unspeakable reaction called fundamentalism.

Orthodoxy too has had a delicate relationship with the modern ecumenical movement. From the beginning, especially because of the Anglican connection, it was thought that the movement might play an important part in healing the breach between East and West. Giant figures such as Georges Florovsky had a formative influence in the Faith and Order Movement, and I am personally indebted to the friendship and ecumenical vision of such fathers as Alexander Schmemann and John Meyendorff. In the years following World War II the ecumenical movement served a number of purposes for Orthodoxy. It provided a measure of international contact, albeit often morally ambiguous, for Orthodox leadership behind the iron curtain; agencies such as the World Council of Churches helped Orthodoxy to maintain a public profile in a West that was and still is all too inclined to forget Eastern Christianity; and the ecumenical movement provided Orthodoxy with other ecclesial connections that could be useful in facing the ever-present reality of Rome—a reality that in Orthodox eyes is frequently perceived to be a threat. However the ecumenical movement might have served the purposes of Orthodoxy, there is no denying that Orthodoxy rendered a most singular service to the ecumenical movement.

At a time when the influence of Protestant neo-orthodoxy had waned, and conciliar ecumenism seemed to be caught up in all the fancies and passions that one might expect to issue from a slogan such as that of the World Council of Churches, "The world sets the agenda for the church," Orthodoxy at least provided ecumenical Protestantism with a bad conscience about the Christian tradition it had so largely abandoned. But the Orthodox ecumenical engagement did more than that. As recently as 1982, for instance, Faith and Order produced at Lima the historic document *Baptism, Eucharist, and Ministry*, an achievement that, it is generally agreed, would have been impossible without the leadership of Orthodox and Roman Catholics.[1]

Whatever may be the new ecumenism that is anticipated in conferences such as this, it cannot be entirely new. There is much in that older ecumenical movement that can be retrieved and built upon, especially in the work of Faith and Order, which at least until recently represented an impressive measure of lower-case orthodoxy—largely because of the participation of upper-case Orthodoxy. The new ecumenism will be very significantly shaped by the already-mentioned resurgence of evangelical Protestantism in world Christianity. While many evangelicals may remain cool to everything that they associate with ecumenism, the imperative toward unity is inherent and irrepressible in Christian existence, as it is also explicit in our Lord's will for those who call themselves his disciples.

Alongside the evangelical resurgence, the great new fact, following the Second Vatican Council and as a direct consequence of the council, is the ecumenical engagement of the Roman Catholic Church. It is by no means accurate to say that the Catholic Church joined the existing ecumenical movement. By virtue of size, scope and tradition, the Catholic Church, with approximately a billion members, would necessarily transform any movement that might attempt to incorporate it. While there were suggestions from time to time that the Catholic Church might join the World Council of Churches, seasoned ecumenical observers believe that that was never a live possibility, and it certainly is not today. Because of its nature and the explicit mandate of Vatican II, the Catholic Church is compelled to chart a distinctive course in ecumenical relations. The reasons for this are evident in the Decree on Ecumenism *(Unitatis redintegratio)* and perhaps even more so in the Dogmatic Constitution on the Church *(Lumen gentium)*. In the latter document the church makes clear its understanding that all who are baptized and believe in Christ are "truly but imperfectly" in communion with the Catholic Church.

However imperfectly it may be expressed, the reality of the church is coterminous with the reality of Christ, the presence of the church is coterminous with the presence of Christ. The Catholic Church therefore understands itself to be ecumenically entangled with all Christians, whether or not they wish to be entangled with the Catholic Church and whether or not Catholics wish to be entangled with them. As was so strongly affirmed in the 1994 declaration, "Evangelicals and Catholics Together," we have not chosen one another, we have been chosen. And because it is the one Christ who has done the choosing, we have been chosen to be his together. Unity is not by our choice. Ecumenism is not optional. Ecumenism is not our effort to achieve a unity that does not exist; it is our response to the gift of unity already given. Like it or not, the gift and the problems that come with the gift are already ours.

In the volume of essays elaborating the meaning and possible significance of "Evangelicals and Catholics Together," Father Avery Dulles presents a useful taxonomy of the ways in which Catholic ecumenical theology and strategy relate to the many parts of world Christianity.[2] Among all those relationships the relationship to the Orthodox churches is unique. The new *Catechism of the Catholic Church* reiterates the statement of Pope Paul VI that the communion with the Orthodox churches is so profound "that it lacks little to attain the fullness that would permit a common celebration of the Lord's Eucharist" (*Catechism* 838). It is perhaps not too much to say with respect to the Orthodox that the main obstacle to full communion is the absence of full communion. In the present pontificate one cannot help but be struck by the persistence, the urgency and the warmth of the expressed desire for reconciliation with the Orthodox Church.

There is also a sense of heightened expectation that such reconciliation could by the grace of God happen soon, enabling the historic patriarchates of East and West to cross the threshold of the third millennium in full communion with one another, as they are in full communion with Christ. John Paul II has spoken about the second millennium as the millennium of Christian division and the third millennium, please God, as the millennium of Christian unity. Again and again he has alluded to the hope that the third millennium will be a "springtime"—a springtime of ecumenism and a springtime of evangelization. Always in his vision, unity and evangelization are inseparably joined. The unity of Christians is a great good in itself but always, as in John 17, it is a necessary part of the invitation to the world to believe in the one whom the Father has sent. As was the case in Edinburgh in 1910, but was then largely forgotten by the movement to which Edinburgh gave birth, ecumenism must always be vivified by the missionary mandate.

It is important that Protestants, and especially evangelical Protestants, understand why the relationship with Orthodoxy must have ecumenical priority for Rome. Not only is that the division that precedes by more than half a millennium the divisions of the sixteenth century, but also it is the division in which the seeds of future division were sown. That is to say, if the disputes that issued in the division of 1054 had been handled differently, it is quite possible that the disputes of the sixteenth century would not have resulted in further divisions. It is between East and West that the healing must begin. As admirably as Orthodoxy has engaged other churches and communions in the modern ecumenical movement, the healing of the breach between East and West cannot be effected by reconciliation with communions that are not themselves reconciled with the church where the breach began, namely, the church of Rome. The remedying of the great divide in world Christianity, that between East and West, presses upon the Catholic Church with peculiar urgency. It is in that light that one should read the apostolic letter of last November, "As the Third Millennium Nears," in which John Paul confesses the sins that Catholics have committed against Christian unity and in which he prays for an outpouring of the reconciling power of God's forgiveness in Christ.

The singular place of East-West relations in Catholic ecumenical thought and strategy, however, should not for one second be mistaken for lack of interest in relations with other Christians with whom Catholics are in true but imperfect communion. On many different fronts Rome simultaneously advances the quest for a fuller expression of the unity that is ours. The ecumenical energy of the sixteen years of this pontificate is truly unprecedented. The media sometimes convey the impression that there is a flagging of ecumenical commitment, but nothing could be further from the truth. I believe that, were one to ask what is the first priority of this pontificate, the answer would be Christian unity. This applies very particularly to the relationship with evangelical Protestants.

The declaration "Evangelicals and Catholics Together" (ECT) was carefully designed to be an independent project. The signers made clear that they did not speak for their churches but hoped to speak responsibly from and to their churches. There is no doubt that the distinguished evangelical signatories have demonstrated that they know how to engage the constituencies of which they are leaders of great credibility. While no one person or group of persons can speak for evangelicalism—indeed, there is considerable disagreement over what is meant by evangelicalism—ECT is assuredly a statement within and to and from evangelicalism that has struck a powerful chord and quite possibly effected an abiding change. So also on the Catholic side. While it is determinedly an independent initiative, ECT and the process of which it is part has received the warm encouragement of responsible parties in Rome, and no one can dispute that some of the signatories are voices of the very highest credibility in the Catholic Church.

Some critics appear determined to overlook it, but ECT underscored again and again that there are significant and abiding differences and disagreements between evangelicals and Catholics. In discussions of the several drafts we wondered if the declaration did not repeat that too often. In view of some of the reactions to ECT, it appears that it cannot be repeated too often. ECT is but a beginning. It is hoped that there will be continuing theological conversations in which the questions addressed will be refined and sharpened. Again, these conversations, like the initiative itself, will be entirely independent. In no way do they intend to negotiate differences between evangelicals and Catholics. They do not possess and they do not desire any authority to act on behalf of others. The sole purpose is to explore ever more deeply and ever more carefully what we acknowledge in common to be the revealed truth of God in Christ. What we come to understand in common will be shared with our several communities; whether this work is received or rejected or ignored is entirely out of our hands, which is as it should be.

ECT and the development that it reflects have stirred both great hopes and great fears. In the book also titled *Evangelicals and Catholics Together,* I suggest that what is happening between evangelicals and Catholics may represent something of a *kairos*—an appointed moment of judgment and promise in which something new is afoot, although we know not quite what. In that essay I try to place ECT within the context of what I understand by the new ecumenism and the hopes of Roman Catholics. I note the concern of one evangelical critic of ECT who says, "Our worry is about the third and hidden *c*." By that he means that ECT talks about "convergence and cooperation" between evangelicals and Catholics, but the worry is that behind such talk is another *c*—conversion. Some of the more strident attacks on ECT have claimed that it is nothing less than a betrayal of the Reformation and an implicit acceptance by evangelicals of the invitation to return to Rome.

Permit me to cite a pertinent section from my essay:

There are, and there will no doubt continue to be, conversions: evangelical Protestants becoming Catholics and Catholics becoming evangelical Prot-estants. Individual Christians must earnestly seek to discern God's will, and then act upon that discernment when it is given. But there is in ECT no hidden agenda of conversion harbored by either Catholics or evangelicals. In addition, any talk about "ecclesial reconciliation" between evangelicals and Catholics at this moment in history is, in my judgment, utterly premature and detracts from the great purpose served by ECT. Only God knows what the relationship between evangelicals and Catholics might be fifty or a hundred years from now. There would have to be very significant developments in both evangelicalism and the Catholic Church to make credible the discussion of ecclesial reconciliation. That is not the task of ECT. That is the task of another generation of evangelicals and Catholics together, if indeed Our Lord does not first return in glory.

As for our historical moment, it is enough that after four centuries of suspicion and hostility we have found one another; it is enough that we are able to address our differences with candor and clarity; it is enough that we are learning to engage one another in mutual respect for the institutions, traditions

and patterns of discipleship that have developed over the years of our separation; it is enough that we discern together and embrace together the great
challenges of moral and cultural renewal; it is enough that we witness to the
world and witness to one another the saving gospel of Jesus Christ; it is enough
that, toward that great end, we can admonish and encourage one another,
always speaking the truth in love (Eph 4:15). It is more than enough. It is
something like a *kairos*.

I began by observing that the well-chosen title of this gathering—"An
Ecumenical Conference for Traditional Christians"—puts squarely before us
some of the questions that we must most earnestly and carefully address. I have
further suggested that one question, the most important question, is also
implicitly answered in the title, namely, we do acknowledge one another as
Christians. The most important affirmation of ECT is this: "All who accept
Christ as Lord and Savior are brothers and sisters in Christ. Evangelicals and
Catholics are brothers and sisters in Christ. We have not chosen one another,
just as we have not chosen Christ. He has chosen us, and he has chosen us to
be his together."

Critics on both the left and the right have challenged that affirmation.
Liberal Christians claim that ECT is no more than a social-political compact
between Christian conservatives. In their view the theological affirmations of
the document are but a veneer thinly disguising an alliance in America's culture
wars. Critics who describe themselves as evangelical or fundamentalist agree
with the liberal critics of ECT, except they claim it is and should be nothing
more than a statement of cobelligerency in the public square. In their view the
theological affirmations of the document are not so much a deceptive veneer
as they are a reflection of the naiveté of evangelicals who were taken in by their
crafty Catholic interlocutors. I am persuaded, however, that the theological
affirmations are the heart of ECT, as I am persuaded that theology must be at
the heart of the new ecumenism proposed to us by this gathering.

Recognizing one another as Christians and recognizing that ecumenism is
inherent in Christian existence, I note that the conference title further suggests
that we are "traditional" Christians. Surely this cannot mean merely that we
are conventional or conservative in our disposition, opposed to change and
determined to preserve the status quo. Some of us may be traditional in all
those meanings of the term, but I take it that the title intends to suggest that
we are traditional in the sense that we are freely bound by a normative tradition

that is the bearer of truth. Our devotion is to tradition and not to traditionalism, remembering the fine phrase of Jaroslav Pelikan that tradition is the living
faith of the dead while traditionalism is the dead faith of the living.

Since the sixteenth century Protestants and Catholics have engaged in
battles royal over the meaning of tradition. Such conflicts have typically been
over the authority of Scripture versus the authority of tradition. The pitting of
Scripture against tradition, and of tradition against Scripture, was certainly not
the intention, but it has all too often been the consequence of Protestant-
Catholic disputes. One may devoutly hope that among the new things in the
new ecumenism that is envisioned is a fresh appreciation of the unity of
Scripture and tradition. In this new circumstance Catholics and Orthodox can
come to understand the Reformation principle of *sola scriptura* as an important
contribution to the tradition, while Protestants recognize that that formula is
itself a tradition within the tradition.

It is necessary to speak of tradition and of traditions. In the first instance,
when speaking of the *paradosis* of what has been handed on from Christ to his
church through time, it may be useful to speak of upper-case Tradition. In this
sense Tradition includes Scripture. Scripture is that part of the Tradition that
possesses a unique authority. As the Tradition is grounded in Scripture, so also
the determination of what is Scripture and the requirement that the Tradition
be grounded in Scripture are themselves grounded in Tradition. Such an
assertion may seem impossibly circular, but that is only because we have
become accustomed to thinking of Scripture and Tradition as two separate
sources of authority and truth. Catholics bear a great measure of responsibility
for this confusion. In response to the Reformation's pitting of *sola scriptura*
against the Tradition, the Council of Trent drew a distinction between the
"written books" and the "unwritten traditions." Although it was probably not
the council's intention, this led to a conventional language about "two
sources" of revealed truth.

At Vatican II an earlier draft of the Dogmatic Constitution on Divine
Revelation (*Dei verbum*) spoke of "Two Sources of Revelation." It is of great
importance that that formulation was changed in the approved text of the
council, which speaks of "sacred Tradition and sacred Scripture" as essentially
connected sources that together "form one sacred deposit of the word of
God." Tradition and Scripture are different in form but are the same in
content. Put differently, Tradition is formally but not materially different from

Scripture. I cannot in the brief compass of this paper attempt to point the way toward an exit from what would appear to be the hermeneutical circle in what must be said about the relationship between Scripture and Tradition. I believe Catholics and Orthodox would be united, however, in urging our Protestant brothers and sisters to consider more seriously than they ordinarily do that whatever we may say about the Scriptures is itself part of the Tradition. Such considerations have a necessary part in any gathering of traditional Christians.

Here too we may build upon achievements of that earlier ecumenical movement. One thinks, for example, of the 1963 Faith and Order statement at Montreal on "Scripture, Tradition and Traditions." The statement asserted, "We exist as Christians by the Tradition of the gospel (the *paradosis* of the *kērygma*) testified in Scripture, transmitted in and by the church through the power of the Holy Spirit. Tradition taken in this sense is actualized in the preaching of the word, in the administration of the sacraments and worship, in Christian teaching and theology, and in missions and the witness to Christ by lives of the members of the church." That formulation hardly answers all the questions about the relationship between Scripture and Tradition, never mind questions about the interpretation of each, but it does, I believe, provide a useful starting point.

Each of us is participant in a specific tradition. The tradition of which we are part, most of us would like to think, is in turn solidly within what might be called the great Tradition that gives definition and form to (lowercase) catholic and (lowercase) orthodox Christianity. Yet the several traditions of which we are part typically demarcate our divisions. The negotiation between these traditions in order to overcome such divisions has been a source of enormous problems in ecumenism to date. In his deservedly praised book *The Nature of Doctrine*, George Lindbeck puts one of the problems in a form both succinct and striking:

> Over and over again in recent years, there have been reports from Roman Catholic, Orthodox, or Protestant theologians engaged in dialogues sponsored by their respective churches that they are in basic agreement on such topics as the Eucharist, ministry, justification, or even the papacy, and yet they continue—so they claim—to adhere to their historic and once-divisive convictions. Those who hear these reports often find them difficult to believe. They are inclined to think that the very notion of doctrinal reconciliation without doctrinal change is self-contradictory, and they

suspect that the dialogue participants are self-deceived victims of their desire to combine ecumenical harmony with denominational loyalty.[3]

Here we come up against the familiar tension between unity and truth. The apostle enjoins us to "speak the truth in love," but in two thousand years of Christian history it seems we have seldom found the way of doing justice to both truth and love. It is commonly suggested that truth directs us to doctrine and love directs us to unity, but if what has been said about Christian unity is right, it should be obvious that the ecumenical imperative is itself a constitutive part of the truth that we affirm together. The new ecumenism, as reflected also in ECT, is adamant that truth and unity must not be pitted against one another, that the only unity we seek is unity in the truth, and the only truth we acknowledge is the truth by which we are united.

As our existing unity is the gift of God, so the fuller expression of that unity will be the gift of God. If we are radically open to the Spirit's leading, we will not attempt to force things; we will not, as has sometimes happened in ecumenism, try to achieve a unity that is finally false to both the truth of unity and the unity of truth. Joseph Cardinal Ratzinger, the prefect of the Congregation for the Doctrine of the Faith, has spoken forcefully on this danger:

> It seems important to me, therefore, looking towards the future, to recognize the limits of what one might term the "ecumenism of negotiation" and not to expect of it any more than it can provide: rapprochements in important human fields, but not unity itself. It seems to me that many disappointments could have been avoided if this had been clear from the start. But after the successes of the early period just after the Council many have understood ecumenism as a diplomatic task in political categories; just as one expects of good negotiators that after some time they will come to a joint agreement that is acceptable to everyone, so people thought they could expect this of the Church authorities in matters of ecumenism.[4]

While it is true that we are all participant in traditions, these traditions are not mere historical artifacts. Their claim upon us is precisely to the extent that they are bearers of the truth. We cannot negotiate between these traditions as though they are little more than accidents that inconveniently divide us. Again Cardinal Ratzinger puts the point sharply: "For if one were to agree completely on regarding all the different confessions simply as traditions, then one would have cut oneself completely loose from the question of truth, and theology would now be merely a form of diplomacy, of politics. Our quarreling ancestors were in reality much closer to each other when in all their disputes they still knew that they could only be servants of one truth which must be acknowledged as being as great and as pure as it has been intended for us by God."[5]

Our unity in the truth is more evident in our quarreling about the truth than in our settling for something less than the truth. At the same time we recognize that, short of the end time, none of us possesses the truth entirely, exhaustively and without remainder. Such possession awaits the consummation when, as Paul says in 1 Corinthians 13, we know even as we are known. Each of us and each of our traditions is held accountable to the great Tradition, including the Scriptures, which is the deposit of the truth. The definitive exegesis of the Tradition is an eschatological event. Along the way of history we try to derive from Scripture and the church's reflection upon its experience the formulae and criteria by which we might better discern that which is biblical, catholic and orthodox. Thus, from the apostolic era onward there have been numerous variations on, for instance, St. Vincent of Lerins's rule of faith: *quod ubique, quod semper, quod ab omnibus creditum est* (what has been believed everywhere, always, and by all). Such formulae are probably inescapable and just as probably will always be inadequate.

But we have no choice but to keep trying. The truth of unity and the unity of truth give us no choice. In contemporary ecumenical discussion Lindbeck has rendered stellar service with his argument for a "rule of faith" or "grammar of doctrine" that can be accepted by all. Accepting the rule or the grammar does not guarantee an outcome of agreement on substantive teaching, but it holds us accountable to the truth and accountable to one another. Among Roman Catholics perhaps the most suggestive treatment of these questions is the 1990 "Instruction on the Ecclesial Vocation of the Theologian," issued by the Congregation for the Doctrine of the Faith. Other Christians will have difficulties with what is said there about the church's magisterium, but all can benefit, I believe, from its thoughtful treatment of the connections among the Tradition, traditions, and the development and discernment of doctrine. Later this year it is expected that the pope will issue an encyclical on ecumenism, and I will be surprised if it does not elaborate on these questions in a manner that will claim the attention of all Christians.

It may be that I have read altogether too much into the reference to traditional Christians in the title of this gathering. But I do believe these questions must be addressed if a new ecumenism is to fare better than the old.

We take up these questions from where they were left, and from where they were too often abandoned, in the earlier ecumenical movement. What none of us should do, it seems to me, is to delude ourselves into thinking that we are not part of a tradition that is, to the extent that it is identifiably Christian, accountable to the great Tradition of Christian teaching, worship and discipleship. It is naive to posit biblical Christianity against the Tradition, for every possible construal of biblical Christianity is but another particular tradition. Similarly, we cannot elevate one piece of the tradition to a position of mastery over the Tradition.

On the last score I have noted with interest the way in which some critics of "Evangelicals and Catholics Together" have seized upon what they view as that document's inadequate treatment of justification by faith. The fact that the declaration does not affirm justification by faith alone, they say, discredits its claim that evangelicals and Catholics are brothers and sisters in Christ. *Sola fide,* they say, is the *articulus stantis et cadentis ecclesiae,* the article by which the church stands or falls. Apparently that precise formulation first appeared in 1718, almost two hundred years after the beginning of the Reformation, and was devised by a Lutheran theologian, Valentius Loescher, in order to attack the Pietists of his day.[6] According to Loescher's Lutheran orthodoxy, *sola fide* condemned, among other things, the claimed necessity of an identifiable conversion experience. There is considerable irony in the fact that, nearly three hundred years later, some evangelicals invoke *articulus stantis et cadentis ecclesiae,* the formula by which Lutheran orthodoxy condemned the common evangelical teaching on faith and conversion.

But that is only one particularly piquant instance of the contradictions encountered when we attempt to turn traditions against the Tradition. Many more might be found in the course of Christian history, the most abiding being variations on the effort to turn the Bible—which is the text of and for the church, canonized as the Word of God by the church—against the church. As the title of this conference indicates, all of us gathered here—Protestant, Orthodox and Roman Catholic—are brought together by a churchly purpose. As we have each been chosen by Christ, so we find ourselves in the community of the chosen. As we find ourselves in the community of the chosen, we recognize ourselves to be chosen. We have in common that we have made an act of faith in Christ, the head, and therefore an act of faith in the church, his body. As in Edinburgh eighty-five years ago, we come together for the sake of the evangelization of the world, in the hope that our life together might give greater credibility to the gospel that we proclaim together.

"Behold, I am doing a new thing," says the Lord. The new thing is not the search for Christian unity, nor is it the recognition of the unity that is already ours as a gift from God. In this century and in every century of the Christian story, Christians have gathered to consider their relationship to the *oikoumenē*, the universal household of faith. Ecumenism, like the faith by which we are gathered, is, in the words of St. Augustine, ever ancient, ever new. What will come of this meeting and similar meetings at the threshold of the third millennium, what will be the genuinely new thing, only God knows. But I am confident that we will not go wrong if we open ourselves to the possibility that we are participating in something like a *kairos*.

A (Somewhat) Protestant Response to Richard John Neuhaus

S. M. Hutchens

*I*n his address Father Neuhaus ponders an anomaly. On one hand he speaks, with Cardinal Ratzinger, of the present stasis and apparent intractability of ecumenical dialogue. On the other there is the educated intuition that despite this the type of people who are gathering at Rose Hill stand poised together on the threshold of an ecumenical *kairos*. He is wise not to resolve the tension, for there is also evidence here of the intuition that if there is a way out of the thicket of disunity, God will provide it, since we have exhausted our own ingenuity. While it is true, as Father Reardon is fond of saying, that much of the midcentury ecumenical movement involved the kind of chummy muddle-headedness that was willing to sell the faith for a mess of collegial pottage, many of its documents are astute and accurate signs informing us that we have reached the end of the road and the bridge is out. Father Neuhaus cites Cardinal Ratzinger's observation that in the days when our ancestors fought each other tooth and nail it was because they still had a kind of hope in the convertability of their erring brethren that we have given up. We stand at the end of a road, and at the end of a day, frustrated because we cannot in good conscience achieve the unity we desire, but also unable to dispose of each other with anathemas, as hard as we have tried. Yes, we Protestants are stuck with you Catholics and Orthodox too. I think the Lord may be telling us that the vows we made to him hold us to each other, and that even if we cannot agree, we still need to stay together for the good of the children.

Let me ponder Father Neuhaus's anomaly in terms that will be recognized as Protestant by Catholics, whether my fellow Protestants hear them that way or not. I cannot recognize Protestantism as based on a dialectical or dialogical principle, as Philip Schaff and Paul Tillich do, but rather as an uncentered conservative resilience to the particular route taken by Roman Catholic doctrinal development. In other words, a Protestant is a protesting Catholic who tried but failed to reform the Western church by halting its movement in directions that it thought unwarranted by revelation. This means that my view of the movement of the two communions (or more accurately, the one communion and the other aggregate of communions) is precisely opposite of Schaff's: Roman Catholicism is essentially progressive and Protestantism is essentially reactionary. Protestantism has no positive principle other than what it shares with Catholicism. All else about it is either medicine for the Catholic body or heresy. The fissiparating sickness of Protestantism, which is the greatest witness against the argument that it has an integrating principle, comes from its attempt to live on corrective medicines as if they could sustain life. Protestant medicines taken without Catholic food are poison; Catholic food taken without Protestant tonics and exercises cause the body to bloat and distort.

Let us note here that *modernist* religious progressivism, both Protestant and Catholic, is the product of capitulation to the spirit of the age's mocking perversion of Catholic development described so carefully by Newman, since Catholic doctrinal development—while we Protestants think some of it may be wrong—is based upon and logically consistent with New Testament teaching. The developed doctrine of the Immaculate Conception, for example, is a distinctively Catholic guardian at the gate of a Christology upon which we agree together while modernism scoffs at us both.

The documents of the Anglican and Lutheran dialogues with Rome in particular underscore that the real Protestant difficulty with the doctrine of the papacy is far less with the primacy or spiritual authority of the bishop of Rome—whom, although estranged, some of us regard as still very much our bishop and listen carefully and respectfully to what he says. It is rather the developed doctrine of the papacy with which we have difficulty. One need not deny the apostolic legitimacy and pastoral authority of Peter's successor to believe also that there is and always has been apostolic authority in the church to rebuke Peter when he cooperates with those who would bring it under the bondage of the law, or when his faith or courage fails, or when he speaks with the voice of Satan, or when he is simply wrong. We Bible Christians, if I may speak now for a certain kind of Protestant, know Peter, love him and would be willing to follow him, but we must first be able to recognize Peter on Peter's throne, and the admission of fallibility—in the sense of admitting error that was once held with all Petrine boldness and conviction—may well be the key to that.

Let me emphasize that I do not by any means think that everything that is commonly regarded by Protestants as Catholic error is necessarily erroneous. Some Protestant error involves the denial or at least culpable ignorance of what Catholics are supposed to believe. Until, however, the day comes when we, looking at Peter's portrait in our Bibles, can actually see Peter in Rome (now we see the emperor—a good, Christian emperor, John Paul II, to be sure, but an emperor nonetheless), the best we can probably do is love the pope, hear his teaching, and follow him where we can. That great shepherd who presently sits on Peter's throne has unquestionably done more than any other pope in the last half millennium to make us long for reunion with the beauty and power of Christ that we see reflected in him. It is time that we turn from gazing upon the demonic face of Rome and look upon the angelic. We have always seen that great city as a symbol of Babylon. It is time we began to exercise righteous judgment to see that it is also a symbol of Zion. The determination to do this, not to approve all things Roman Catholic, for we doubt we can do that, but to love everything in Rome that we can, is, I believe, what is behind "Evangelicals and Catholics Together" (ECT).

Polarizations Within Evangelicalism

This brings us to the evangelical problem of which Father Neuhaus spoke at such length. In the first issue of the promising new journal *Regeneration*

Quarterly, Kevin F. Offner writes that this movement to which he belongs is "adrift with amnesia." "Whether," he writes, "our eyes are fixed backwards on fundamentalists (how not to be like them), or forward on contemporary culture (how to be similar), the root problem remains the same: American evangelicals have forgotten who they are" (p. 6). Whether evangelicalism has ever known itself is a matter for debate, but here Offner has in short order identified both the cultural and theological poles between which it is suspended. This tension between fundamentalist traditionalism and modernity that James Davison Hunter has chronicled so extensively has determined the shape and course of the movement from its first moments of self-awareness in the 1940s, and is at the root of the problem of why Christians who have a strong sense of history and the authority of tradition have such a difficult time communicating with evangelicals.

Let me observe that these poles, fundamentalist traditionalism and modernity, are both decidedly modern. The movement contemplates and evaluates itself by turning its gaze into one of two mirrors, either that of its own short past, by which it tends to interpret all of church history and doctrine (its systematic theologies are typically attempts to define the teachings of evangelicalism), or into the supremely tempting image of itself as successful, respectable and smart in the eyes of the modern world. The vision it sees in the first, since evangelicalism has rejected fundamentalist rigor, is of insufficient strength, quality and depth to impose the old fundamentalist zeal for orthodoxy onto its secularizing vision of itself; so while it is presently becoming visibly wider, Offner compares the width to the Potomac, which in places is several miles across but only a few feet deep. And the strength of the secularizing vision is such that I see nothing to stop this river from descending into the same swamp in which the Protestant mainline churches are presently floundering. Those who are watching the evangelical colleges and seminaries know how quickly this descent is now taking place, principally through the feminist/inclusivist rapids.

The dialectic by which evangelicalism makes this movement between fundamentalism and modernism involves a subtle interaction between the intelligentsia and the people in the pews. The latter, as one might expect, are typically more conservative and tend to resist innovation in church doctrine and practice. But they too are faced in the course of their everyday lives with powerful temptations to worldliness and the cognitive dissonances these create in Christians, especially in Christians who read the Bible, and they look to their leaders to help them cope. They may appreciate permission, for example, to use politically correct patterns of speech, since the public square is demanding it of them with ever greater intensity.

The intelligentsia, for their part, are under even greater pressure, for the similar requirements of the prestige academy and its press have become nearly absolute within the last generation. As a result the intellectual's suspension between the old faith and modernity has become almost unbearably taut. As the academic world grows ever more hostile to Christianity, anything resembling Christian orthodoxy is now called fundamentalism, and is regarded (rightly) as irredeemably antipathetic toward the mind of the new world order and as non grata at its ivied well-shrines. More than ever before capitulation to the *Zeitgeist* is the price of the doctor's degree, and more than ever this capitulation is the dark secret of the doctors of philosophy at the evangelical schools. The troubles of which one is reading with radical teachers, feminists in particular, in these colleges and seminaries are the inevitable result of payment for the degree with surrender to the spirit of the age and the conflicts those who have done it have with people who managed to retain their intellectual virginity.

Although this may at first sound odd, I would place far more emphasis on certain evangelicals' dislike of ECT in this sphere of bad conscience rather than in traditional disagreements between Protestants and Catholics on the economy of salvation. I have come to believe that there is a deep intuitive fear of catholicism of any type among a large and growing number of evangelical intellectuals. Having eschewed fundamentalism with the greatest possible vigor, they find the two major paths of creative and reflective labor that open before them are the essentially catholic and the essentially modernist. While some still hesitate between them and others are at least somewhere on the catholic path (where I would place strongly confessional Protestants), a great many have struck out quite firmly on the modernist way. (This includes, it appears, many who took the "Canterbury trail," becoming Episcopalians. Caught up in that denomination's rapidly changing life, they are in danger of becoming ceremonial modernists.) The evidence of this is that the institution that forms their intellectual horizon is the academy and not the church, and the criteria of judgment they employ are increasingly progressivist and antitraditionalist. Evangelicalism was pregnant with this change from its inception.

The terrible, gnawing desire of intelligent fundamentalists for the intellectual respectability that was taken from them in the early years of this century is the mad wife in the attic of the evangelical academy. While she is hated and her presence is hardly ever admitted, she in fact weighs on its mind at all times and controls the directions it takes.

So then, the negative reaction to ECT is of at least two kinds. One is that of those more catholic Protestants to whom Cardinal Ratzinger referred when he spoke of our battling ancestors who we can now recognize as closer to each other than they knew. Their heirs are still with us; they represent the traditional theological disagreements between Catholic and Protestant believers. These differences turn on questions of fact upon which we still have no resolution, but those who hold them may be able to come to the place where they recognize each other as brothers, and for now that may be victory enough.

The other is those whose anticatholicism arises from another quarter of the spirit. When these appeal to justification by faith alone they are appealing to the revivalist soteriology of the evangelical masses, who associate the doctrine with their belief that once one has a punctiliar conversion experience, one's soul is eternally secure. But their deeper concern, I fear, is that these masses not take the right fork toward church and tradition when they have taken the left toward the strongholds of the spirit of the age. These are hard, blunt words, I know, but these are my own people and I think I know them, and I do not think Roman Catholics in particular will be able to understand the evangelical reaction to ECT unless they understand the divided mind of the movement. The fundamentalist side, as retarded and unattractive as it may appear, is the repository of the catholic mind of evangelicalism. It is unshakably creedal (although it would not say it this way), antimodernist Christianity that is willing to die for the faith, and it is regarded with high disdain in the centers of evangelical culture and learning. The other side is nearing the end of a gradual conversion to everything the early fundamentalists opposed.

The Identity of the Church

Protestants who have actually attempted to understand Roman Catholicism tend to sputter in frustration when they see the massive and entirely plausible impregnability for which the term "the church" stands in the Catholic mind, against which their picayune objections to certain points of doctrine and their spiritualizing conception of the church (backed as it is by nothing more impressive than two thousand squabbling sects) seem so paltry. Those of us who have allowed themselves to be struck by the glories of Rome cannot but come away with the troubling intuition that we, despite what we still think are legitimate objections to Roman Catholicism, are (as the Orthodox typically see us) really only little Romans ourselves. Rome has traditions; we do too. Every denomination has hundreds of them, and they have every bit as much authority as an ex cathedra pronouncement. Rome has popes; so do we—thousands of them. Rome is an ordered episcopal hierarchy in which the priests and the laity are of different orders. So are we, only it is all unofficial, and our real priests are the professors. The first and only fundamental Protestant objection to Roman Catholicism, I would venture, is not to the parts but to the conception of the whole, and for that perspective I have come to agree with the Orthodox that one must step outside the Western church.

For this reason also I agree emphatically with Father Neuhaus's observation that the first in the order of ecumenical priority must be the relationship between Orthodoxy and Rome, for only in the resolution of their differences can the first and fundamental objection of Protestantism to Roman Catholicism, which has to do with the identity of the church itself, be addressed. These two communions, to the eyes of Protestants its older sisters, must decide between themselves who is the church, for in doing so they cannot help but begin to decide at the same time what is the church, which is the decisive ecumenical question. My own indelicate way of putting the matter is that when these two great ladies can agree between themselves who is the real Mrs. Jesus, faithful Protestants could join them under the terms of the agreement, for the real ground issue that divides the West would in that agreement, if it were true, be decided.

"If it were true" is an important proviso, for such an agreement could also produce an antichurch. Indeed, the Scriptures tell us to expect such a thing and to expect it to be ecumenical, and so to my final comment on Father Neuhaus's *kairos*. I think I see it too, but it frightens me, for the shape of the world these days is such that the true union of Christians may finally be consummated on this earth by a mingling of their blood, not just in separated regions but, as in the days of Diocletian, in all places where there are Christians, as the shadow of the dark wing falls over the whole earth in a way that it never has before.

The history of the church in the world appears to me a great crescendo-diminuendo, rising from the pianissimo of the pre-Constantinian age to the fortissimo of the imperial church, and now again piano, and hasting toward a final pianissimo of which perhaps our Lord spoke when he asked, "When the Son of Man returns, will he find faith on the earth?"

For me the calculus of how far we must progress together as Catholics, Protestants and Orthodox does not reach deeply into our disagreements, but only to the place where we can recognize each other as Christians—the importance of which Father Neuhaus repeated a number of times. That is enough to bring us to the place where we can die together, and to establish the conditions for this I believe to be our principal duty to the next generation.

3

PROCLAMATION & PRESERVATION
The Necessity & Temptations of Church Tradition

Harold O. J. Brown

*A*t many times in the history of God's dealings with his people, they have been confronted with the demand to make a choice. Moses told the Hebrews, "Choose life" (Deut 30:19), and Joshua demanded, "Choose you this day whom ye will serve" (Josh 24:15). The choice between the Lord and idols, between God and Baal, is clear. But there are times when the choice one is offered is a bad choice, one that one would prefer not to have to make: the choice in Utah between hanging and a firing squad, for one sentenced to death; the choice in the Netherlands—sometimes preempted by quick-thinking physicians—between dying slowly in great pain, because methods for the management of pain are ignored, or dying quickly by presumably painless suffocation at the hands of a physician. Christians and their churches today are impaled, so to speak, on both horns of a dilemma: the one horn, being pressured to choose between two essentials, when one needs both; the other horn, being forced to take one, presumably the lesser, of two evils, when both alternatives are intolerable.

Many bad choices are offered in the realm of religion, sometimes between false alternatives, when one really ought to take both, sometimes between Scylla and Charybdis, or in the modern vernacular version, between the devil and the deep blue sea, when neither alternative permits viability for the church or the Christian. We are asked to choose between the false alternatives of doctrine and practice—they need not, should not, be mutually exclusive alternatives; between the pope and the "paper pope," that is, the Bible; Scripture or tradition; Scripture or church; faith alone or faith plus works. The problem with these choices is that either they are not real choices or they are not real alternatives. Sometimes the alternatives are not mutually exclusive— right doctrine or right conduct—and one could conceivably have both; sometimes neither is acceptable, and one ought to reject both.

A False Alternative: "Dogma" Versus "Life"

We have all been frequently told to reject dead orthodoxy for living faith. This choice would not be hard to make: it is self-evident that we ought to choose living faith. But if the choice were put: "You can have either orthodoxy or living faith," we would have to refuse to choose, or demand that we be allowed to choose both. Sometimes the choice one is asked to make is not presented in categorical terms, but one is merely asked to set a priority; this may be legitimate, but it can also be a rhetorical device consciously or unconsciously intended to make us disregard something of great importance. Sometimes assigning top priority becomes in effect a choice for one and a rejection of the other.

A bad choice is frequently offered to us today—not the worst of the bad ones we shall examine, but bad enough. That bad choice is a false alternative: right doctrine, or orthodoxy, to use the familiar term, and right conduct, or orthopraxy, to bring in the fashionable neologism. This question implies that faith and practice are opposites, or at least that they are in tension with one another. I remember that this was suggested when I first began the study of theology at the University of Marburg in Germany—the stomping ground of Rudolf Bultmann, where he encountered Martin Heidegger and José Ortega y Gassett. (Unfortunately for the future of theology, Heidegger made more of an impression on him than Ortega y Gasset.) After we were informed of all the critical questions, doubts, uncertainties, and the like that were supposed to pervade the New Testament, the professor of practical theology came to raise our spirits, he thought, by saying, "Now that you have heard the theory, let's hear what practice has to say." There were dangerous implications in this approach, which seemed to suggest first that what the New Testament really means will necessarily conflict with the life of the church, and second that the practical minister has to ignore theology, "die wissenschaftliche Theologie," as the Germans like to put it.

This supposed conflict or opposition between doctrine and life, faith and practice, orthodoxy and orthopraxy, runs through both the liberal-ecumenical and traditionalist-orthodox camps, although it takes on different forms in each. In liberal, ecumenical circles, the term *orthopraxy* has been developed as an alternative to orthodoxy. The tension is presented as one between theory and practice, faith being considered a theory and therefore assumed to be of little use to people who are starving or suffering political or economic oppression. First they have to be given practical help in the form of food, freedom, jobs, and the like.

This false alternative is rhetorically quite clever. Because *orthos* means "right," most Christians will have scruples about throwing "ortho-"anything away. However, if we can find another ortho-word to put in its place, the very theological and right-sounding word *orthopraxy*, we may be able to make the transition without distressing too many traditionally or conservatively minded members of our flocks who otherwise might think that we were abandoning the gospel for social action.

The implications of this alternative are clear: one has the choice between believing right (theory) and acting right (practice). Jesus himself laid the emphasis on doing the will of God (Mt 7:21), that is, on orthopraxy. The implication is apparent: it makes no difference what you actually believe, as long as you are working for world peace, social justice—and perhaps for gender equality and politically correct language.

In more conservative circles the tension is usually seen not as one between thinkers and dreamers on the one hand and doers and movers on the other hand, between theoreticians and practitioners, but rather as a tension of a different kind, the question about what is acceptable and pleasing to God. It is not, Should we give priority to thought or instead to action? but rather, How can we be saved? Is it by faith alone, or are good works necessary?

The apostle Paul is usually cited as the great advocate for justification by faith alone, and this citation is clearly correct (Rom 3:28). In addition he is also said to contradict James, who is interpreted as claiming that we can be saved by good works and thus as flatly contradicting Paul. Does James actually speak for works righteousness, and does what he means contradict Paul's message? It is true that James tells us, "Faith without works is dead" (Jas 2:20), but is Paul so different? Paul himself warns that "neither circumcision availeth any thing, nor uncircumcision; but faith which worketh by love" (Gal 5:6 KJV). James writes, "I will show you my faith by what I do" (Jas 2:18 NIV). To the best of my knowledge, no reputable Roman Catholic teacher has ever asserted that one can be saved through good works without faith, and it is unusual, although it happens, to find an evangelical saying that there is such a thing as true, saving faith that is devoid of works. This is another example of the kind of forced choice between false alternatives that will tend to mutilate either our faith or our Christian life or both.

Another important false alternative with which we are often presented is the alternative between pope and paper pope, a clever rhetorical device. Inasmuch as America, historically a kind of Protestant culture, has a long tradition of suspicion of papal authority, of "popery," those who oppose the concept of binding authority in religion find it easy to discredit the historic Protestant view among unreflective American Protestants by claiming that the doctrines of inerrancy and infallibility make the Bible into a paper pope. Thus they easily gain support for a repudiation of authority in religion altogether. It would be more sensible first to ask the question of whether the Christian religion really is based on divine revelation, authoritatively and reliably given, or not. This is a matter of historical as well as spiritual truth. If the answer is yes, then one can ask where this authority is to be found, whether in the papacy, church councils, the Scripture, academic theology or someplace else, and which of these or which combination of these is sufficient to guarantee the truth of a doctrine. But if the answer is no, then one need ask no further. The alternative, pope or paper pope, begs the question.

"Orthopraxy versus orthodoxy" and "pope or paper pope" are cries that we still hear from time to time, but for us there are two more significant pair of false alternatives being presented today: the first is Scripture or tradition, the second, Scripture or church. It is more than appropriate to ask the question, How are we to rank these, in their order of priority or authority, Scripture, tradition and church? It is inappropriate and misleading to demand that we choose between Scripture and tradition, Scripture and church (or even tradition and church).

These pairs are not mutually exclusive or mutually contradictory, or at least they need not be. Even those of us who say *sola scriptura* and consider the Bible the *norma normans* cannot do without tradition, nor can we do without the church. Both Eastern Orthodox and Roman Catholic liturgy and life are permeated by Scripture: both are unthinkable without it. The question is not whether they hold it to be authoritative or even infallible and inerrant. (Traditionally both Eastern Orthodoxy and Roman Catholicism took the infallible authority of Scripture as a given, although now both great confessions harbor representatives of various critical views, and some Catholics seem determined to repeat all of the mistakes made and to some extent already repented by Protestants in their attitude toward the authority and reliability of the Bible.)

Both the Orthodox and the Catholics may be seen as teaching not *sola scriptura* but "Scripture plus." The Orthodox, if I understand them correctly, have always affirmed the primacy of Scripture and understood tradition as interpreting Scripture. The tension between this view and that of the Protestant Reformers is less marked than that between Protestantism and Roman Catholicism. Prior to the Reformation it was permissible to advocate a view of Scripture like that of Luther and Calvin within the Roman communion. At the Council of Trent, however, it was made mandatory—and remained so until the Second Vatican Council—for Catholics to acknowledge two equally authoritative sources of divine revelation, Scripture and tradition, which created a clear conflict with Protestantism and to a lesser extent with Eastern Orthodoxy. Tradition as a source of revelation was supposedly derived from the oral teachings of Jesus during the forty days between his resurrection and his ascension. One difficulty inherent in this supposition is the fact that many doctrines and practices that came to be accepted as part of tradition appeared centuries after the time of Christ. One needs to postulate a Spirit-guided development of doctrine, as the leading Roman Catholic convert of the nineteenth century, Cardinal John Henry Newman, taught.

Today the approach of most conservative Catholics seems not very different from that of Eastern Orthodoxy on this point, coming to look upon tradition as the interpretation of Scripture rather than as a second source and deemphasizing elements of popular piety that are supported only by tradition with no clear basis or even hints in biblical revelation. Modernistic Catholics are not so different from the most "liberal"[1] varieties of Protestants: both tend to reduce Scripture to at best a human witness and response to God's revelatory activity; both have no use for tradition—except for the pseudoscientific, academic traditions they themselves develop.

A Personal Excursus

One of the problems that we confront in theology and the churches today is that many serious, godly Christian people, the ones who support our institutions and promote evangelism and missions, do not think in terms of either theology or the church. Some of them can debate relatively precise points of doctrine, such as the relationship of the rapture of the saints to the great tribulation—a particular interest of evangelical and fundamentalist Protestants, for any who may not be familiar with the issue. They do not see the broad scope of theology, which touched upon all of reality, God and man, time and eternity. During the summer of 1994 I was able to take part in a seminary-sponsored tour of the main centers of the Protestant Reformation. The participants were all committed Christians from our evangelical churches—I almost said "traditions"—and were all familiar with the Bible and well-informed concerning what we call the plan of salvation. They were all impressed by Wittenberg, the Castle Church where Luther posted the Ninety-five Theses and preached, and by the quiet, modest Preachers' Seminary where he once taught and lived. But what surprised me, as I lectured to the participants, was the fact that they missed two of the main points—Luther's points, as he preached and taught, and mine, as I tried to make them plain to my audience.

First, with respect to theology our good evangelical churchmen and churchwomen did not think of Christian theology as a system or a structure of truth that spans the universe and refers to the totality of human experience. They thought more in terms of individual doctrinal statements to which they gave heartfelt assent, but not only did they not have what Calvinists like to call the Christian world and life view, they were hardly aware that there is such a thing and certainly did not think one important, not to say essential. Whereas earlier in the century Christians of many denominations vigorously opposed the doctrine of evolution with its naturalistic and atheistic implications, the situation today has changed. It is not so much that most Christians have been persuaded that evolution is true and can be reconciled with faith, but rather that they have comparmentalized both, so that they not only do not conflict with one another, but do not even come into contact. Perhaps if our group had had weeks instead of days to discuss this point, I could successfully have shown them that biblical truth does indeed imply a rather comprehensive world and life view, but at the time this way of thinking was unfamiliar to them. They did not reject it; they were simply not aware of it.

Of course everyone has some kind of a world and life view, some kind of a *Weltanschauung,* but with many, perhaps most people, it is implicit, unconscious, neither clearly worked out nor capable of being clearly stated. To use a term made popular by Harry Blamires, most of our people do not have a Christian mind nor even think about having one. Thus, for my group, Luther's great theological achievement lay in simplifying the plan of salvation, telling us what we must do to be saved (only believe), not in reforming theology and the comprehensive Christian view of reality to correct the deformations that had accumulated during a dozen centuries.

The first problem is by no means confined to my small tour group, but is found all over Christendom. It is a lack of awareness of the fact that biblical and theological truth relates to God's whole universe, not merely to individuals and their personal salvation. As David Wells writes in his book with that title, there is *No Time for Truth.* The second problem, also widespread among Christians, is a failure to understand the nature of the church in the sense in which Luther did. For Luther the church still was what it had always been: a transcendent structure extending across both space and time. Instead the church came to be seen only as an association of individuals, a sort of religious Rotary Club. In attempting to tell them that what Luther was trying to do was to reform the church, I ran into the problem that the group members did not see church for what it is, the body of Christ, "the blessed company of all faithful people," with its origin in Eden[2] and its future in heaven. They did not think of it as having a form that could be deformed and need to be reformed. They thought that Luther only wanted to eliminate some abuses, to change some forms of worship, to redirect the spiritual life of individuals, to eliminate some practices seen as superstitious or idolatrous, and of course to preach the gospel of salvation by faith alone. They did not seem to understand the church as a transcendent, historical and suprahistorical reality, and that it was this church that Luther wanted to look different after he finished his reforming work. They thought in terms of personal reformation, not of the transformation of an institution.

If we follow the thinking of Karl Barth in *Protestant Theology in the Nineteenth Century,* this limited idea of the church is the result of the excessive individualism that came into the church, as it did into Western society as a whole, with the Enlightenment. It is particularly widespread in the United States, where individualism is one of the few truly sacred articles of American faith. Without implying any disrespect—for my fellow travelers were serious, godly Christian people—I think that they considered the church rather as one might consider a golf club. A man or woman might be an enthusiastic golfer, play golf every Saturday and perhaps on Sunday as well, read golfing magazines, take golf lessons, go to golf resorts and know all of the famous golfers past and present, but would hardly think of himself or herself as belonging to an eternal Golf founded by the First Golfer and stretching through the centuries until all its members reached the great Eighteen Holes in Eternity. And while golf may become an obsession, very few people would think that there is a golfing world and life view or a golf mind.

A Common Mind

This little excursus points up the lack of something that we need if we are even to talk seriously together, not to speak of working together and fighting as allies, namely, a common mind, and specifically a common Christian mind. We do not all need to think absolutely identically, but until and unless we come to share many of the same ways of thinking and understanding, we shall never be able to share ways of work and worship, and we will certainly not be able to form a common front against the onslaught of secularism and modernity. The creation of a common Christian mind will inevitably clash with the mentality of our late twentieth century, with our postmodern age.

In our efforts to discover or create a common mind we run up against the sort of obstacle described by the late Allan Bloom in *The Closing of the American Mind,* by Neil Postman in *Amusing Ourselves to Death,* as well as by many others. It was foreseen by Ortega y Gasset in *The Revolt of the Masses* and by Pitirim A. Sorokin in *The Crisis of Our Age.* For Ortega y Gasset, "luxury" produces stupefaction, and three generations of stupefaction produce generalized stupidity. It becomes hard to teach people to think alike when they lose the knack of thinking at all.

Faith and Salvation

A crucial New Testament verse for us today is the words spoken by Peter to the Sanhedrin: "There is no other name under heaven given to men by which we must be saved" (Acts 4:12 NIV). There are so many pernicious tendencies abroad in Christendom that it is hard to say which one of them is the worst, but the loss of Peter's conviction certainly ranks in the forefront. Indeed, there is no reason for us Christians of varying stripes and colors to wrangle with one another about doctrines and practices unless what Peter said really is true, that there is no other name but that of Jesus by which we can be saved. Because we are convinced that salvation comes only through Christ, it becomes tremendously important to know him by faith (see Jn 17:3). In order truly to know him, it is evident that one must hold a true faith—not necessarily a vastly extensive faith, with primary and secondary fundamental and nonfundamental doctrines, the whole lot, but certainly a true faith.

Faith, Christian faith, gospel faith, is clearly the *sine non* of salvation; it is a necessary condition. Let me use a metaphor to characterize some of the problems of the high liturgical fellowships, Catholicism and Orthodoxy, and of the more talk-oriented, *kērgyma*-centered Protestant fellowships. If we consider faith as a climber trying to scale a snowy mountain peak, the one group will have him so packed in flowing garments that he can hardly move, while the other might have him naked and barefoot—or to be more decent, in shorts and sneakers—and in imminent danger of hypothermia.

We might ask whether faith is a sufficient condition, as Luther proclaimed by adding the word *allein* (alone) in his translation of Romans 3:28: "justified by faith alone." The word *alone* is not there in the Greek; Luther acknowledged this but argued that in German it is necessary to add *allein* in order to make the meaning clear. But, to return to our metaphor, the faith by which we can find eternal life is no naked faith. Elsewhere, as already noted, Paul speaks of "faith which worketh by [is active in] love" (Gal 5:6): there is no bare faith. We should have no difficulty agreeing. A merely formal faith, intellectual assent to the truth of the gospel message without a transformed life, cannot be saving faith. But if we do not want a bare faith, with what should it be clothed, and when do the clothes become encumbrances?

One need not necessarily take the Bible physically into one's hands, but there is no way to come to faith without hearing and accepting its message. We need not entangle ourselves with the question of election and free will.

Scripture states quite clearly, "Faith comes from hearing the message, and the message is heard through the word of Christ" (Rom 10:17 NIV). There is no possible substitute for proclamation of the gospel message of salvation through faith in the person of Jesus the Christ and in the atoning sacrifice that he made for our sins, for the sins of the whole world (1 Jn 2:2). Christian faith involves the communication, comprehension and acceptance of a message with very definite contents, a message that can be paraphrased, expressed orally, expounded in preaching, summarized in tracts, but one that is basically contained in normative form in the written text of the Bible.

There can be no question that the Bible, the Word of God, is of the utmost importance for Christians and for the church. It is the means or tool to which we naturally turn in order to proclaim the gospel message today. The Reformation and especially the Pietist movement produced massive printing and wide distribution of the Bible, which now is universally available in all developed, free countries: more Bibles and Bible portions have been printed, in most of the human languages, than any other book. The book itself, the actual printed text, can be the agent that brings people to faith in Christ, although more often a human witness or witnesses will be used by the Holy Spirit to bring the message home to the heart of the seeker.

If the Scripture is normative, how did it come to be normative? On a naive level Roman Catholics may argue that the church—the Catholic church—gave us the Bible and that church authority authenticates it. Protestants answer that it is the Scripture that creates the church. It certainly is true that it is the Word that creates the church, which is built on the foundation of the prophets and apostles (that is, on their word), but it would be a historical anachronism to say that the Bible created the church. This is true only to a certain extent even for the churches of the Reformation and for some of those of more recent origin. Not one of the great Reformers or founders of newer fellowships came to the Bible cold, as it were, but each had been exposed to the Christian message and to forms of Christian life before being "reformed" by the text of Scripture.

Liberal biblical criticism used to date the books of the Testament as late as possible, but in recent decades the tendency has been to date the Gospels, Acts and Epistles ever closer to the time of Christ himself. Still, there is no way to make the New Testament older than the church. It is evident that Christians were preaching, baptizing, witnessing and frequently enduring martyrdom for years before the written Gospel texts were in circulation, and that the church was there a century or more before the whole of the New Testament became available. The message of Jesus was proclaimed and handed down in oral form even before the final versions of the Gospels were put into writing and long before the New Testament as a whole was available. But does this mean that it was the church that produced the Scripture and the authority of the church that authenticated it?

No, that would be saying too much. The counterargument also makes sense. New Testament books were accepted as the Word of God and placed in the New Testament canon because the churches of the time recognized them to be the Word of God; the work of the Holy Spirit enabled the human writers to write God's words, and it is this work of the Spirit that makes the Scriptures divinely authoritative and preserves them from error. In addition the Holy Spirit was active in the early congregations and councils, enabling them to recognize the right Scriptures as God's Word and to reject others, such as the apocryphal Gospel of Thomas, as inauthentic.

While acknowledging that the Bible is younger than the church, Protestants see the providential hand of God active in the fact that the Gospels and other New Testament messages were set down in written form and thereby made available to Christians through the centuries and across the continents. When the Scripture is acknowledged to be the very Word of God, it necessarily becomes the *norma normans,* the "norm that norms" the other standards, such as creeds, catechisms or manuals of discipline.[3]

The Sufficiency and Insufficiency of Scripture

It is a bit unfair, but one might say that for some—Orthodox and Catholics— the question seems to be, How much can we add to the message? whereas for others—the Protestants—the question is, How much can we pare away from it? Four attributes of Scripture are emphasized in our Reformation tradition: authority, sufficiency, clarity, and, especially among Reformed or Calvinist Protestants, autopisty or self-authentication. There is hardly any quarrel among traditional Christians, Catholic, Orthodox or Protestant, about the first of these attributes, authority. The other three are all challenged to varying degrees and for different reasons.

The concept of the autopisty of Scripture is particularly emphasized in the Calvinist or Reformed tradition. Calvin maintained that just as the individual books of Scripture authenticated themselves to the congregations and councils of the early church, the text of Scripture imposes itself on the believer as God's Word without the need of ecclesiastical authority or even of human arguments. Calvin's view was that while many arguments can be brought forward to persuade us of the authority of the Bible, in the last analysis it is the Word itself that must persuade us that it is the Word of God. The Holy Spirit moves in the reader to create an awareness of the divine origin of the Bible. Thus Calvin sees a parallel phenomenon to the acceptance of the books of the Bible by the early church in the acceptance of the authority of the Bible by believers today. Just as the Holy Spirit persuaded the early church to acknowledge the right texts as Scripture and to reject the others, so today he moves in the life of the individual to create conviction that the Bible is God's Word, fully authoritative and completely reliable.[4]

The concept of the clarity or perspicuity of Scripture is also hotly debated. Roman Catholicism in particular was hesitant about putting the Bible in the hands of ordinary believers. The church maintained its authority by keeping the texts that might have challenged it out of the hands of most Christians. Even though that hesitancy has been largely overcome in the twentieth century, Catholicism still has a latent suspicion of the ability of the ordinary Christian, without the aid of the church's teaching authority, the magisterium, to read and understand Scripture without falling into serious errors and confusion.

It would be good if we "Bible-believing Christians" could say that the perspicuity of Scripture is sufficient to enable everyone to recognize errors and false doctrines. The way in which sects and heresies have proliferated among people who profess biblical inerrancy and assume that they understand the Bible correctly lends plausibility to this Catholic apprehension. The solitary study of Scripture—a Gideon Bible in a hotel room, for example—has led many individuals to a saving faith in Christ, but solitary study, cut off from the fellowship of believers seeking the guidance of the Holy Spirit and lacking any awareness of the faith of the church through the ages, is often a source of serious error.

It is the remaining attribute, the sufficiency of Scripture, that creates the greatest problem among our three confessions. I think that it is fairly easy to defend the concept of the sufficiency of scriptural teaching for salvation. We can readily find what we need to know to accept and trust Christ and his sacrifice for the forgiveness of our sins in the text of Scripture itself. Stories abound of people who have been converted through a simple encounter with the Bible—a Gideon Bible in a hotel room, for example.

The difficulty comes after individuals have come to saving faith in Christ: where do they go from there? They have to "go to church." Let us think first of worship, then of the common life of the congregation. In using these terms we implicitly accept the notion that the Christian is called to membership in a body; that just as no baby is physically born solo, but always has at the very least a mother that it needs to nurture it and to permit it to grow, no one is born again as a child of God alone, but must always have a spiritual mother to bear and nourish him or her.

Contemporary Protestantism tends to have a defective view of the fundamental significance of the church. The early Reformers were very different. We have already mentioned Luther. For Luther one becomes a Christian by faith and *eo ipso* a member of the invisible church, so by this tautology there is no salvation outside the church. Calvin too echoes the medieval view: *extra ecclesiam nulla salus,* no salvation outside the church. Of course he does not mean this in the sense of Pope Boniface VIII in the bull *Unam sanctam,* which asserts that it is "absolutely necessary for every human creature for salvation to be subject to the Roman pontiff." For Calvin the church is existentially vital for salvation, even if it is not a formal requirement in the sense of Pope Boniface. Calvin's view was rather a practical, experiential one, based on the fact that it is the church that offers the message of salvation, teaches the Word of God, and provides the environment in which a believer can be strengthened and admonished and grow spiritually. Calvin would have considered the placing of Gideon Bibles in hotel rooms commendable but hardly sufficient. In any event it is rather a truism of all Christian bodies that the individual believer needs to be part of a believing and worshiping community. One of the cardinal features of any human community is the development of tradition, a mechanism that enables the community to identify itself and to distinguish those who belong to it from those outside of it. There is no such thing as a community without tradition, whether it formally recognizes it or not.

The Inevitability of Tradition

It is commonly said that Luther's goal in his revision of worship was to purge the church of every inherited traditional element that is unscriptural; the

English Reformation proceeded in a similar way. Calvin sought to restructure Christian worship using only what he considered required or illustrated in Scripture; this is why his church is called "reformed": it was reshaped, or at least the attempt was made to reshape it, strictly on scriptural principles. Churches in the Reformed tradition like to think of themselves as having recovered a New Testament style of worship, and perhaps at the outset they were close to it. (Reformed and free church worship today has been greatly influenced by the Enlightenment, with its interest in education and edification, leading to a situation in which many Protestant services resemble academic lectures with a musical introduction and ending.) At the time of the Reformation, even Calvinist services retained many structural elements taken over from the Catholic Mass. Various liturgical reforms since then have given rise to a kind of high Calvinism with many clear similarities to Catholic worship. It is very difficult to create a form of truly Christian worship that does not to some extent resemble forms of the past.

Since Vatican II, changes in Roman Catholic practice have increased the similarity between Protestant and Catholic worship. For example, the fact that the Roman Catholic priest, now called the celebrant, stands behind a table facing the congregation, rather than with his back to the worshipers, facing an altar against the wall, makes the Catholic Mass look like many Protestant communion liturgies. There are symbolic values in both postures: the priest who faces the altar with his back to the worshipers symbolically leads them before the throne of God and represents them before God. The minister who stands behind the table facing the congregation symbolically offers to them the gifts of God in Word and sacrament, "the gifts of God for the people of God." Should one or the other be mandatory? I think not. It ought to be evident that all of these forms of worship draw from a very old tradition; hardly a detail is literally prescribed in the Bible. If we depend only on data to be found in the Bible to organize our worship, we might well be limited to something like the Lord's Prayer and the words of institution of the Lord's Supper.

There are two things to be observed about these aspects of Christian worship: first, it is evident that even though the New Testament can "make you wise for salvation," as Paul wrote to Timothy (2 Tim 3:15 NIV), it does not tell us how to worship; it does not even tell us that there ought to be organized and fixed forms of worship. Second, it is also evident that in most Christian groups, unwritten tradition has had a major role in creating forms of worship. The worship of the first Christians carried over elements of Jewish worship. It is also apparent, from what we now know of the worship of the early Christian communities, that in spite of adversity, persecution and limited resources and facilities, from a very early date they had a rather structured form of worship, one that we would characterize as liturgical rather than free.

If we look at the free churches in the Protestant communions, even those which claim to have "no creed but the Bible" show that they have plenty of tradition, though they may formally disdain the concept. Sunday school is not in the Bible, and Sunday school for all ages has become a virtual sign of fidelity to the Bible. Sunday evening services and Wednesday night prayer meetings are going the way of the Roman Catholic priest with his back to the congregation, but their loss has been painful, and many pastors and parishioners have felt that their disappearance is a sign of decline, loss of faith and loss of spiritual zeal. In many circles personal devotions, the "quiet time," is regarded as mandatory. Of course neither the Sunday evening service nor the prayer meeting is mandated in the Bible; Sunday worship is not mentioned, and the closest thing to a command to engage in common worship is the line in Hebrews, "Let us not give up meeting together, as some are in the habit of doing" (10:25 NIV). The change of worship from the Jewish sabbath to the Christian Sunday, and the application of the fourth commandment, referring to work on the sabbath, are both traditions, not demonstrable from Scripture. Several Christian groups virtually mandate abstinence from tobacco and alcohol, although the one is not mentioned in the Bible and use of the other is actually encouraged, in moderation of course. Sophisticated believers and pastors in such groups generally acknowledge that the Bible does not mandate teetotaling and agree that the Lord turned water into an alcoholic beverage, wine, as his first miracle, although some go so far in their condemnation of all alcohol that they claim that what he produced was unfermented grape juice. For the rest, prudential arguments are cited, often in such a way as to become commandments. Specific and clear commands of Scripture may be ignored, among them the commands relative to going to law before unbelievers (1 Cor 6). Christians do in fact go to court against one another, and it is seldom that Christians who criticize others for this going to court before unbelievers will take upon themselves the responsibility spoken of: "Is it possible that there is nobody among you wise enough to judge a dispute between believers?" (1 Cor 6:5 NIV). It should be apparent that although the simple message of the gospel is sufficient for salvation, it is not sufficient for Christian worship, fellowship, community and life.

The Danger of Traditions

James wrote that faith without works is dead (2:17). It appears that faith without a surrounding matrix of tradition is naked. The difficulty is that the essentials of the faith are lean and sparse. Every life, both the life of the individual and community life, such as that of a congregation, needs to develop a structure of forms and conduct in order to function. No human being can order his or her life about one simple injunction (such as "Be all you can be!"). Of necessity everyone learns and develops ways of doing things, from brushing teeth to choosing clothes; people establish patterns such that their friends and neighbors can recognize them by those patterns. In a similar way every community necessarily develops forms and behavior patterns of many kinds, from the way its members recognize one another to the things that they can expect from one another as mutual duties and responsibilities.

In Matthew 15:9, citing Isaiah 29:13, Jesus warns against teaching as doctrines the commandments of men. In many respects the gospel message is, if we may say so reverently, too simple for us: "Believe on the Lord Jesus Christ, and thou shalt be saved" (Acts 16:31). Once I have believed, what then? Consequently we fill out and amplify the gospel message with the *mandata hominum,* the commandments of men. This is inevitable and necessary, as we have argued. But it is also dangerous. When tradition proliferates it may obscure the vital truths of the gospel. Where traditions lead the naive to trust in some human idea—a holy relic or a particular pious devotion, for example—rather than in the atoning sacrifice of Christ, they may imperil their own salvation. This is the personal danger of tradition.

The organizational danger of tradition lies in the fact that as traditions help confessions to identify their own members, far more than the message itself it is the traditions that come to divide Christian confessions from each other. We can all recognize this when we realize that on the popular level, conflicts between confessions are often expressed in terms of things that are minor if not irrelevant: Why does the priest have to speak Latin? He doesn't any more, and so now traditionalist Catholics ask, Why can't the Mass be in Latin? (It can, subject to a number of conditions.)[5] The clash of traditions is not limited to such simple misunderstandings, however: it involves major theological differences, such as the invocation and intercession of the saints, the understanding of the Eucharist, the teaching authority of popes, bishops and church councils.

Our problem is that we need traditions to live; the Bible itself, the undisputed source of Christian truth, does not provide us with enough content to fill out our worship, not to say our lives. This fact has been too little recognized among Protestants, like the pious fiction "No creed but Scripture!" Sooner or later in different communities and at different times our traditions always proliferate to the point at which they conflict with one another. How can we maintain a rich community life, which necessarily develops traditions out of which it lives, without creating conflict with other Christian communities whose traditions develop differently?

The nature of our answer must differ depending on the group to which it is addressed. From the Protestant perspective it is necessary to tone down the polemic against tradition as though it were necessarily a falsification of simple Christian truth. To do this we must recognize and acknowledge the role that tradition plays in our own worship and life. This should help us gain a tolerance for the importance of tradition in other communions. Inasmuch as we ourselves cannot live and worship without it, we need to acknowledge that the thing in itself is not only not evil, but a necessity. We need to accept tradition in principle, and at the same time we need to be critical of traditions, both our own and those of others, lest they become the "commandments of men" about which Jesus warns us.

For Catholics and Orthodox it is necessary to recognize the human factors in the growth of tradition. Traditions do grow and proliferate, and they may be rich and helpful or rife and suffocating. Beware of placing the *mandata hominum* even alongside of the Word of God as though they were equal to it, and certainly never place them above it. Do not require of others what your traditions, but not God himself, require of you. "In my Father's house," Jesus said, "are many mansions" (Jn 14:2; "rooms" in contemporary translations). Different mansions probably will have different furnishings. One can live in an Oriental palace; one can also live with Scandinavian modern furniture. It is hard, although not altogether impossible, to live without any furniture, and it certainly is not very nice.

Essential to Christianity is faith; this is why the term *faith* can be used to stand not merely for the content of the message believed, as well as for the believer's trust in God, but even for the totality of Christianity. Faith does take on forms; indeed it must. Part of the genius of the Christian message is that God in his providence has left us considerable freedom in developing the forms that outline our worship and our lives. Some things are constant and firm. The church must be an *ecclesia audiens,* a listening church, ever attentive to the Word of God.

I am reminded of the words of the late Dutch Christian philosopher Herman Dooyeweerd, which he wrote in a personal letter to me after a lecture tour that I organized for him, a tour that taxed his health: "I thank God that he has permitted me once more to bear witness to the reforming power of his Word, even for science and philosophy." We experience the formative power of that divine Word in worship and life; we must also bear witness to its reforming power for our theology, our liturgy, our tradition. The church can never be merely *ecclesia reformata* without also being *ecclesia semper reformanda.* Paul speaks of our having the treasure of the knowledge of the glory of God "in earthen vessels" (2 Cor 4:7). We usually assume that Paul is referring to himself and to us as his fellow stewards of the gospel, but do his words "earthen vessels" or "pots of clay" not also apply to our institutions and to our traditions?

The late Pitirim A. Sorokin, with whose work I have been much preoccupied in recent months, was a Russian Orthodox Christian; according to his son Sergei, a college friend of mine, he observed the great feasts but was not active in any particular congregation. In a number of works he called for and actually anticipated a great spiritual renewal to bring us out of what he called the crisis of our age. In order for the churches to become the motive force of such a renewal, in his view it was necessary for them to do two things. First is to rediscover the vital presence of the living God.[6] This is something that cannot be manipulated or engineered; in both liturgical awakenings and the charismatic renewal of our days, we may be experiencing a beginning of this rediscovery. The second requirement can be stated rather simply: the churches must practice what they preach. The simple instruction of Micah 6:8, to "do justly, and to love mercy, and to walk humbly with thy God," was affirmed by Jesus himself, who warned that heaven is not for those who say, "Lord, Lord," but for those who do the will of his Father in heaven (Mt 7:21). I pray that a great revitalization of theology and a fresh appreciation of the rich traditions that surround the life of God's people will not be limited to the intellectual realm, but will once again produce the lives of witness, sacrificial service, self-giving love, and where necessary, martyrdom, that enabled the Christian church to spread across the entire globe.

There is an earthiness, a humanness, if you will, about our traditions in which the gospel is embedded and, we hope, properly framed but not hidden. We may observe these traditions and honor them as suitable, acceptable and even necessary, but we must avoid claiming that they are mandatory, determinative or obligatory. There is a vital lesson here to be learned for all of us: tradition can possess grandeur but also pose temptation. We need it; we cannot live without it. We cannot hold oil or wine in our hands, at least not much of either: we do need vessels. Perhaps gold or crystal vessels are the most desirable, but clay pots will do as long as they are solid. Containers are necessary and not to be scorned, as otherwise the precious contents will be lost. But the contents are more precious than the containers.

I venture to hope that these meetings that we are having will contribute both to reformation and to formation, for all of us. Tradition: we cannot do without it, but we must take care not to let it do too much to us.

A Response to Harold O. J. Brown

Father Andrew (Isaac Melton)

*A*s a member of the Orthodox Catholic Church for nearly seventeen years, and now as a monastic and the editor of a small magazine, I have been asked to respond to Dr. Brown's paper. While I am enthusiastically Orthodox, I have also been around long enough to be fully aware of the existential weaknesses and problems of modern Orthodoxy, which awareness tends to temper any triumphalism. One sometimes marvels at the survival of the Orthodox Church into the late twentieth century, not only in spite of centuries of vicious persecution but also in spite of betrayals by some of its own people, both clerical and lay. In this regard I recall the half-joking lament of Anglican traditionalist Dotty Faber, whom some of you will remember. "I'm gonna found a church without people," she would often exclaim, "because it's people that cause all the problems."

The survival of the Orthodox Church and its recent rapid growth is surely nothing less than a wonder worked by the Holy Spirit. But precisely because of this ongoing wonder of divine grace, as well as the Lord's promise to be with his church, Orthodoxy still presents the fullness of apostolic and patristic teaching and therefore has very much to offer to the modern world.

I was introduced to the thinking of Harold O. J. Brown some thirty years ago as a young deacon in the Episcopal Church when I read an article by him in, I believe, *Christianity Today*. So impressed was I by that article that I clipped it out, took advantage of the amazing new Xerox copy machine acquired by the local bank, whose president was one of our vestrymen, and shared the article with quite a number of friends. I would not be surprised if I still have a copy of that now antique photocopy packed away in some box.[1]

So I approach responding to Dr. Brown's thesis with a strong bias in his favor, a bias of some thirty years' standing. His paper only confirms that positive bias and my respect for him. I find myself in total agreement with where he wishes to lead us in his paper, namely, both to a common Christian mind and to a renewed appreciation of the place of Tradition. Those two goals are of course closely related.

Dr. Brown notes that Christians and Christian communities are often impaled on both horns of a dilemma, as false choices are offered in religious questions. From the Orthodox viewpoint these false choices derive from the strong penchant in medieval Western Christian thought to rigidly categorize aspects of theology and of church life in general, a penchant that was passed on intact to the Protestant confessions at the time of the Reformation. Dr. Brown quite rightly recognizes that we need to get past these false choices, and in so doing he echoes the primitive theological balance preserved in Orthodoxy. Rigid categorization goes far beyond ecclesiastical bounds: it is, for instance, the major reason many of the same people who fervently shout "never again" with regard to the Holocaust at the same time see no connection whatsoever between euthanasia, abortion and Nazi eugenics.

In Orthodox teaching there are many distinctions and for that matter many paradoxes, but there are no dichotomies between the invisible church and the visible, concrete body of Christ on earth (the latter being the earthly icon of the former); or between faith and practice; faith and life; religion and life;

orthodoxy and orthopraxy; faith and works; grace and *synergeia* (graceful response to grace); Word and sacrament; sacrifice and memorial; the liturgical priesthood and the priesthood of the people of God; liturgy and life; contemplation and action; liturgy and contemplation; mysticism and dogma; or formality and informality; and so on. All of these pairings are seen as dynamically related to each other and as interdependent aspects of a whole. That from time to time and from place to place dichotomies do appear on the practical level in the Orthodox church is the result not of Orthodox theology but rather of human frailty and blindness, and also, in many cases over the past four hundred years, the result of the adoption by some, often unwittingly, of non-Orthodox tendencies toward minimalism, reductionism, rigid categorization and modern secularism.

Dr. Brown wants to avoid a false choice between Scripture and Tradition, and he clearly sees their interdependence, but he continues to view Scripture and Tradition as totally distinct categories. That is the issue that I wish to focus on in this response. Let me suggest that what I offer today from the Orthodox viewpoint is a shift in perspective rather than a corrective to Dr. Brown's paper. This perspective should shed different light on the issue of tradition, leading us further down the road toward a common Christian mind.

Vatican II attempted to clarify the Western medieval notion of Scripture and Tradition as the dual founts of revelation, but perpetuated the dichotomy between them. The Protestant Reformers had reframed that medieval Roman Catholic concept into the question "Scripture or Tradition?" and so it remains in the Western denominations to this very day. But this split between Scripture and Tradition is not found in the writings of the fathers, Eastern or Western, nor, as we shall see, in the Holy Scriptures themselves.

St. Irenaeus of Lyons was a second-century bishop in Gaul and a native of Smyrna in Asia Minor. He represented in his person and his teaching the one worldview of both Eastern and Western early Christian thinking, and he echoed the whole patristic tradition when, in about A.D. 180, he equated the Tradition with the Christian faith itself:

> While the languages of the world are diverse, nevertheless, the authority of the Tradition is one and the same . . . For the Faith is one and the same, and cannot be amplified by one who is able to say much about it, nor can it be diminished by one who can say but little. (*Against Heresies* 1.10.2)

Ironically the same Reformers who framed the question "Scripture or Tradition?"—undoubted lovers of the Scriptures—failed to note, it would seem, that not only is the word *tradition* itself very scriptural, but so is the early Christian usage of the word *tradition* to refer to the total Christian package. I would like to review quickly the place of the word and the concept *tradition* in the New Testament, not to instruct my hearers in what you very likely already know, but simply to underscore this point.

The Greek word for tradition, *paradosis*, means "that which has been given over." The English word *tradition* derives from the Latin *traditio*, which also means "that which has been handed over." "Tradition" in the New Testament refers to teaching or practice that has been handed over.

Like some other New Testament words such as *flesh* and *world, tradition* in certain places has a negative meaning, but in other passages it has a very positive meaning. The New Testament clearly distinguishes between mere (and sometimes negative) "traditions of men" (see Col 2:8; Mk 7:3) and that Tradition which comes from God. For instance, in 2 Thessalonians 2:15 we read: "Therefore, brethren, stand fast and hold the traditions which you were taught, whether by word or our epistle." In this verse the phrase "by word" indicates that there are traditional teachings and practices not specifically spelled out in the Bible; the words "by our epistle" provide clear biblical witness that Scripture is itself written-down tradition.

The term *tradition* is used in the same positive sense in 2 Thessalonians 3:6: "But we command you, brethren, in the name of our Lord Jesus Christ, that you withdraw from every brother who walks disorderly and not according to the tradition which he received from us." In this highly positive and godly sense, the term *tradition* is found even more often in the New Testament in a verbal form. That verbal form does not have an equivalent in normal English usage, in which the word *tradition* is employed only as a noun. In the Greek New Testament, however, the verbal form *paradidōmi* (to tradition) is used over and over. Let us note that this highly positive and godly usage of the words *paradosis* and *paradidōmi* has specialized significance in the New Testament—it connotes not merely the passing along of some information, but rather the solemn and sacred delivery of grace-filled faith and practice. John 19:30 gives us a feeling for the solemnity associated with this concept of traditioning. There both the verb *paradidōmi* and the noun *pneuma* are used with two-layered meanings. This verse is translated in the New King James Version as "He gave up His spirit," that is, he died, and clearly that is one level of meaning John wished to convey. But in John's typical fashion he purposely uses the verb *paradidōmi* to convey as well an even higher meaning. For the phrase can be equally translated, "he *traditioned* his Spirit," indicating the death of the Lord was in effect a proto-Pentecost. The solemn significance of tradition and traditioning is also seen in Matthew 11:27 and in Luke 10:22, where Jesus tells us that all things are traditioned to him by the Father.

In Romans 6:17 we read of the "form of doctrine which was traditioned to you" (my translation). In 1 Corinthians 11:23 Paul speaks of the account of the institution of the Eucharist that he had received from the Lord, which in turn he had traditioned to the church in Corinth. Later, in 1 Corinthians 15:3, he reminds the Corinthians that he had traditioned to them the teaching about the Resurrection that he had received from others. In 2 Peter 2:21 the writer speaks of the holy commandment traditioned, obviously referring to the Christian way of life. Jude 3 translates literally, "the faith once for all traditioned to the saints."

Since in biblical usage "tradition" in the good sense refers to the gifts that God has handed over to his church, the Tradition in its fundamental reality is nothing less than the Father's twofold gift to us of his only begotten Son and his Holy Spirit. All else in holy Tradition manifests, communicates and is imbued with that fundamental and ongoing traditioning of the Son and the Holy Spirit. In this regard let us make note of the fact that the Orthodox Church does not consider any authentic part of Tradition to be merely human tradition. Without believing that every iota of Orthodox practice is immutable or on the same level as the sacraments, the Scriptures and other core elements in the Tradition, the Orthodox Church nevertheless regards all aspects of holy Tradition as Spirit-inspired. This includes the relatively less important customs of Tradition (sometimes called "traditions with a little *t*," which we will discuss at the end of this response), which therefore, even given their possible mutability, are nevertheless honorable and worthy of respect, to be treated reverently and not to be laid aside lightly.[2]

Dr. Brown has noted that Orthodoxy and the Roman Catholics[3] may be seen as teaching not *sola scriptura* but "Scripture plus." From what we have seen, however, it is clear that Orthodoxy does not in fact so view the Scriptures. In the Orthodox view Tradition does not add to the message—Tradition is the message. The New Testament Scriptures are the canonized, written, basic expression of the Christian Tradition, the message in one form. (The Old

Testament records the pre-Christian preparatory Tradition.) For that very reason the contents of the holy Tradition other than the Scriptures are not seen as some kind of plus, but rather as other expressions of the same faith in different forms. From the Orthodox perspective, therefore, the Reformation dogma *sola scriptura* implies the wrenching of the Scriptures from their God-given context, which is the whole Tradition.

In the Orthodox Tradition it makes no sense to rank the Scriptures and extrascriptural Tradition, nor is it an issue which came first temporally, the New Testament Scriptures or the church. For the church from the beginning has manifested the basic teachings found in the New Testament, and at the same time the New Testament expresses the basic teachings of the church. We may indeed distinguish between Scriptures and the rest of the Tradition, but the Scriptures without the rest of the Tradition, which together define the way of life of the living church, have their proper meaning clouded.[4] If pressed, we would have to affirm with Dr. Brown that all extrascriptural Tradition in effect interprets Scripture, but then we would immediately have to add that by the same token extrascriptural Tradition is also interpreted by the Scriptures. This affirmation, however, is made with the dichotomy of Scripture and Tradition lurking in the background, and there exists the danger that making such a response might contribute to the perpetuation of the dichotomy. In the purely Orthodox context it would not so much as occur to anyone to make such an observation, since for us it would not be unlike saying, "An icon symbolizes the person depicted therein, but by the same token the person depicted therein is symbolized by the icon."

Dr. Brown likens high liturgical faiths to climbers so packed in flowing garments that they can hardly scale a snowy mountain peak. One appreciates his concern, but this also implies another dichotomy that is not found in the Orthodox Tradition. For Orthodoxy high liturgy is no more foreign or opposed to pure and simple faith in Jesus Christ than is the Bible, which is itself highly complex, often difficult to understand, and frequently couched in what to some might appear to be obscurantist poetry designed to befuddle the credulous.[5] The answer to these parallel challenges is not the elimination of or selective excisions from either the Bible or the Liturgy in the name of "simple faith." The answer in both cases is the message at the heart of the apostolic *kērygma* that personal faith in and commitment to the Lord Jesus Christ is the continuing first step in Christian living. This primitive *kērygma* has not lost its force in the Orthodox Church with the passage of the centuries, for that personal faith is found in millions of modern Orthodox believers, faith in Christ mediated to them in a variety of ways, such as through reading and hearing the Scriptures, by the testimony and example of their parents and grandparents, by catechesis and by the Liturgy itself. Immersing oneself in the midnight service of Pascha, that is, Easter, it is evident the worshipers indeed know the risen Christ. Countless twentieth-century Orthodox Christian martyrs have expressed their personal commitment to their incarnate Lord, not in a "decision for Christ" during a revival service, but before a firing squad or in a Siberian death camp. When this basic prerequisite of personal faith in Jesus Christ is met, then the flowing garments of liturgy, no matter how high, like the flowing robes of Holy Scripture, no matter how obscure, are neither a straitjacket nor an albatross, but rather the wedding garment of salvation.

The traditional Orthodox attitude toward the Tradition is not minimalistic, and this fact is important in our discussion. As an example of this, the Orthodox approach and attitude toward liturgy is maximalistic: the unspoken motto is, Do as much as is feasible,[6] but with understood emphasis on the word *feasible*. The liturgical practice of the Great Church (Agia Sophia) in Constantinople in its golden age remains the liturgical ideal in Orthodoxy. Orthodoxy's inherent maximalism, however, is tempered by prudent pastoral recognition of personal limitations and present circumstances, so in the here and now we approximate the Liturgy of the Great Church as best we can.[7] On occasion that could even mean that a lone priest must serve the Divine Liturgy out of doors, with no more than one singer who alone constitutes the congregation.[8] But such circumstantial minimizing is never ever taken to be normative.

A number of modern Orthodox, however, particularly in America, have perhaps inadvertently moved toward a certain minimalism with regard to the Tradition by emphasizing the distinction between Tradition with the capital *T* and traditions with a little *t*. In modern English we often use the word *tradition* as a synonym for custom, and one supposes that those who take great delight in the distinction are trying to differentiate what they think of as mere customs from the Tradition itself. But why do they feel such an urgent and pressing need to make this distinction, where do they propose to lead us, and where exactly does one draw the line between the Tradition and a putative mere custom? They seem to be asking, How much can we abandon and still call ourselves Orthodox? One would wish they were asking something to the effect of, How much loss can we suffer before we lose our Orthodox *Weltanschauung*?

As we have seen, one can of course make distinctions within the Tradition. Traditions such as clerical beards or kissing the hand of the priest, for instance, obviously do not rank with the Scriptures or the Eucharist. But does that make the former merely traditions? They are widely so regarded, at least in North America. For that reason many American Orthodox maintain that traditions such as clerical beards, or even the scriptural admonition that women cover their heads in church, can be abandoned without doing any violence to the Tradition. As another example, in Orthodox history a number of other traditions, mainly liturgical customs, have changed over time. Do we therefore identify those as traditions with a little *t*?

History also reveals that with the passing of time, for one reason or another, on occasion a particular tradition may paradoxically even begin to violate the principles of the Tradition. At that point a change in the particular tradition will therefore be called for by the Tradition itself. The most obvious case of this is the question of liturgical language. A consistent historical principle of the Orthodox liturgical tradition is that the Liturgy is to be served in the literary language of the people. That traditional principle begins to contradict what has become traditional practice then the traditional language of a community is no longer understood by that community. One might therefore legitimately come to the conclusion that particular liturgical languages are traditions with a little *t*, but the principle that the language of worship should be understood by the worshipers is itself part of Tradition. In the traditional Orthodox view, however, even traditions (unless obviously and clearly contradictory to and/or deleterious to the Tradition and therefore not authentic traditions), however small, seemingly insignificant and even if legitimately replaceable, whether liturgical customs or disciplinary standards, are nothing less than closely related tiles, large and small, in the great mosaic icon of the Lord Christ that is Orthodoxy. Those who experience that icon with faith will not find it less than "the House of God and the Gate of Heaven."

For that reason I have a problem with the distinction between big- and little-*t* tradition. Such a distinction can be made, although that is not always the simple task some imagine it to be, and one should not rush into assuming some practice is merely a little-*t* tradition. One can argue quite convincingly that this change and that change would be valid and useful in what are identified, perhaps much too quickly, as little-*t* traditions, but in my own experience the motivation and principles underlying the push for change in customs or discipline are more often than not faulty if not downright destructive. As one small contribution toward achieving a common Christian mind, I would like to close with a look at several of those faulty motivations and principles. These adversely affect not only the Orthodox Church but all of us who value the faith. It needs to be noted that most of these principles either gave birth to or are characteristics of modern secularism. Those who hold these faulty principles tend, perhaps unawares, to espouse them as life-giving dogmas. They cling to these non-Christian dogmas with the rigidity and fervor of an evangelical fundamentalist. The secularist worldview created by these principles indeed functions as a religion for those who adhere to it.

In the mid-1960s I cravenly listened to friends who found my "fundamentalist tendencies" laughable, and as a result I chose to abandon several of my earlier conservative Christian beliefs. In other words, I swallowed some of these faulty principles and then I put them into practice in my life: the results were painfully destructive. Today I harbor no illusions whatsoever that these principles might be valid.

Minimalism. The minimalism and reductionism (which I like to call "merely-ism") that underlies many strident calls for change in Orthodox Church traditions, and sometimes calls for change in what is quite likely the core Tradition itself, has pervaded Western thought since the Middle Ages. This same minimalism underlies calls for changes in other Christian bodies as well. Such merely-ism gladly sets aside as "merely this" or "merely that" anything that gets in our way or that we find inconvenient. One motive for adopting a minimalistic approach in Orthodoxy is the desperate desire of people of immigrant background to be accepted in the social mainstream, but for more academic-minded Orthodox, the craving is to be accepted by one's secularist, non-Christian peers, so one begins to shed what is perceived of as "mere tradition." Aiding and abetting this minimalism is an unexamined acceptance of

Upside-down incarnationalism. In verse 35 of the ancient Western hymn known as the Athanasian Creed, we read that the incarnation was accomplished "not by the conversion of the Godhead into flesh, but by taking of the Manhood into God." Very many today have this upside-down. They focus so intensely and one-sidedly on God's self-lowering that they lose sight of fact that in the incarnation Christ came down to earth and emptied himself precisely in order to initiate immediately, from the bottom up, so to speak, a process of human and cosmic transfiguration and glorification, and that by way of crucifixion and death. Because of the incarnation, there are necessary ascetic, converting, purifying and transforming dimensions in Christian living. But the upside-down view seems to believe that by his incarnation Christ sets his divine seal of approval on the base, the tawdry, the mundane and even the corrupt. In a manner of speaking, upside-down incarnationalism therefore tends to baptize without converting. At its least pernicious it promotes the use of the street vernacular and tasteless music in the liturgy, but taken on to its logical term, inverse incarnationalism singles out even the blatantly perverse as a candidate for consecration. The most extreme but quite revealing example of this I have ever encountered was in a National Public Radio program I heard in 1985. A Roman Catholic priest (who most certainly lacked his bishop's *nihil obstat*) informed his interviewer and his audience that anonymous homosexual "acts of love" in a San Francisco gay bathhouse were for him the apex of incarnational spiritual experience. The only "incarnational experience" that took place in the baths was the repeated enfleshing of the AIDS virus in the immune cells of its victims.

"Tail-wags-the-dog-ism." Upside-down incarnationalism quickly leads to a tail-wags-the-dog mentality, in which the world, precisely in the sense where the New Testament uses the term *world* pejoratively, is viewed as having become in effect the incarnation of Christ and the sacrament of the Holy Spirit. For that reason this world is understood to set the agenda for the church, which agenda the church must follow to remain relevant, in touch, or however one might express it. In my own experience it is often middle-aged clerics, desperately grasping at relevance and hoping to prove they are still young at heart, who most easily fall into this mentality. A classic manifestation of this is the pathetic rationale offered by Archbishop George Carey of Canterbury for female priests in the Church of England: In society all jobs are open to women and the church will look foolish if it does not follow suit.

Secularism. The sheer unadulterated secularism of our times, eagerly blessed by Christians espousing upside-down incarnationalism, proclaims with a totally blind act of faith that "this world is it, and what you see is all you get." That underlies many calls for abandonment of tradition, both big *T* and little *t.* Why should we fast, be chaste or embrace simplicity of life, people ask, if this is it? Grab all the gusto you can while you can, since we pass by this way only once.

Darwinism. For more than a century and a half a Darwinist mentality has molded our thinking. Darwinism's underlying philosophical naturalism, which has roots in medieval merely-ism, is fundamentally atheistic and is a major source of modern secularism. Darwinism has also made the idea of continual and necessary progress dominant in our thinking. That has given rise to a rather arrogant intellectual Darwinism that demands that if one wishes to be *très chic,* it is de rigueur to be au courant with the ever-evolving intellectual fashions. New is better, new is to be preferred, for "newer is truer." Intellectual Darwinism has infected many a Christian, and that malady in part underlies the call for the abandonment of certain traditions as well as for changes in the core Tradition itself.

Nominalism. Merely-ism, that is, minimalism and reductionism, often joins hands with old-fashioned medieval nominalism—no thing and indeed no part of the human body has inherent value or significance. All things are whatever we would like them to be. Little surprise that a recent move by some gay liberation activists is to have the anus medically reclassified as a sex organ.

An impoverished concept of holiness. Resulting from merely-ism, nominalism and secularism is the almost wholesale loss of the concept of holiness in Western culture. Nothing is sacred about old people, marital fidelity, family ties, or very much else. Even among some Christians the Bible becomes merely a book, the liturgy of the Word is merely a pedagogical event and the Eucharist is merely a fellowship meal. As I once heard Father Alexander Schmemann of blessed memory comment, such Christians "think that if they sit down to chicken à la king and Chianti, they are making Eucharist!"

Subjectivism. The merelyistic-nominalist mentality also leads to wholesale subjectivism—if you feel it is true, then it is true for you, and that is all that counts.[9] Such subjectivism is the foundation of the still-flourishing drug culture, as well as the underpinning of the many sex-related questions of our times. For example, a fetus is merely a bit of tissue, because that is what we feel it is.

Egalitarianism. Most of us would find solid Christian bases for the political notion that we all equally have the basic rights to life, liberty and the pursuit of happiness. But egalitarianism is taken by many to an extreme that eschews any form of order or hierarchy and abhors the idea that one person might have more authority than another. Under the influence of Marxist thought (in particular through liberation theology), a new twist in the egalitarian mindset since the late 1970s is to see all human relationships in terms of oppressor and victim, or more recently in terms of codependency, unless all parties in the relationship are totally equal and autonomous. That is the basis upon which the radical feminists have called traditional marriage "institutionalized rape."

Just as philosophical Darwinism has given birth to intellectual Darwinism, so political egalitarianism has spawned a sort of intellectual egalitarianism that sees any sort of personal distinction as unjust discrimination. As but one example, this way of thinking is manifest in the many studies that purport to prove that all differences between boys and girls, other than the "merely biological differences," are purely the result of unfair social conditioning. The ever-evolving *Zeitgeist* is slowly emerging out of that highly unscientific view, but the strongly felt idea that distinction equals unfair discrimination remains a major force in much feminist commentary. Intellectual egalitarianism gets carried so far that even the distinctions necessary in logical thought become suspect.

Insufficient analysis. One encounters a refusal, born of egalitarian lack of respect for authority and a poor concept of holiness, to consider the possibility that the little-*t* traditions some people propose to abandon have much more positive significance and value than one could suspect. The question of clerical beards and covered female heads, for instance, might well have far more relevance than we ever imagined in a society being overturned by gender confusion. Here is but one result when a few of the foregoing faulty principles operate in concert. The au courant intellectual Darwinist fascination with myth à la Joseph Campbell is based squarely on the unspoken assumption that secularism is probably physically true, but what really matters is what you feel is true for you, not what might have roots in nature or express historical reality (and who knows what reality really is anyway). This means that as long as you sincerely believe your own truth, all myths are equal, which in turn means you are free to create your own meaningful, equally valid personal myth. One obvious problem with this approach is that potent myths like Aryan superiority therefore must also be accepted as valid, not to mention the mythology that inspired the Oklahoma City bombers! If we wish to discredit those destructive myths, we then must bid a fond adieu to the strawberry fields of subjectivist merelyism.

When so-called reforms in the church, based on a combination of such faulty rationales, are carried out, the result is not improvement but impoverishment. Much unnecessary pain and confusion have thereby been inflicted on millions, and it has all been in the name of making the church more meaningful and relevant for the people.

True traditionalism respects, applies and tries to live the Tradition in spirit and in truth, without being ridiculously picky or supercorrect. As we have seen, the Orthodox tradition includes within it awareness that moderation is often called for and an awareness that not every detail accepted as tradition is necessarily a sine qua non of Orthodox faithfulness. In fact those who do not recognize those moderating elements in the Tradition, and even worse, those whose traditionalism is only superficial, give traditionalism an undeserved bad name. Such "traditionalists" do as much harm for traditionalism as people who espouse the foregoing faulty principles. Faithful response to the *kērygma*, one needs to stress, is the basic element in authentic traditionalism: one must indeed repeat and believe in the name of the Lord Jesus in order to be saved. When that prerequisite repentance and faith is present, then Pelikan's aphorism about Tradition being the living faith of the dead, but traditionalism being the dead faith of the living, while losing none of its cuteness, does lose most of its validity.

Traditional Orthodox maximalism tempered by pastoral prudence is also apostolic and patristic maximalism. It is the balanced maximalism of Christ himself, who has called us to perfection, even as he decries legalism, for legalism itself is but a form of minimalism (e.g., what's the least I can do and still be saved?). If we all adopt this maximalistic approach to the whole Tradition as we have received the same from the fathers, which is our common heritage, we will be well on our way to a common Christian mind.

4

FATHER, GLORIFY THY NAME!

Patrick Henry Reardon

*T*here persists among Christians today a disposition to talk of God apart from Christ. I do not mean that Christians, at least serious Christians, explicitly theorize that the true God can be known without Christ. I am referring rather to a tendency to describe even the true God, the God of the Christian revelation, in very general, abstract terms not rooted in the living experience of God in Christ. It seems that some Christians, having found God in Christ, feel free to separate him from this unique font of revelation and to discuss and describe him in terms that are hardly related at all to the vision of his glory manifest in the face of Christ. They take their ideas about Christ and God and then run off to elaborate them, as it were, on their own.

A chief and disturbing instance of this disposition, I submit, is what I venture to call today's *via negativa vulgaris,* or popular apophaticism. Speaking of God as mysterious and incomprehensible has become very much the style in certain quarters. In my opinion it is most often just another symptom of modern murky thinking, however, and I plan to argue that it has nothing to do with what the church has traditionally called apophatic theology. At the hands of this cultivated modern obscurity, God is not exactly the *mysterium tremendum et facinosum*. He is something far less dangerous, foggier and more user-friendly. Let us call him the *mysterium nebulosum sed multum flexibile et valde accomodans*. That is to say, the climate of this theology may be described as overcast, but it predicts no storms.

The formulation of this popular apophaticism tends to run along the following lines: "God is very, very obscure. God transcends all of our conceptual images of him and all the language in which we speak of him. In thinking about and discussing God at all, we constantly run the danger of idolatry. All references to God must be as indefinite as possible, because every description of God, in the measure that it is dogmatically clung to and insisted upon, may become a graven or molten image." An attempt is sometimes made at this point to justify this apophatic vigilance against doctrinal formulation by some vague and very caliginous reference to those fathers of the church especially known for their emphasis on the *via negativa*. The latter appeal is apparently supposed to quiet any scruple that Eastern Orthodoxy may feel about the whole process.

Our popular apophaticism then goes on to contend that the contemporary theological task is twofold. First, we are informed, one must maintain a strict caution. Mysterious means blurry, so when one speaks of God it is imperative not to say anything very clear or precise. One must be constantly aware of the peril of identifying him with any concept descriptive of him, for such descriptions are only symbolic and metaphorical. Inasmuch as the new *via negativa* ultimately negates the whole theological pursuit anyway, theology should glory in being hazy, haphazard and provisional.[1]

Thus, according to this popular apophaticism, when the creed speaks of God as Father, theology must recognize that we are dealing only with a metaphor. All positive statements about God must then be negated. A proper respect for this consideration should prompt us to say that God is also not Father, for the image of fatherhood must be apophatically transcended. If God is Lord, the same reasoning insists, he also surpasses the category of lordship, and that image too only testifies to its inadequacy.

Second, according to the *via negativa vulgaris*, precisely because all imagery descriptive of God is merely metaphorical and provisional, a proper evangelical solicitude will prompt theology to balance and condition such descriptions in various ways in order to make God more attractive. For example, recognizing that the proclamation of the gospel may be hindered by its inclusion of images perceived as negative or oppressive, it says that theology should endeavor at the least to neutralize these images or perhaps even to expunge them altogether. In this way theology can be made more relevant to the contemporary concerns of feminism, political liberation and other just causes. Sometimes this process of reinterpretation is described as a "development of doctrine," and rather shaky allusions are made to the thought of John Henry Cardinal Newman. This last move is apparently supposed to quiet any misgivings that Roman Catholicism may feel about the whole process.

We may illustrate this procedure by the same examples. Because the modern apophaticists associate the terms *Father* and *Lord,* by which we have traditionally spoken of God, with the oppressive patriarchies of the past, something must be done about them. And since the *via negativa vulgaris* has already pronounced them to be inadequate and possibly misleading, there should be no problem about dealing with them decisively. If God is not really Father, then "Father" is no more appropriate a name than "Mother." So why not employ both names, or perhaps neither? As for "Lord," the word is nearly Nietzschean; it so smacks of oppression that maybe it should be dropped altogether or at least neutralized with a less masculine equivalent like "sovereign."

The impact of this development is already being experienced by some Christians in their congregational worship. Whether in the new Methodist service book in use for the past three years or so, or the so-called trial liturgies inflicted from time to time on those long-suffering Episcopalians, or the various new hymnals adopted by several of the major and mainline churches, traditional references to the Persons of the Holy Trinity are rapidly disappearing. They are being replaced by such expressions as "Grandfather, Great Spirit," "God, our grove," "Jesus our Mother," "our father and mother God" and (everybody's all-time favorite) "Bakerwoman."[2] Moreover, the same license with regard to altering language about God also characterizes several so-called translations of the Psalms intended for congregational use.[3]

Diverse Forms of Obscurity

Now what are we to say to all of this? Mystery and incomprehensibility certainly are appropriate terms when we speak of God. God is mysterious; God is incomprehensible. The ancient worship language of the church describes him as *aphatos, ineffabilis.* But does this mean that all language about the living God is equally meaningless? If an apophatic principle in Christian theology makes it finally impossible to take seriously the defined affirmations of the creed, then what is distinctive about the Christian faith? Other great religions, such as Islam and Hinduism, likewise describe the divinity as incomprehensible. Are we Christians only saying the same thing as they? Do we have in Jesus a knowledge of God not otherwise available, or only a somewhat more advanced God-talk? If we Christians may no longer with a quiet conscience refer to God using the names *Father* and *Son,* are we really talking about the Christian faith?

We should suspect here the presence of some terribly perverse thinking that needs to be cleared up. A critical reexamination of Christian apophaticism would seem to be the proper way of tackling the problem, and I suggest that we start by being apophatic about apophaticism, that is to say, that we commence by examining what Christian apophaticism does not mean.

First, Christian apophaticism is not primarily an epistemological affirmation. When we Christians call the true and living God incomprehensible, we are saying something about God himself and not simply describing the limitations of our knowledge. It is not as though we knew where God was, so to speak, but were obliged to confess our inability to get there. The difficulty of getting to God is a statement more about God than about us. It is not as though we human beings, by dint of deeper reflections, more lucid musings or improved heuristic patterns, might somehow attain closer to the summit. That we do not know the living God describes him, not us. The difference between God's inner truth and our knowledge is not one of degree. Even to say that God transcends our concepts is inadequate, inasmuch as it suggests some relationship between our concepts and God, whereas Christian apophatic theology insists that there is no such relationship.

For that reason quantitative assertions of human ignorance here are only metaphorical. In speaking of God as immeasurable (*ametrētos*), we are affirming infinitely more than the inability of our minds to take his measure. The difference between God's truth and human thought is not merely dimensional. In Christian apophatic theology we are not simply asserting that the human mind is insufficiently capacious to contain him. If that were the case, references to God's incomprehensibility would have only an anthropological significance. It would be an apophaticism owing more to Feuerbach than to St. Basil.

Second, Christian apophaticism is not a merely logical reference. The incomprehensibility of the living God is revealed truth, not a fact available to unaided reason. I believe it very important to insist on this point. Left to its own lights, philosophy too can certainly affirm an incomprehensibility of "God" in the sense that that concept is plainly tautological. If, as Aristotle wisely taught, understanding is the knowledge of things in their causes, then the principle of causality is the basis of understanding. And if the concept *God* excludes his having a cause, then philosophy itself may properly speak of the incomprehensibility of God.

Such a tautology is characteristic of the standard cosmological arguments, such as Aristotle's Unmoved Mover, for example, which becomes the Prime Mover in Maimonides and the *ens necessarium* both of Avicenna and of the Third Proof of St. Thomas Aquinas. I submit that a philosophical *via negativa* is even more pronounced in the entirely negative formula of St. Anselm's ontological argument: *aliquid quo nihil maius*, something than which nothing greater. It is no less true, I think, of Descartes's thesis that the concept of God, inasmuch as it cannot be causally traced, must be assumed as a principle independent of any other. The philosophical concept of God, because it outruns, as it were, the principle of causality, is tautological and as such defies understanding. But this consideration is still infinitely short of what Christian theology means when it calls the true and living God incomprehensible *(akatalēptos)*. Philosophy required no special revelation to know that a tautology is logically inaccessible.

Third, Christian apophaticism is not Neo-Platonic ecstasy. Plotinus too writes of the divinity as incomprehensible, but this is his way of identifying that divinity as The One *(to hen)*. Observing that discursive reason necessarily introduces a distinction between the knower and the known, Plotinus recognizes it as an exercise in multiplicity. That is to say, I cannot really know The One if I remain distinct from The One, for in that case he is not The One; he is rather the other. So the goal of Plotinus's mystical quest is a union with The One *(to hen)* in which the distinction between objectivity and subjectivity is removed. What the Neo-Platonist pursues is an absolute simplicity *(haplōsis)* by which is dissolved the difference between the knower and the known, and this is accomplished by way of the ecstatic experience of "unknowing." Inasmuch as it eliminates the essential difference between God and the soul, however, the Neo-Platonic unknowing is obviously not to be identified with Christian apophaticism.[4]

Even earlier than Plotinus, expressions of this mysticism of absorption are also found in Hindu monistic literature as variants of the famous phrase *Tat twam asi,* That art thou, from the *Chandogya Upanishad.* For example, the *Maitri Upanishad* says that Brahman has two forms: Brahman formed and Brahman formless, manifest and unmanifest, Brahman He and Brahman It. To the extent that the *atman,* or soul, remains distinct from and relates to the Brahman, the Brahman is He, personal, manifest and formed. But the mystical goal of this *Upanishad* is the absorption of the soul into the Brahman, as the drop becomes lost in the sea or the ray of light returns to the sun. Individuality disappears. There is no longer Brahman He; there is the formless, the unmanifest, the impersonal, but ultimately real, Brahman It. Brahman and *atman* are one, so that there is no more distinction between objective and subjective.[5]

Christian Apophatic Theology

The similarity of such Hindu speculations to Plotinus's ecstatic unknowing is obvious enough, but I am more struck by their affinity with a certain doctrinal aberration rather often found among Christians. Let me identify the aberration by posing this question: Is God ultimately It or He? What is first in God, so to speak, essence or person? Using the classical terms of Christian theology, is God first *ousia* or *hypostasis, essentia* or *persona?*

It is unfortunately customary to dismiss such questions as excessively speculative. To raise them is to risk being indicted for unnecessary Byzantine subtlety. Nonetheless, how this question is answered will make a great deal of difference to our analysis of apophatic theology. If the "font of divinity"—the *pēgē theotētos,* to borrow an expression from St. Maximus the Confessor—if the font of divinity is the divine essence, *ousia,* then God is ultimately impersonal. That is to say, there is in God a priority of It to He.

In fact one runs across this idea rather often among Christians. I have lost count of the times that I have read in Christian theological literature such lines as "the one divine being, who subsists in three modes of existence." In other words, *ousia* precedes *hypostasis.* I am calling this a theological aberration because it does not conform to the ancient creedal formulas of the church. The Apostles' Creed, for example, does not begin with the divine essence but with the Person of the Father: *Credo in Deum, Patrem omnipotentem.* The Nicene Creed likewise does not make God first *ousia* but *hypostasis,* not *essentia* but *persona:* "I believe in one God, the Father almighty."

In identifying God first as the Father and then affirming that the Son is begotten of the Father and that the Holy Spirit proceeds from the Father—in holding, that is, that the *patēr* is the *archē*—then we necessarily affirm patriarchy in the Holy Trinity. Indeed, inasmuch as all the Christian dispensation is trinitarian, there is a necessary inference that "all of the Christian revelation is patriarchal."[6]

This, the Father without origin, *ho patēr ho anarchos,* is the God whom "no man hath seen . . . at any time." We would not know him at all, except that the only begotten, who is in the bosom of the Father, has revealed him to us (Jn 1:18). The Son can reveal this Father to us because he is in the bosom of the Father; he and the Father are one (10:30); he is of the same essence *(homoousios)* as the Father. This, the Holy Trinity, the Father and the Son with the Holy Spirit, is the truly incomprehensible God.

When one says that God is incomprehensible because we are unable to conceive of the divine essence, that is correct; but I believe that it is still an inadequate way of describing Christian apophatic theology. Christian apophaticism, unlike the impersonal apophaticisms of Hindu monism and Neo-Platonism, is first an apophaticism of person. What Eastern Orthodox theology calls the "root of divinity" *(rhiza theotētos)* is not the divine *ousia* but the Person of the Father. Christian apophatic theology, then, stresses primarily the incomprehensibility of the *hypostasis,* the divine *prosōpon,* not even known to be unknown unless revealed, unknown only as revealed, and revealed as unknown. It is the Person of the Father who, in the fullness of his hypostatic freedom, is the source of the Son and the Holy Spirit.

To hear some Christians talk, you would think that we all along knew exactly who God was and then, "in these last days," identified Jesus by reference to this God whom we knew all along. One might imagine that we were dealing with a long-time and very familiar friend who finally got around to telling us that he also had a son that he had been keeping secret from us and had at last decided to come clean about it. Or it would be as though Jesus, when he revealed himself to us as God's Son, expected to be greeted by the words "Oh yes, we already know your Father. Isn't it strange that he never mentioned you!" And then we would go on to investigate how to manage the proper damage control for our monotheism.

The truth is that we do not know the true God except in the Son who reveals him. Indeed, "whoever denies the Son does not have the Father" (1 Jn 2:23 NASB). And the Son reveals this Father to us as eternal mystery, as infinitely incomprehensible, as the Father who lives in unapproachable light.

If Christians speak of the incomprehensibility of God, it behooves them to be certain that they are talking about the true and living God manifest in Jesus Christ, not some philosophical Unmoved Mover or *ens necessarium,* not some general, all-purpose divinity. *Ho Ōn,* the living God, is not the *ens necessarium* to which clear thinking may reason its way. He is rather the personal God whose glory shines on the face of our Lord Jesus Christ. Philosophy cannot reach nor does it even begin to guess at the real incomprehensibility of God. The true God is infinitely more inaccessible than any philosophy ever suspected.

The incomprehensibility of the true God is a very specific and utterly unique mystery, not a general obscurity that we must somehow manage as best we can by juggling our metaphors. When Christians speak of the incomprehensibility of God, they are not talking of darkness but of light. According to Holy Scripture, this unapproachable light *(phōs aprositon)* "no man knows nor can know." The name of him who abides in this light is the Father (1 Tim 6:16).

So when we invoke God as the Father we are pronouncing only what we know in Christ. It is solely in the Holy Spirit that we call out "Abba, Father" (Gal 4:6; Rom 8:1, 5),[7] and it is imperative that we do not second-guess the Holy Spirit. "Father" is the ultimate apophatic pronouncement; there is no way for it to be further apophaticized. At no time is it good theology to say that the Father of Jesus is not the Father.

Therefore to pretend that in teaching us to call him Father "God adopted patriarchal concepts in order to reveal his will and purpose to the human race"[8] is to make a claim about God for which there is no warrant in Holy Scripture. Where is the ground for taking such a stand? This is purely private theology. It has nothing to do with either the Bible or the church. There is no theological justification for thus attempting to get beyond the Father. Such an endeavor scarcely differs from Meister Eckhart's pursuit of a "God beyond God."

A Figure of Speech?
Patristic literature asserts that in God the name *Father* is not titular but real. It is a "proper" name,[9] pertaining to God as God and not simply to God's relationship to us. Before he is our Father outside the Trinity, he is the Son's Father within the Trinity (see Jn 20:17).

Although it is difficult (and ultimately futile, one suspects) to classify God's name *Father* (his Christian name, so to speak), within normal rhetorical and literary categories we should at least avoid reducing it to a mere figure of speech, for such a reduction is the very opposite of apophatic. It is just one more endeavor to conceptualize a mystery. Indeed, to classify Revelation's language about God at all, to cramp it into rational categories of any sort, is the attempt to bring divine truth under human control. Moreover, it appears to me that classifying the Father's proper name as only metaphorical is not, in practice at least, to explain it; it is to explain it away. It makes God's revelation nothing more than a restatement of our ignorance of him, so that we are back where we started, as though there had never been a divine revelation in Jesus Christ.

Nor is it my point to distinguish between a metaphor and a simile, for the difference between the two is only a matter of grammatical configuration. Constructed on a comparison, both have the same conceptual content; a metaphor is only an implicit simile. In either case, whether explicitly or by inference, we are asserting that one thing is like another.

A legitimate example of such a figure of speech is referring to God as a mother, a reference justified by Holy Scripture (see Is 49:15; Mt 23:37) and favored by some of the saints. Whether expressly or by implication, this usage is founded on an analogy; it is a comparison to motherhood as known through human experience. One is asserting that God's relationship to us has certain maternal characteristics.

In no wise would it be theologically correct, however, to call God the Mother in any sense comparable to calling him the Father. Even some defenders of the traditional faith miss the point here by drawing attention to how God's relationship to us is more fatherly than motherly. Such arguments from propriety *(ex convenientia)* are inadequate and even misleading. To refer to God as Father is not simply to assert that God's relationship to us has certain fatherly characteristics, as distinct from motherly characteristics. It is not as though God somehow reminds us of dear old Dad, or even what dear old Dad should have been.

Such attempts to explain how God is our Father represent a failure to accept the apophatic force of Christian theological language, an endeavor to reduce the mystery to human dimensions. When we invoke God as our Father, however, we transcend all that we know of fatherhood in this world; we make a formal departure from the purely figurative realm, surpassing pious metaphor to an absolutely unique and personal mystery. As the solemn introductions to the Lord's Prayer in both the Roman and Byzantine liturgies indicate, to call out that holy name *Father* into the mystery of God, "the unapproachable light," requires an ultimate boldness. It is a deed of enormous daring, for which nothing in this world prepares us.

Our God is not a father; even less is he like a father. He is the Father, the one "from whom all paternity in heaven and on earth is so named" (my translation, Eph 3:15). We are speaking in strictest propriety here, not mere analogy, inasmuch as this Father has begotten us in Christ, who is God's Son in an absolute and eternal sense. The invocation "our Father" reflects the fact that, in Christ and only in Christ, we ourselves have become "partakers of the divine nature" (2 Pet 1:4 NASB).

Because of this incorporation into Christ, we are not simply *called* the children of God; we *are* the children of God (see all the major manuscripts and most translations of 1 John 3:1). Indeed, because of our participation in the divine life, it is even more proper to call God "Father" than to give this name to our own earthly fathers. Truth to tell, in comparison with this Father, no one on earth should even be so called (Mt 23:9).

Some Christian thinkers have at times expressed this mystery rather boldly. St. Thomas Aquinas, for example, citing Ephesians 3:1, 4-5 as his authority, speculates that the name *Father* pertains more properly to the First Person of the Holy Trinity than to any other instance of paternity. Indeed, he goes on explicitly to deny that calling God "Father" is a metaphor at all, saying of the Lord and his Father: *proprie et non metaphorice dicitur Filius; et ejus princip-ium, Pater*—"properly and not metaphorically he is said to be the Son, and his origin *(principium = archē [!])*, the Father."[10] Other theologians, particu-larly Eastern Orthodox, will find St. Thomas much less apophatic in this respect than the Cappadocian fathers. Doubtless they are right, but I believe that his speculations here, rooted as they are in Holy Scripture and the dogmatic affirmations of the church, are worthy of reverent consideration. The Angelic Doctor's remarks are not on a par with the irresponsible neo-gnostic speculations noted previously.

A Feminine Father and Son?

Some Christians, nonetheless, bothered that God is invoked by so obviously a masculine noun as "father," continue to look for ways of softening or neutralizing that word by recourse to more feminine images. It is even alleged that the Christian tradition itself encourages such a pursuit by providing suitable models.

The major ancient text occasionally adduced in support of this thesis comes from the Eleventh Council of Toledo in 675, which said of the Son that "he was begotten or born from the Father's womb—that is, of his substance" *(de Patris utero, id est, de substantia . . . genitus vel natus).*[11] Some writers, making much of this conciliar reference to the "Father's womb" (*Patris uterus*), are also impressed by the juxtaposition of the participles *begotten* and *born.*[12] Fathers, after all, beget, and mothers give birth. So it is claimed that Toledo XI, in its employment of such language, was striking out on some new and bold theological venture. Jürgen Moltmann, for example, describing the conciliar statement as "daring," goes on to speak of Toledo's "bisexual affirmations" and "radical denial of patriarchal monotheism."[13]

Such enthusiastic conclusions are premature. Indeed, I believe that they would greatly bewilder the venerable fathers at Toledo, and with a view to sparing them such bewilderment I propose the following four points for consideration. First, no one in the whole conciliar and creedal tradition regarded the word *father,* when used in reference to God, as having any sexual connotation whatsoever. The Cappadocians in particular had already gone to some length to say that paternity and sonship in God possessed no sexual reference.[14] So the bishops at Toledo, endeavoring to respect the traditional affirmations, were certainly not trying to correct those affirmations by the deliberate introduction of feminine language. It was the thing furthest from their minds.

The very idea of sexuality in God, to say nothing of bisexuality, is more than slightly silly. It is not simply that God's eternal fatherhood transcends sexuality; it transcends any consideration of sexuality, even the denial of sexuality. It is not related to sexuality at all, not even in transcending it. Sexuality offers no avenue to the mystery. The dogma of God's fatherhood must be approached entirely on its own terms. It can be approached only within the context of its revelation, the glory of God shining from the face of Christ. Christians are not free to go off and develop the idea on their own.

Second, the juxtaposition of "begotten" and "born" in reference to the Son was not Toledo's attempt to balance doctrinal language with masculine and feminine words. When used of the Son's relationship to the Father, those two words, each equally inadequate to express the divine and eternal mystery in question, had for a long time been employed interchangeably and in parallel construction in church teaching, whether in councils or in other contexts.[15]

Third, far from being daring and innovative, Toledo XI's reference to the "Father's womb" was rather conservative. In fact the authors thought it was biblical. Sunday by Sunday since at least the third century,[16] the entire Latin church had been starting vespers with Psalm 109 (110 in Hebrew and most English translations) in verse 3 of which they found the following reference to the Son's eternal generation from the Father: *ex utero ante luciferum genui te* (from the womb, before the daystar, I have begotten thee). So God's "womb," however modern scholarship may judge its accuracy as a biblical translation, would hardly have struck anyone as particularly bold in the late seventh century.[17] The bishops of the council comfortably employed the word because they had all along been using it with the same reference in worship every Sunday and major feast day for four centuries or more.

Fourth, it is significant that this reference to the Father's womb, found in both the Latin and Greek Psalters, was never exploited for its feminine possibilities in the entire Christian tradition, East or West. If ever anyone had thought it important to find a feminine side to God's paternity, Psalm 109:3 was readily at hand to assist in the effort. The opposite, however, was true. That is, except in liturgical texts where a more poetic form rendered it appropriate, Christian theology tended generally not to draw attention to the *uterus Patris*. For example, St. Augustine's *De Trinitate*, which cites that line from the Psalter dozens of times, invariably leaves out the reference to the womb. Similarly, in his *Enarrationes in Psalmos,* Augustine interprets it as a metaphor for the divine *substantia*, exactly as Toledo XI does, without drawing any attention to its feminine character. The few other references to the paternal womb in Latin Christianity follow suit.[18] In sum, Toledo XI does not say what Moltmann and others would like for it to say.

Our inherited doctrinal statements about God the Father are paralleled with affirmations about his Son. In speaking of Jesus as the Son of God, we Christians insist that this is not a purely biological assertion. That is to say, he is not called Son simply because he assumed human nature in the masculine gender. One frequently hears it asserted that God's eternal Word became his Son only by the incarnation. Those who venture this assertion invariably regard his sonship as a mere circumstance of biology, and they normally go on to claim that Jesus might just as well have been born as a little girl.

Such speculations are excellent examples of what I earlier described as thinking about God apart from his revelation in Christ. They are purely imaginative, even idolatrous attempts to get past the God actually revealed in Jesus Christ. Rooted in neither Holy Scripture nor any other component of holy Tradition, their theological value is zero. To take such speculations seriously, to grant them even the faintest claim to valid consideration, is to summon forth once again, from the deep sepulchers where St. Irenaeus of Lyons long ago consigned them, the demonic specters of Gnosticism; it is to depart from the ancient creedal confession that has re-echoed down through history in the hymn Te Deum, where our Lord Jesus Christ is addressed: *tu Patris sempiternus es Filius,* Thou art the everlasting Son of the Father.

Come to the Father

So what is revealed in Christ is not the mere name *Father* as a description of God. What is manifested is the invisible Father himself. It is a matter more of vision than of language. "And he who sees me sees him who sent me" (Jn 12:45 RSV). The invisibility of God is revealed in the Son. "Have I been with you so long, and yet you do not know me, Philip? He who has seen me has seen the Father" (14:9 RSV). God's eternal Son is "the effulgence of his glory and the impress of his person" (*charaktēr tēs hypostaseōs* [Heb 1:3]). He is "the icon of the invisible God" (*eikōn tou theou tou aoratou* [Col 1:15]).

This eternal iconography, made visible in the incarnation, I take to be the heart of Christian apophatic theology. It is not primarily a way of talking but of seeing. St. Paul calls it "the Gospel of the glory of Christ who is the icon of God" (2 Cor 4:4). We do not see the Father except in the Son, and then only by reason of the Holy Spirit who is poured into our hearts. So no one comes to Jesus unless drawn by the Father (Jn 6:45), because no one knows the Son but the Father (Mt 11:27). But if we know the Son we know the Father also (Jn 8:19), because no one knows the Father but the Son and he to whomsoever the Son will reveal him (Mt 11:27). "Now this is eternal life: that they may know you, the only true God, and Jesus Christ, whom you have sent" (Jn 17:3 NIV). "For God, who said, 'Light shall shine out of darkness,' is the One who has shone in our hearts to give the light of the knowledge of the glory of God in the face of Christ" (2 Cor 4:6 NASB).

On his way to martyrdom in the year 107, St. Ignatius of Antioch wrote to the church at Rome of his inner experience of the Holy Spirit. "My earthly desire is crucified," he said, "and the love of material things no longer burns in me. There is, rather, a living water speaking inside and saying within me: Come to the Father!"[19] This, the Father who dwells in inaccessible light, is the goal of the Christian life. Christians are those who pray with Christ: "Father, glorify thy name" (Jn 12:28 RSV).

While apophatic theology is an attitude governing all of the Christian life, it has chiefly to do with worship and contemplative love. It is primarily doxological. Its major expressions are adoration and longing. It prays with St. Isaac the Syrian, "Behold, Lord, the waves of thy grace close my mouth with silence, and there is not a thought left in me before the face of thy thanksgiving."[20] The direction of this silent adoration is eschatological. It holds a firm course finally to that throne before which worships the church in glory, that heavenly church described by the world's greatest poet as the "White Rose." There arises from that anagogical church, with whom we join our voices here on earth, the great hymn of apophatic praise: "Glory to the holy, consubstantial, life-creating and undivided Trinity, the Father, the Son and the Holy Spirit, now and ever, and unto ages of ages. Amen."

Trinitarian Theology & the Quest for Ecumenical Orthodoxy: A Response to Patrick Henry Reardon

William J. Abraham

*I*t is a great pleasure to respond to Father Reardon's paper. Father Reardon has provided us with a crisp and substantial thesis concerning the current status of trinitarian doctrine among Western Christians, and he has challenged us to explore the possibility of Christians from different backgrounds joining in collective witness to a common faith designated as "ecumenical orthodoxy." The whole thrust of his paper is devoted to the first of these projects; presumably it is his hope that agreement on the doctrine of the Trinity will have to be a crucial element, if not the crucial element, in any account of classic Christian faith. Hence he concentrates his energies on exposing a false apophaticism that he judges to be profoundly mistaken, on tracing indirectly origins of this false apophaticism, and then on calling us to the true apophaticism of Scripture and tradition.

I want to say at the outset that I think that this is a profound paper. We should not be misled by the folksy and polemical pose sometimes adopted by Father Reardon. He takes us into some very deep waters that deserve the most careful pondering and reflection. I am especially interested in the philosophical proposals that surface in his paper. As it stands I am not entirely convinced by what Father Reardon has to say on this score. My concern is not to deny what he asserts but to query what he denies. More generally I would like to explore the place of epistemic proposals in the life of the church.

I shall not go further than merely raising this question in this paper, but I would like to record that I have become increasingly convinced that Western forms of Christianity have been bedeviled by a tendency to transpose the canonical heritage of the church into an epistemological heritage that is then taken captive by the philosophical proposals of the day. Hence I am intrigued by Father Reardon's resolution not to get entangled in philosophical proposals about God that do not fit with the church's canonical teaching. I completely share his concerns at this point. Yet I wonder whether he himself does not get into the kind of epistemic commitments that will have precisely the same result, namely, that they will lead eventually to the kind of philosophical captivity that Paul and many of the fathers eschewed. Leaving that aside until I raise it again at the end, let me organize my remarks around three questions.

1. Are we now witnessing the most serious attack on the doctrine of the Trinity since the fourth century, and is that attack driven first and foremost by a false apophaticism?

2. Are there any difficulties in the alternative apophaticism proposed by Father Reardon?

3. What are the implications of our discussion for the way we think about ecumenical orthodoxy?

False Apophaticism?

1. Are we now witnessing the most serious attack on the Trinity since the fourth century, and is that attack driven first and foremost by a false apophaticism? Frankly I do not know the history of trinitarian doctrine well enough to answer this question. My own sense is that trinitarian doctrine was in trouble from the outset within the Protestant tradition. While the Reformers read and even loved the fathers and hence had ready access to the canonical tradition of the church on the Trinity, and while the Protestant Scholastics were clearly keen to explore the details of trinitarian doctrine, two impulses tended to get in the way of a full appropriation of trinitarian material. First, there was almost an obsession with the doctrine of the Christian life represented by the doctrine of justification by faith. This focus involved an anthropocentric turn in the whole tradition, that is, a turn away from an interest in God himself toward an interest in personal salvation and experience of God. In my judgment this development has had disastrous consequences across the centuries. The Reformers began looking at God in all his majesty and glory in the face of Jesus Christ, but their followers ended up looking more at themselves and their salvation. The theological intentions were valid and the corrective was sorely needed at the time, but eventually we lost our theocentric bearings and various attempts to fix the damage have never really worked.

Second, and more important, the whole attempt to derive everything from Scripture in a logically binding manner called everything into question. As a corrective and as a heuristic device the slogan *sola scriptura* was invaluable in recovering neglected treasures of the gospel, but as an epistemology of theology, which is what it effectively became, this principle led quickly to a point where any doctrine of the Trinity became a kind of speculative option or tended to idle in the background. In the long run it cast doubt and suspicion on the whole patristic heritage and hence on the trinitarian doctrine developed therein.

In the light of this we should not in the least be surprised that the doctrine of the Trinity is such a precarious doctrine among academic theologians formed within the Protestant tradition. I see no cure for this other than a whole new analysis and appropriation of the full canonical heritage of the early church. This in no way entails a rejection of the centrality of Scripture for the economy of faith; on the contrary it has precisely such a place in the canonical developments of the patristic era. What is needed is an acknowledgment that the canon of Scripture was surrounded by other canonical material without which we suffer irreparable damage in the long haul.

In the light of this we should not in the least be surprised that the doctrine of the Trinity continues to evoke such sustained criticism. The current tendency to invoke various apophatic proposals is in my judgment merely a device to clear the decks for the replacement of trinitarian doctrine by a favored alternative. The real intent in much contemporary theology is to rid the church of what are thought to be oppressive forms of discourse and replace them by supposedly liberating discourse. In this context using some kind of apophatic doctrine is merely a device that is plucked from the tradition to unsettle those elements of the tradition that get in the way of the desired changes.

I seriously doubt apophaticism is a specific thesis that is all that well supported in the contemporary literature, even though there are a wide variety of ways of developing an apophatic account of religious discourse. The fact is, if an apophatic critique did not work, another critique would soon appear to do the job. The real drive is to find a way to use theology as a discourse of liberation, that is, as a kind of instrument that will further certain moral and political goals that are more often than not derived from Enlightenment sensibilities. The appeal to apophaticism is simply a good tool to clear a way for such discourse.

That I may be right about this is suggested by the fact that the apophaticism is quickly forgotten once the doctrinal decks have been cleared. One cannot begin to make sense of a theology of liberation without extended claims about divine action in history. Hence all sorts of cataphatic materials are invoked. Equally, all sorts of images or metaphors other than that of father are applied to God. These images are sometimes taken in a nonrealist sense; to use the language of Janet Martin Soskice, they are not taken as reality-depicting.[1] But this is not the whole story. De facto the new predicates are often taken as descriptive of God in the same way that the more common image of father was taken as descriptive. Hence the cataphatic is always lurking in the neighborhood. So the use of the apophatic strikes me as halfhearted and even incoherent, for the apophatic has always been balanced by the cataphatic, and it is extremely difficult to survive intellectually and spiritually on the merely apophatic.

The reason this convoluted appeal to the apophatic takes place in the first place stems from the amazing degree to which so much of Christianity in the

West is still committed to trinitarian doctrine. In that sense I do not think the crisis is endemic in the church as a whole. There is indeed a large group of theologians who have no time for the doctrine of the Trinity other than as a historical curiosity. However, this is not the whole story, for there is also a revival of interest in trinitarian doctrine in academic theology that extends far beyond the impetus provided two generations ago by Karl Barth.

We can also agree that there is indeed considerable confusion and ignorance about the details of trinitarian doctrine in local churches. Yet what impresses me is that so many church members are keen to make up for this deficit in their formation. Many are also keen to stand up for the trinitarian faith of the church. It was a matter of some delight to me to hear so many in the recent Confessing Movement Conference at Atlanta call for a clear commitment to the trinitarian heritage of the church.[2] The focus of the Confessing Movement has rightly been on christological matters, but it was pressure from the ground up that insisted that this could not be divorced from the full trinitarian faith of the church, and adjustments were made in the final declaration to make this manifest. Thus while we should not underestimate the forces at work to invade the theological and liturgical life of the churches in the West, we should equally not underestimate the way in which the ordinary faithful have enormous reserves of resistance against such developments.

To summarize: There is considerable opposition to trinitarian doctrine, but this should not be seen in apocalyptic terms. This is a long-standing feature of academic theology since the Reformation, and its current incarnation complete with the appeal to the apophatic should not surprise us. Such developments could well lead to the recovery of trinitarian doctrine rather than its demise. Might we not hope and pray that it will lead to the renovation of Christianity in the West through a new appropriation of patristic faith?

Difficulties with Reardon's Alternative Apophaticism
2. Are there any difficulties in the alternative apophaticism developed by Father Reardon? Obviously this is a very complex matter, so I can only hope to make appropriate gestures here. We are given three fascinating theses.

1. Christian apophaticism is not primarily an epistemological assertion. That is to say, it is not a metaphor for the inadequacy of human thought. When we Christians call the true and living God, we are saying something about God himself and are not simply describing the limitations of knowledge.

2. Christian apophaticism is not merely a logical reference. The incomprehensibility of the living God is a revealed truth, not a fact available to unaided reason.

3. Christian apophaticism is not Neo-Platonic ecstasy. Speaking positively, the Christian apophatic tradition has its own content and roots. It involves a resolute rejection of the idea of a divine essence that is then displayed as subsisting in three modes of being. The Nicene Creed affirms belief in one God, the Father almighty from whom the Son is begotten and from whom the Spirit proceeds. The Person of the Father is the "root of divinity"; he is the source of the Son and the Spirit. This Father is made known only by the Son through the Spirit. It is this God, the Holy Trinity, who is the truly incomprehensible God.

The beauty of this formulation of the issue is that it completely undercuts the attempt to use the apophatic tradition to undermine talk of God as Father, Son and Holy Spirit. To put it in vulgar language, it does this by playing the cataphatic card before it allows one to play any apophatic card. It is only as God is already identified as the blessed Trinity, as He rather than It, that this God is then described as incomprehensible.

Moreover, the incomprehensibility of God is affirmed through divine revelation, not through reason, experience, intuition, inference and the like. This is the second way Father Reardon cuts off the appeal to the Christian apophatic tradition by those who use it to displace trinitarian doctrine. Where contemporary apophaticists and ineffabilists base their proposals on a theory of language, or a theory of knowledge, or a metaphysical theory, or a theory of religious experience, the tradition bases its apophatic proposals on divine revelation. As Reardon puts it: "Christian apophatic theology stresses primarily the incomprehensibility of the *hypostasis,* the divine *prosōpon,* not even known to be unknown unless revealed, unknown only as revealed, and revealed as unknown."

This is a brilliant little exercise in polemical theology. Things are murkier, however, when we examine the supplementary material growing in and around these astute observations. I want to raise three issues for further reflection.

First, is it the case that trinitarian doctrine entails the kind of patriarchy that is so much an issue for contemporary theologians? If we affirm God first as the Father in the way specified by Father Reardon, do we "necessarily affirm patriarchy in the Holy Trinity"? Do we have to say "all of the Christian revelation is patriarchal"? The short answer will of course be yes, because the content of Christian revelation will be a revelation of God first as Father, and from this it follows that there is patriarchy in the Holy Trinity and that Christian revelation is patriarchal. I presume this is how Father Reardon is thinking.

However, does this then entail commitment to the thesis that females are inferior to males, that women should be treated as second-class citizens in the church and the world, that various forms of discrimination should be upheld and defended? Father Reardon remains silent on these matters, and hence he leaves us uncertain as to how to construe precisely what he means by patriarchy or patriarchal. His earlier remarks might lead us to infer a wider meaning than I have attributed to him, but this would be premature. I hope this is the case, because it is surely obvious that the form of patriarchy we encounter in God could be profoundly subversive of the kinds of patriarchy we encounter in the world, just as encounter with the sovereignty of God may totally undermine the kinds of human sovereignty to which we are accustomed. Or, to make it more explicit, encounter with the fatherhood of God may totally transpose our understanding of what it is to be a human father. All this can be said before we even explore the implications of the equality of the divine Persons for human life and conduct, a matter omitted from the exposition but one that surely qualifies any simple way of enumerating patriarchy within the Trinity.

Second, is it the case that Christian apophaticism entails that there is no knowledge of God outside of Jesus Christ? I am not sure Father Reardon makes this claim, but there are certainly hints that could be taken that he does. His target, I suspect, is any attempt to derive a doctrine of God from philosophical speculation, and I have every sympathy with his reservations about some Unmoved Mover or *ens necessarium*. Yet we must be careful not to deny the fact that God was indeed known in Israel before he was known as the triune Mystery revealed in Christ. In fact I would argue that identifying Jesus Christ as the Son of God logically presupposes that God was already known in some manner and to some degree, for otherwise the reference to God would be vacuous. The term *God* in the sentence "Jesus Christ is the Son of God" would be an unknown x without any content.

It was at the right and proper time that the fullness of the revelation was given to us, and acknowledging that fullness is not exalted by disparaging the crucial revelation vouchsafed to Israel and made available in the Old Testament. The same applies *mutatis mutandis* to what has been made known of God in creation, that is, in nature and in conscience. To do justice to the subtleties of such revelation we cannot revert to the Christomonism of the early Barth. We need a deep and rich account of the development of the doctrine of God in Israel and in early Christianity.

Third, is it the case that to call God "Father" is not a metaphor but a mystery? My question is whether we have to choose the kind of either-or implicitly proposed here. The predicate *father* as applied to God is surely a metaphor. But as Janet Martin Soskice and other recent writers have shown, it is wrong to assert that we cannot use such a metaphor to depict accurately the reality of God. What counts here is not some general theory of metaphor but those speech acts in which we use metaphorical discourse to describe reality. This would be entirely in keeping with the claim that the name *father* is not titular but real. Equally we can use various metaphors to describe God without in any way claiming that these metaphors exhaust the reality of God or that they eliminate the mystery of God. God forever remains mysterious to us no matter how we depict or describe him. Hence playing off metaphor against mystery is as misleading as playing off metaphor against reality.

Moreover, that our language about God is primarily doxological does nothing to dislodge this claim. On the contrary, our doxological usage presupposes that our descriptions of God, including our metaphorical descriptions, are true. It is in part because we know God as father that we gladly praise his name in the congregation of the faithful. Furthermore, I take it for granted that we come to know God through the working of the Holy Spirit. My concern is to insist on the cataphatic dimension of theology. When we express what we know in metaphors, using metaphors is not some kind of inferior way of describing God that needs to be replaced with better, nonfigurative language. Metaphor is a thoroughly proper way to express what we know about God in Christ through the working of the Holy Spirit.

Implications for Theology

3. What are the implications of our discussion to date for the way we think about ecumenical orthodoxy? I have presumed that one of the reasons Father Reardon sees the doctrine of the Trinity as so pivotal is that it is an obvious candidate for inclusion in the ecumenical orthodoxy or in the classic Christian faith he is seeking to foster on a wider front.

There are those who find this whole notion of "mere Christianity" divorced from the ecclesiological home in which it is lodged incoherent and unworkable. I do not count myself among those who think like that. I agree entirely with C. S. Lewis that the idea of mere Christianity, of "classical or ecumenical orthodoxy," is both coherent and religiously valuable. I have argued the case for that elsewhere.[3] Here, however, I am prompted to develop an additional and complementary line of thought prompted by Father Reardon's concern with current attacks on the doctrine of the Trinity.

The deep issue facing us in the West is not just an attack on the Trinity but a wider attempt to create new canonical material. We should be alerted to this by the fact that the doctrine of the Trinity expressed in the Nicene Creed was not just an option applauded by the church: it was an option formally adopted by the whole church and made binding for future generations. The rule of faith was developed alongside the canon of the New Testament to preserve the riches of the Christian heritage and ultimately to make possible the salvation of our souls. In and around this material the church also canonized the Chalcedonian definition, a network of liturgical practices, an iconographic tradition, a list of teachers or fathers, a system of episcopal oversight and various disciplinary canons for organizing the life of the community. The point of these canonical materials and practices is not to furnish us with a theory of knowledge but to initiate us into the kingdom of God. They are gifts of the Holy Spirit to create in us the mind of Christ and to make us truly holy. In and through them we are to become by grace what Christ was by nature. Their purpose is soteriological. Hence these gifts cannot be properly received and used without humility, repentance and faith on the one side and without a profound immersion in the life of the Holy Spirit on the other. Through this process we are intended to come to know the true God, Father, Son and Holy Spirit. Yet in coming to know this true God we can never fathom the divine essence: we are in the end reduced to silence before the light and glory of the triune God.

I am proposing that to speak of classical orthodoxy is not enough. Such notions as ecumenical orthodoxy, mere Christianity, traditional Christianity, classical orthodoxy and the like are invaluable. They pick out and highlight common doctrinal and moral commitments that are embedded in the various Christian communities that exist across the world. Yet these are merely heuristic devices that we need for purposes of identification and scholarly discussion. We need also to think through these common commitments in terms of their place in the canonical heritage of the church. This way we can move from a purely secular kind of designation to one that forces us to examine our own relation to historic developments in patristic Christianity.

One immediate advantage to this shift in perspective is that it enables us to designate our differences in terms of different renderings of that canonical heritage or in terms of laying hold of different aspects of that heritage to the neglect of others. Thus we might see the division between East and West as in part a divergence in developments related to the creedal canon, as is most easily represented in the addition of the *filioque* clause to the creed. Equally we might begin to see the whole matter of the papacy in a new light, interpreting it as a particular rendering of the institution of canonical oversight, pulling it in a new epistemological direction. We might also see the Reformation as a massive attempt to engage in canonical reform that ultimately failed because it reduced the canonical heritage to Scripture and, following Aquinas, turned the canon of Scripture into an item in the epistemology of theology.

The most interesting gains from this analysis, however, relate to what is currently happening among us. What is at stake is not just an attack on the doctrine of the Trinity. What is really at issue is the creation of new canonical materials. As Ellen Charry has forcefully argued,[4] a new body of literature is designated as Scripture. In and around this literature are developing new liturgies, a new community designated as womanchurch, new forms of pastoral care, new forms of homiletics, new forms of institutional oversight, new conceptions of seminary life and new ways of rendering the internal content of the Christian faith originally laid out in the creed. What we are witnessing is the emergence of a new creed, a new moral code and a new cult, that is, the invention of post-Christian religion. In this new religion to be a sinner is to be in bondage to patriarchy; to be redeemed is to be set free from patriarchy; to be born again is to cease to be a victim; and to be sanctified is to join in the struggle for liberation.

Examining these developments in the light of ecumenical orthodoxy and related terms enables us to see them merely as an attack on this or that part of the tradition. This is certainly valuable in its own right. However, taking stock of them in terms of the canonical heritage of the early church enables us to map them more accurately. We can see the attack for what it truly is, namely, the intentional invention of a new religion. This perspective also helps ordinary

Christians conceptualize the profound unease they have long felt but have not been able to name accurately. This way of viewing the situation also provides a perspective for mounting a deep critique that we sorely need in order to prevent the wholesale takeover of our churches and to reform and renew the canonical traditions we currently own and deploy.

One additional observation is in order. This way of construing the data also prompts us to examine very carefully where and to what extent epistemic proposals fit into the life of the church. To what extent have the various churches of Christendom canonized particular theories of knowledge? It strikes me as fascinating that the early church did not canonize a theory of divine revelation or divine inspiration, but it did canonize trinitarian and christological doctrine. Various epistemic suggestions show up in the Scriptures and in the canonized teachers of the church, many of which remain to be fully explored by philosophers and theologians. Yet I suspect that the church was extremely reluctant to give any epistemology of theology canonical status. This kind of material was left hidden in embryonic form in the bosom of the community. Hence as I read the various epistemic suggestions that crop up toward the end of Father Reardon's paper, I am prompted to ask how far he sees these as representing his own attempts to articulate the scattered insights of the canonical tradition and how far he sees these as actually canonical. How we answer this question has far-reaching consequences for our construal of the canonical heritage of the church and for the hopes we can entertain regarding unity in our faith together.

5

THE TRINITY
Heart of Our Life

◼

Kallistos Ware

The whole round world is not enough to fill
The heart's three corners, but it craveth still:
None but the Trinity, who made it, can
Suffice the vast triangulated heart of man.
CHRISTOPHER HARVEY, *Schola Cordis (1622)*

Let us love one another that with one mind we may
confess Father, Son and Holy Spirit, the Trinity
consubstantial and undivided.
FROM THE DIVINE LITURGY OF THE
ORTHODOX CHURCH

When I say God, I mean Father, Son and Holy Spirit," states St. Gregory of Nazianzus (329?-390?), or Gregory the Theologian as he is known in the Orthodox church.[1] His approach is not abstract but specific. For St. Gregory God is not a hypothesis or a philosophical postulate but a communion or *koinōnia* of three persons: the living, personal God with whom we humans enter through prayer into a living, personal relationship. Such also is our approach when we confess our faith in the words of the Nicene-Constantinopolitan Creed. After the opening phrase "I believe in one God," we do not continue, "I believe in an Ultimate Ground of Being, in Primordial Reality, in an Unmoved Mover, an Uncaused Cause" (although such statements are doubtless legitimate); but in common with St. Gregory we affirm, "I believe

in one God, the Father . . . and in one Lord Jesus Christ the only begotten
Son . . . and in the Holy Spirit."

For traditional Christians the doctrine of the Trinity is not just a possible
way of thinking about God. It is the only way. The one God of the Christian
church cannot be conceived except as Trinity. Apart from the Father, the Son
and the Holy Spirit, God cannot be known in the truth and reality of his being.
The doctrine of the Trinity is not an embarrassing complication, a piece of
technical theologizing of no importance for our daily existence. It stands at
the very heart of our Christian life.

Or so at least it ought to. For in fact how central is the Trinity to the
experience and thinking of the majority of Christians? What practical difference
does the threefoldness of the one God make to most of us most of the time?
Can we say in all sincerity that it has a drastic effect upon our understanding
of human personhood, of society and politics? Has faith in the Trinity any
relevance to the way in which, for example, we take the chair at a committee
meeting or fill out our tax returns? With good reason Karl Rahner laments that
in practice all too many Christians are just "monotheists"; all references to the
Trinity could be omitted from most Christian books, and yet the author's
argument would be virtually unaffected.[2] When in 1989 the Study Commission of the British Council of Churches issued its report on the Trinity,
appropriately it used as its title *The Forgotten Trinity.*[3]

It is interesting in this connection to compare the views of two Western
patristic scholars. Writing in 1940, G. L. Prestige asserted, with particular
reference to St. Athanasius (c. 296-373) and the Cappadocians: "The problem
of the Trinity is the one theological question of absolutely fundamental
importance which has ever been pressed to a positive and satisfactory answer.
. . . The doctrine of the Trinity . . . is unique . . . in having brought to
Christendom a final solution of the vital problem with which it deals."[4]
Eighteen years later, however, C. C. Richardson concluded on a far less
optimistic note: "The doctrine of the Trinity . . . is an artificial construct. . . .
It produces confusion rather than clarification; and while the problems with
which it deals are real ones, the solutions it offers are not illuminating."[5] It has
to be admitted that most contemporary Christian thinkers agree with Richardson rather than with Prestige.

How are we to cleanse the doors of our spiritual perception and to recover
once more our sense of wonder before the living truth of the Trinity? How

are we to renew our awareness of trinitarian doctrine as nothing less than a saving revolution in human thought? Let us ask ourselves three questions (the first of these will occupy most of our time):

1. When reflecting on the triune character of God, what images or analogies bring us closest to the deep truth of the mystery?

2. What difference does faith in the Trinity make to our appreciation of the human person?

3. What can we do to make our personal prayer more fully trinitarian?

A Mystery Revealed

We have spoken of the Trinity as a mystery and such indeed it is. This is something that we must keep constantly in view. "Let things ineffable be honoured with silence," insists St. Basil the Great (d. 379).[6] There are limits to our comprehension beyond which we cannot pass. The trinitarian nature of God is a truth that exceeds our understanding, "a cross for human ways of thought," in the words of the Russian theologian Vladimir Lossky (1903-1958).[7] As St. Gregory the Theologian points out, the meaning of God's triunity is not to be attained through human powers of critical analysis, but it is known solely by those to whom the triune God chooses to reveal himself; the divine and eternal Trinity is accessible only to such as theologize "not in the manner of Aristotle but of the fishermen" *(alieutikōs, ouk Aristotelikōs)*.[8]

From this it follows that no statement in human language and no similitude or image drawn from human experience can exhaustively express the significance of the Trinity. Any conciliar definition, however correct and irrevocable—for instance, the affirmation that God is one essence *(ousia)* in three persons *(hypostaseis, prosōpa)*—does no more than act as a signpost pointing toward the transcendent truth. To alter the metaphor: In our definitions we set a fence around the mystery, but we cannot fully delineate its content in words. Our language about God, even when that language is given to us in divine revelation and sealed by the church's worship, never provides an exact and literal description of "the One Who Is" (Ex 3:14 LXX). All statements about the Divine are necessarily analogical.

When, for example, we say that God is Father and Son (and not Mother and Daughter), we speak the truth; and yet we must immediately add that God is Father and Son in a manner infinitely surpassing all human notions of paternity and filiation. Divine fatherhood is not to be interpreted literally, as

St. Athanasius pointed out to the Arians when the latter argued that because a father is older than his son, God the Father therefore preexists God the Son. Likewise, when we say that God is He and not She, once more we speak the truth; and yet we must at once qualify this by saying that in himself God is neither male nor female, for he transcends all gender and sexuality, just as he transcends everything else.

At the same time our approach to God the Trinity is cataphatic as well as apophatic. A mystery, in the proper theological sense, is much more than a conundrum or an inexplicable puzzle. A mystery is something revealed to our understanding (see Eph 1:9; 3:3-4) yet never completely revealed, for it extends beyond our understanding into the limitless darkness of God (Ex 20:21; Ps 18:11). Where then do we find the mystery of the Trinity revealed? We find it revealed in Christ Jesus. More specifically it is disclosed in the five central moments of New Testament salvation history, within each of which there is evident a basic trinitarian structure:

1. Annunciation: the Father sends down the Spirit upon the blessed Virgin Mary, who in this way conceives the Son (Lk 1:35).

2. Baptism: the Father's voice is heard from heaven, bearing witness to the Son, as the Spirit in the form of a dove descends from the Father and rests upon the Son (Mt 3:16-17). This is the most explicitly trinitarian event in the life of Christ.

3. Transfiguration: as at the baptism, the Father speaks from heaven, testifying to the Son, while the Spirit descends upon the Son, on this occasion not in the form of a dove but as a cloud of light (Lk 9:34-35).

4. Cross and resurrection: after Christ's crucifixion and death, God the Father raises the Son in and through the power of the Spirit (Rom 8:11; cf. Rom 1:4).

5. Pentecost: the Son sends down upon the church the Spirit that proceeds from the Father (Jn 15:26).

In these five moments of salvation history, taken together, we see the reciprocity, the mutual *diakonia,* that prevails between the Second Person of the Trinity and the Third. Each sends the other. At the annunciation and the baptism it is the Spirit that makes the Son manifest to humankind, as happens also in the Divine Liturgy at the eucharistic *epiclesis,* while at Pentecost it is the Son who sends the Spirit.

Next to these five moments in the New Testament, the guidelines for our trinitarian thinking are provided by the *lex orandi* of the church, by its worshiping practice. The doctrine of the Trinity is liturgical and doxological, not philosophical. It is no coincidence that the three clearest references to the Trinity in the New Testament all occur within a context of prayer and worship: one of the three passages refers to the church's mission to baptize (Mt 28:19), while the other two form part of an initial or a final blessing (1 Pet 1:2; 2 Cor 13:14). Other triadic formulas in the New Testament have also, explicitly or implicitly, a liturgical flavor: the Three are mentioned in close juxtaposition with thanksgiving to God (2 Thess 2:13-14), then (as before) with baptism (Eph 4:4-6) and also with gifts of grace and ministries (1 Cor 12:4-6). The words of Father Georges Florovsky (1893-1979)—"Christianity is a liturgical religion. The Church is first of all a worshipping community. Worship comes first, doctrine and discipline second"[9]—apply par excellence to the church's trinitarian faith. The dictum of St. Irenaeus of Lyons (d. c. 200) remains normative for our theology of the Trinity: "Our opinion agrees with the Eucharist, and the Eucharist confirms our opinion."[10] Any theology of the Trinity that does not interpret the mystery in terms of praise, blessing and the giving of glory has gone gravely astray.

Dim Shadows

Keeping in view this trinitarian dimension of the main events of salvation history, what analogies and images can we find that will make the doctrine of the Trinity come alive for us? So far from being mutually exclusive, these analogies need to be used in their full diversity, so that they balance each other; any single analogy is bound to prove misleading in isolation. Here certainly there is safety in numbers. Let us be maximalists, not minimalists. At the same time we should not ask of any image more illumination than it can legitimately provide, for all alike are no more than "dim shadows," to use St. Gregory the Theologian's phrase:

> I long to be in that unshaken dwelling-place
> Where my Trinity is found in the gathered brightness of its splendor—
> The Trinity whose dim shadows exalt me.[11]

Three main types of analogy can be found: from sight, from sound and from the human person.

Sight. Since light was felt in the ancient world to be the least material thing in the visible creation, it is natural that the trinitarian images most frequently employed from the realm of sight should involve light or radiance, the sun or the element of fire. The analogies take two main forms. First, the Trinity may be envisaged as three torches, the second and third being kindled from the first. This is an image found in the second-century apologists Justin Martyr[12] and Tatian.[13] The advantage of this image is that the light of the first torch is not diminished when the other two are kindled from it; similarly, in the Trinity each person possesses the totality of the Godhead in its undiminished wholeness, not just a third of that totality. The disadvantage is that the image is too tritheist; it does not convey a sufficient notion of the organic unity of the Godhead, for even when kindled from each other, three torches remain three separate things.

On the whole the fathers prefer a second, more unitary analogy: Father and Son are to be likened respectively to the disk of the sun and to the ray or effulgence that shines out from it. There is obviously a scriptural basis here, for in Hebrews 1:3 the Son is described as the "radiance of [God's] glory." In addition to the analogy of a torch, Justin also uses this sun-radiance analogy,[14] while Tertullian (d. c. 225) gives it a triadic form, likening the Father to the sun, the Word to the ray shining from the sun's disk and the Spirit to the apex or illumination point on which the ray falls.[15] The analogy is taken up in the Nicene-Constantinopolitan Creed, when the Son is affirmed to be "Light from Light." The advantage of the sun-radiance analogy, compared with that of three torches, is that it suggests more persuasively a distinction without separation.

St. Gregory of Nyssa (d. c. 394) provides a pleasing variant of the analogy of light when he compares the Trinity to a rainbow, in which "the brilliance is both continuous and divided." Within the rainbow there is a multiplicity of colors that are not confused but distinct; yet there is no interval between each color, and together they constitute a single undivided rainbow.[16] Perhaps this is the least inadequate analogy from light.[17]

There are, however, manifest shortcomings in all analogies from the realm of sight, as St. Gregory the Theologian was careful to point out.[18] Even when delicately qualified they still project upon God notions of physicality and spatial extension. Light may be indeed the least material thing in the visible world, but it remains a physical reality. What is more, analogies from the realm of sight do not in themselves convey the personal character of the trinitarian God. There is a danger that they may turn God into an object rather than a subject, into an It rather than a Thou (but in many of the visions of divine light granted to the saints—for example, to St. Symeon the New Theologian [959-1022]— the light has in fact possessed a strongly personal, christocentric character).

Sound. How far do we avoid the shortcomings in these analogies from light if we take sound instead of sight as the basis of our imagery? Scripture itself suggests an analogy from sound when it designates the Son as God's *logos,* his word or speech (Jn 1:1). St. Ignatius of Antioch (d. c. 110) takes this up when he refers to Christ as "the unlying mouth through which the Father spoke," "the Father's word, coming out from silence."[19] The Father is silence, God hidden and transcendent, while the Son is Word, God revealed and incarnate. Marius Victorinus (fourth century), the Neo-Platonist who deeply influenced St. Augustine, provides a more elaborate scheme: the Father is "silence eloquent," Christ is the Word or mouth and the Spirit is the voice that utters the word, the breath *(pneuma)* or sound that makes the word audible.[20] It is perhaps surprising that among the analogies from sound, more use has not been made of musical harmony. "You are music," says St. Hildegard of Bingen (1098-1179) to the Trinity, but she does not develop the idea.[21]

These analogies from the realm of sound—with God the Father likened not to the sun's disk but to a speaker and with God the Son likened not to a ray of light but to a spoken word—are certainly less physical and more personalized than the analogies from the sense of sight. But will not the nonmaterial, personal character of the Deity be conveyed yet more effectively if our analogies are based not just on the act of speaking but more directly on our inner human experience of what it is to be a person? Let us look more closely at this possibility.

Personhood. We humans are created in the image and likeness of God (Gen 1:26-27), and that means in the image of God who is Trinity; looking inward we can find within our soul what St. Augustine (354-430) termed "vestiges" of the Trinity. These trinitarian analogies from human personhood can take two forms, unipersonal and interpersonal. The Trinity may be likened either to the interaction of faculties within a single person or to the interrelationships within a community of persons.

The best-known instances of unipersonal analogies are in St. Augustine, who proposes two "trinities of the mind," likening Father, Son and Spirit first to mind, knowledge and love within the human psyche, and then to memory, understanding and will.[22] But such analogies are by no means restricted to the

Latin West. St. Gregory the Theologian, for example, compares the three hypostases of the Godhead to the three faculties of intellect *(nous)*, reason or word *(logos)* and breath or spirit *(pneuma)* within a human being.[23] The scriptural basis here is somewhat clearer than it is with the two "trinities of the mind" in St. Augustine, at least as regards the comparison between the human *logos* and the Son and between the human *pneuma* and the Holy Spirit. It is true, however, that when St. Gregory envisages God the Father as divine intellect, the analogy owes more to Greek philosophy than to the Bible. Trinitarian analogies from the human psyche recur in a series of later Byzantine authors.[24] Perhaps the most interesting example is in St. Gregory Palamas (1296-1359), who compares the three persons of the Godhead to the faculties of intellect *(nous)*, reason *(logos)* and love *(eros)*.[25]

Unipersonal analogies of a different kind have been advanced by twentieth-century authors. For C. G. Jung the Father symbolizes the deep Self, the Son symbolizes the Ego or conscious and revealed Self, while the Spirit symbolizes the Ego-Self axis, the energies that pass between the two. He also likens the Father to the stage of the child, the Son to the process of self-individuation and the Spirit to the embracing of the unconscious and the taking up of Ego-consciousness into a greater and more comprehensive totality.[26] Jung, it must be remembered, is speaking as a psychologist, not as a theologian or a historian of Christian doctrine; his concern is with the "God-idea" or the "God-image," with the human experience of God, not with the formal dogmas of the church. More illuminating, in my view, is the analogy drawn by Dorothy L. Sayers between the Trinity and the process of human creativity. As she sees it, the Father corresponds to the creative idea initially present in an author's mind; the Son represents the creative energy or activity of the author, the book that he actually writes, his idea in material and communicable form; and the Spirit signifies creative power that flows back to the author from his own activity—his own idea, revealed to him in a way that causes him to respond and rejoice.[27] In different ways both Jung and Sayers are drawing here upon St. Augustine's notion of the Spirit as the *vinculum amoris,* the bond of love between the Father and the Son.

The disadvantage of all such unipersonal analogies is that, if used exclusively, they fail to convey the sense of personal diversity, of mutual interplay and interpersonal response, that exists among the three members of the Trinity. The analogies envisage God as an I but deprive him of his true depth and fullness as a threefold I-and-Thou. Unless balanced by interpersonal schemes, they can easily lead to modalism or Sabellianism; and then the all-essential *koinōnia* of the divine life will be lost. To restore a true equilibrium to our trinitarian exegesis, we need also to invoke models that represent the Trinity in social terms, as a community of several persons in relationship. It is significant that St. Augustine, who is most commonly remembered for his unipersonal trinities of the mind, counterbalances these in his work *On the Trinity* by also advancing an analogy of interpersonal love. To this now let us turn.

Before proposing his trinities of the mind, St. Augustine suggests a bipersonal analogy: the Father is the lover *(amans)*, the Son is the beloved *(quod amatur)*, while the Spirit is the love that passes reciprocally between lover and beloved, uniting them each to the other.[28] Most writers on Augustine assume that this Trinity of love is less important for him than his two Trinities of the mind, to which certainly he devotes much more space; but he returns to his interpersonal analogy of love at the end of his work *On the Trinity* and seems to consider that among all the different analogies it is the least incomplete.[29]

The disadvantage of St. Augustine's analogy of love is that it likens the Trinity to two human persons, not to three; for while lover and beloved are both persons, the mutual love passing between them is not a third person additional to the other two. In this way the analogy is in danger of depersonalizing the Holy Spirit, although this was certainly not St. Augustine's intention. Another Western writer, Richard of St. Victor (d. 1173), corrects this defect by giving the analogy of love a fully tripersonal expression. Father and Son, Richard maintains, in their mutual love for each other long to share their love with a third: "The affection of the two persons is fused into one affection by the flame of love for a third." So Richard terms the Holy Spirit the "co-beloved" *(condilectus)*.[30] On this scheme the Spirit is not merely *amor*, the quality or feeling of love, but is a fully personal subject, loved by the other two and loving them in return.

This interpersonal analogy of shared love, as developed by Richard of St. Victor, is not so very different from the understanding of the Trinity prevailing in the Christian East and upheld most notably by the Cappadocians: in the words of St. Basil, "The unity of God lies in the communion *(koinōnia)* of the Godhead."[31] Divine unity, that is to say, is not to be interpreted primarily in abstract or essentialist terms, as a unity of nature or substance; but it is to be interpreted in personal terms, as a unity expressed through the interrelationship or *koinōnia* of the three hypostases. In the words of John Zizioulas, Metropolitan of Pergamon, "The being of God is a relational being: without the concept of communion it would not be possible to speak of the being of God."[32]

What is more, the analogy of interpersonal love has powerful support from Scripture, in particular from the Johannine writings. "God is love" (1 Jn 4:8): among all the realities in our human existence, it is the experience of loving and being loved that brings us closest to the life of God. As Christ's high-priestly prayer at the Last Supper affirms in plain and direct terms, there is a correspondence between the unity-in-diversity of human love and the unity-in-diversity of the divine love subsisting between Father and Son: "May [they] all be one; even as Thou, Father, art in Me, and I in Thee, that they also may be in Us; that the world may believe. . . . I in them, and Thou in Me, that they may be perfected in unity" (Jn 17:21, 23).

"Even as": it is our highest human vocation to reproduce on earth the *perichōrēsis*, the unceasing movement of shared love, that flows from all eternity among the three members of the Holy Trinity. Developing the same idea in the subapostolic epoch, St. Ignatius of Antioch sees the unity of the church on earth as an icon of the divine unity in heaven: "As the Lord was united to the Father and did nothing without Him, neither by Himself nor through the apostles, so should you do nothing without the bishop and the presbyters."[33] The same analogy between the Holy Trinity and the mutual love of human persons is emphasized in the Divine Liturgy, when the deacon says to the people just before the recitation of the creed, "Let us love one another that with one mind we may confess," and the people take up his words: "Father, Son and Holy Spirit, the Trinity." Without mutual love there can be on our part no true confession of faith in God the Trinity, for the Trinity is mutual love.

The Holy Trinity as Self-Giving and Response

Without discounting the other analogies mentioned earlier, for they also have their use, let us dwell particularly on this notion of God the Trinity as shared love and interpersonal *koinōnia*. Even though this too is no more than a dim shadow of the transcendent truth concerning the triune God, it is perhaps the least misleading of the images with which we seek to convey the mystery of the Trinity; and it serves as the best means at our disposal for making that mystery seem relevant to the anguish and tragedy of the contemporary world.

"God is love" (1 Jn 4:8). But self-love—the love of one, turned inward, self-centered, excluding others—does not express the fullness of human love. There is indeed a good form of self-love, as St. Augustine points out.[34] In Christ's words, "You shall love your neighbor as yourself" (Mt 19:19); for unless we have some sense of the true value and meaning of our own self in God's sight, unless (that is to say) we love in ourselves that which God loves in us, we cannot enter into an authentic relationship with others. There can be no I-and-Thou relationship unless there is an I as well as a Thou; if we are to relate to others, we need to be in touch also with our own inwardness.

Modern Christian thinkers, both non-Orthodox and Orthodox, often make a contrast between the individual *(atomon)* and the person *(prosōpon,* literally "face"). The individual, it is said, signifies the human being in isolation, in separateness, as competitor; the person signifies the human being in relationship, in communion, as coworker. This is a helpful approach, but it is important to add that when an individual develops into a person-in-relationship she or he does not cease to be an individual; as we grow into personhood, our individuality is not obliterated but enhanced. If we employ the polarity individual-person, it is vital to insist that the first term of this polarity, the individual, is not canceled out but taken up and contained by the second term, the person.

Self-love can be good, and yet it does not constitute the total breadth and depth of love. Love in its plenitude needs to embrace others, and so it can exist only where there is a plurality of persons. We do not want to be like Napoleon in Walter de la Mare's poem:

What is the world, O soldiers?
    It is I:
I, this incessant snow,
    This northern sky;
Soldiers, this solitude
    Through which we go
        Is I.[35]

Egocentricity is a denial of true love. The lover is the one who learns to say "we" as well as "I," who, unlike the old woman in Dostoyevsky's story, seeks to share the onion with others.

The doctrine of the Trinity is a way of affirming that this applies not just to us humans but also to God, although at an immeasurably higher level, since God in his perfection infinitely transcends our human ideas of love and personhood. God, so the doctrine of the Trinity is telling us, is not just self-love but shared love. God is not a single person, loving himself alone. God is a triunity of persons loving each other, and in that shared love the persons are totally "oned" without thereby losing their personal individuality. In the phrase of St. John of Damascus (d. c. 749), the Three are "united yet not confused, distinct yet not divided."[36]

In a fine paradox the Anglican writer Charles Williams (1886-1945) asserts, "It is not good for God to be alone."[37] God is not like de la Mare's Napoleon; he says "we" as well as "I." God is not just personal but interpersonal, not just a unit but a union. God is social or dialogic; there is within him a timeless dialogue. From all eternity the First Person addresses the Second: "Thou art My beloved Son" (Mk 1:11). From all eternity the Second replies to the First, "Abba, Father; Abba, Father" (Rom 8:15; Gal 4:6). From all eternity the Holy Spirit, "who proceeds from the Father and rests upon the Son,"[38] sets the seal upon this interchange of love. It is this timeless dialogue that is movingly depicted in St. Andrew Rublev's icon, which shows the Trinity in the form of the three angels who visited Abraham (see Gen 18:1-16). The three angels in the icon are not just gazing out into space or looking at us, but they are looking at one another. Joining the three together—marked out through the inclination of their heads and the lines of their shoulders, legs and feet—there is in the icon an enfolding circle: the great *O* of love.

Such then is the primary meaning of the mystery of the Trinity, so far as it can be grasped by the human mind and expressed in human language. God as love is self-giving, sharing, solidarity, reciprocity, response. If that is indeed what the doctrine of the Trinity affirms, then surely it is very far from being a merely technical topic of interest only to specialists. On the contrary, for all of us it involves in a direct and literal way matters of life and death.

Walking Along a Ridgeway

In common with every other analogy, the analogy of shared love needs to be restricted and offset by checks and balances. What was said about the unipersonal analogies—that, unless qualified, they will lead to modalism—applies in a corresponding way to the interpersonal analogy. Unless this latter is also qualified, it will lead to an equal imbalance on the opposite side: repudiating modalism, we shall find ourselves lapsing into tritheism. In trinitarian theology we are always walking along a ridgeway with a precipice on either hand, and it is never easy to keep to the midpoint between the two.

What kind of qualifications are required in the case of the interpersonal analogy? First, when we speak of God as three persons, it is essential to ask how far our modern understanding of personhood, in a post-Cartesian era and still more in a post-Freudian and post-Jungian world, corresponds to what the Greek fathers meant by *hypostasis* and *prosōpon*. Our twentieth-century sense of being a person lays a heavier emphasis upon inner subjectivity, upon our awareness of being a distinct center of self-consciousness, than is the case with the patristic terms *hypostasis* and *prosōpon*.[39]

Second, whether we are thinking in terms of the patristic or the modern sense of the person, the apophatic approach to God as mystery is to be kept continually in view. God is not a person, or rather three persons, in the same sense that we are persons. The divine reality surpasses anything that we humans can comprehend. Certainly God is not less than what we mean by personhood; he is incomparably more. But this means that we cannot simply project upon the uncreated Godhead our created sense of being personal. There is an all-important distinction of levels. An analogy does not signify identity.

The Cappadocian fathers, when they compared the Trinity to a community of three human persons,[40] were well aware of this distinction of levels. They recognized that the union of love between the three divine *hypostases* is altogether closer and stronger than any union prevailing between humans; and to underline this crucial difference they drew attention in particular to three things.

The "monarchy" of the Father. This is a notion of fundamental significance in Orthodox trinitarian theology. The ground and basis of unity within the Trinity is not simply the shared essence *(ousia),* the divine nature that is common to the three. There exists also a personal ground of unity: the *hypostasis* of the Father. In the words of St. Gregory the Theologian, "The three have one nature, God. And the union is the Father, from whom and to whom the order of the persons runs its course."[41] The Father, that is to say, is the *archē* or *principium* within the Godhead, the sole source or principle of origin. The Father is the unique cause or *aitia*, while the other two persons are caused by him. The Father is the "fountainhead" within the Trinity, so that the Son and the Spirit find their unity in him and are defined by their relationship to him: the Son is "begotten," the Spirit "proceeds."

Certain modern authors have suggested that in this Cappadocian emphasis on the monarchy of the Father there may be detected a lingering tendency toward subordinationism. But this is unjust, for the Cappadocians repeatedly insist that even though there is a *taxis* or order among the persons of the Trinity—such that the Father is first, the Son second and the Spirit third—at the same time the three are from all eternity irreducibly coequal. Orthodox writers have often suspected that the Western teaching on the *filioque* undervalues the importance of the Father's monarchy.[42]

Coinherence. Developing the idea of divine *koinōnia* or communion, the Cappadocians regularly affirm that the three persons indwell one another through a movement of reciprocal love. Each is totally open and transparent to the other two and totally interpenetrated by them in a union without confusion. In the words of St. Gregory of Nyssa, "All that is the Father's is seen in the Son, and all that is the Son's belongs also to the Father. For the whole Son abides in the Father, and in His turn He has the whole Father abiding in Himself."[43] The same is to be affirmed, *mutatis mutandis,* concerning the Holy Spirit.

St. Maximus the Confessor (d. 662) sums up this principle of coinherence by saying,

> The whole Divinity is in the whole Father, and the whole Father is in the whole Divinity. The whole Divinity is in the whole Son, and the whole Son is in the whole Divinity. The whole Divinity is in the whole Holy Spirit, and the whole Holy Spirit is in the whole Divinity. . . . The whole Father is completely in the whole Son and Spirit; and the whole Son is completely in the whole Father and Spirit; and the whole Holy Spirit is completely in the whole Father and Son. Therefore the Father, the Son and the Holy Spirit are one God. . . . None of the hypostases or persons either exists or is intelligible without the others.[44]

To indicate this mutual receptivity and indwelling of the three persons, St. John of Damascus employs the Greek term *perichōrēsis* (the Latin equivalent is *circumincessio*). Literally the word means "cyclical movement" and so "interchange" or "reciprocity." The all-embracing circle marked out in Rublev's icon of the Holy Trinity is precisely a visual expression of this *perichōrēsis*. Taking certain liberties with the strict etymology, we may speak of the "round dance" of the Trinity.[45]

Single energy. By virtue of the *koinōnia* expressed in this mutual indwelling, Father, Son and Holy Spirit have only a single energy or operation *(energeia)* and a single will. "The identity of operation," writes St. Basil, "on the part of Father, Son and Holy Spirit plainly indicates the complete unity of the nature."[46] According to St. Gregory of Nyssa, "The Father never does anything on His own in which the Son does not co-operate, nor again does the Son ever act on His own without the Spirit. On the contrary, every operation which extends from God to creation has its origin in the Father, proceeds through the Son, and reaches its completion in the Holy Spirit."[47] This is a primary axiom of Cappadocian triadology: in all their actions toward the world, the three persons invariably operate together, and no one of them ever does anything in isolation. The divine operations *ad extra* are always shared in common by all three hypostases.

On Cappadocian principles, then, creation is to be regarded as a trinitarian act: the cosmos is created by the Father, through the preeternal Logos, in the Spirit (Ps 33:6; Jn 1:3; Gen 1:2). The same is true of all the events of our salvation and sanctification. The crucifixion, for example, has a trinitarian dimension; while it is the Son who suffers and dies upon the cross, and not the Father or the Spirit, yet at the same time the Father and the Spirit consent to the sacrifice of the Son and participate in it. By the same token it is bad theology to say that in baptism we receive Christ, while in confirmation (Chrismation) we receive the Spirit; for we cannot receive Christ without the Spirit or the Spirit without Christ. The Second and the Third persons of the Trinity are both alike present in the two sacraments of baptism and confirmation, although the manner of their presence is different in each sacrament. Again, in Holy Communion there is a "real presence" of the Spirit as well as of Christ, but as before the manner of this presence differs; for the Spirit did not become incarnate and so we cannot speak of receiving the body or blood of the Spirit.

In maintaining that the three persons of the Trinity have only a single energy and a single will, the Cappadocians make it abundantly evident that the interpersonal *koinōnia* of the Trinity is indeed unique. Three human persons may choose to cooperate in a joint project, but each retains her or his individual energy and his or her individual free will. In the case of the Trinity this is not so. Every divine operation is one and undivided, and the Trinity has but one will and not three. In this manner the three persons of the Trinity are one in a way that three human persons can never be.

Through this insistence upon the monarchy of the Father, upon the mutual indwelling of the three persons and upon the single energy and will of the three, the Cappadocians seek to counterbalance any danger of tritheism and to safeguard the uniqueness of the divine unity. They would have been the first to admit that none of these three ways of speaking adequately explains the full significance of God's unity-in-diversity; but then no human language can ever do that. God remains always the *mysterium tremendum et fascinans,* the mystery before which we tremble in awe, yet which draws us to itself with love. But, despite the shortcomings of human language, the intention of the Cappadocians is unmistakable. They believed that any personal communion on the created human level, however deep and rich, falls infinitely short of the perfect and uncreated personal communion that exists from all eternity in the round dance of the Trinity.

"Transcripts of the Trinity"

Although all forms of human communion fall infinitely short of the plenitude of the divine *koinōnia,* there is still an analogy between the two levels. Did not Christ say, "Even as Thou, Father, art in Me, and I in Thee, that they also may be in Us" (Jn 17:21)? Our human communion may be no more than a dim shadow of the trinitarian life, yet at its best, by God's mercy and his free grace, it is nevertheless a true reflection. We are indeed icons and "transcripts" of the Trinity, to use Charles Wesley's term: "You whom He ordained to be / Transcripts of the Trinity."

Let us turn, then, to our second question. The Trinity, says Jung, is "a revelation not only of God but at the same time of man."[48] In what way? What light does the doctrine of the uncreated Trinity shed upon our created human personhood? What does it mean that we are made in the image of God who is three-in-one? What practical consequences does our trinitarian faith have for our personal, social and political life?

"In our image, after our likeness" (Gen 1:26). If "God is love," as St. John affirms (1 Jn 4:8), then William Blake is right to add, "Man is love."[49] "As in heaven, so on earth": the Trinity, in the words of Williams, is the "primary act of love,"[50] and we humans are called to be earthly expressions of that primary act. All that was said earlier about God as Trinity applies also to us humans:

"United yet not confused, distinct yet not divided": such is divine person-hood, and such also are the human persons-in-relationship, according to God's image.

God is self-giving, sharing, solidarity, reciprocity, response: such also is the human person.

God is not self-love but shared love: such also is the human person.

God is coinherence, *perichōrēsis*, the round dance of love: such also is the human person.

God expresses himself from all eternity in a relationship of I-and-thou: so also within time does the human person. The trinitarian image in which we are created is not possessed by any one us in isolation from our neighbor. The image comes to its fulfillment only in the "between" of love, in the "and" which joins the I to the Thou. Because I am a transcript of the Trinity, I need you in order to be myself. As Williams insists in his poem "The Founding of the Community," the actions of "exchange" and "substitution" are fundamental to the Christian doctrine of the person:

its cult was the Trinity and the Flesh-taking . . .

it exchanged the proper self

and wherever need was drew breath daily

in another's place, according to the grace of the Spirit

"dying each other's life, living each other's death."

Terrible and lovely is the general substitution of souls.[51]

It is certainly no coincidence that in the account of creation, immediately after the words "and God created man in His own image, in the image of God He created him," it is then stated, "male and female He created them" (Gen 1:27). The divine and trinitarian image is not given to the man alone or to the woman alone, but to the two of them together; it is to be found in the "between" of love that draws them each to the other in a union without confusion. Only within an interpersonal communion can the triune image be properly realized. It is a relational image, reflected in the shared life of man and woman, in the primordial social bond of marriage that is the foundation of all other forms of community.

If we humans who have been created in the image of the Trinity repudiate the relationship of mutual love, we cease to be truly human and we become subhuman. (I do not say "bestial," for the animals frequently live in closely knit communities.) Without mutual love each of us is not a person but an "unperson," not a man but an "un-man," to use the term in C. S. Lewis's *Perelandra*. And if we choose to carry that repudiation to its ultimate extreme, we shall deprive our life of all joy and all meaning. In a chilling and literal sense we shall anticipate hell. As Lossky says, adapting a phrase from the priest-mathematician St. Paul Florensky (1882-1937?), "Between the Trinity and hell there lies no other choice."[52]

In this way faith in God as Trinity, so far from being speculative and theoretical, has an immediate and transfiguring effect upon the way in which we live our daily life. In the words of that eccentric but shrewd Russian thinker Nicolas Fyodorov (1828-1903), "Our social programme is the dogma of the Trinity."[53] Belief in a God who is three-in-one, whose characteristics are sharing and solidarity, has direct and practical consequences for our Christian attitude toward politics, economics and social action, and it is our task to work out these consequences in full detail. Every form of community—the family, the school, the workplace, the local eucharistic center, the monastery, the city, the nation—has as its vocation to become, each according to its own modality, a living icon of the Holy Trinity.

When as Christians we fight for justice and for human rights, for a compassionate and caring society, we are acting specifically in the name of the Trinity. Faith in the trinitarian God, in the God of personal interrelationship and shared love, commits us to struggle with all our strength against poverty, exploitation, oppression and disease. Our combat against these things is undertaken not merely on philanthropic and humanitarian grounds but because of our belief in God the Trinity. Precisely because we know that God is three-in-one, we cannot remain indifferent to any suffering, by any member of the human race, in any part of the world. Love after the image and likeness of the Trinity signifies that, in the words of Dostoyevsky's *starets* Zosima, "we are responsible for everyone and everything. The phrase of Williams, "dying each other's life, living each other's death," is cosmic in its scope.

Such is the compelling relevance of the doctrine of the Trinity for the life and action of every one of us. Without the Trinity none of us can be fully a person. Because we believe in the Trinity, each of us is a man or woman for others; every human being is our sister or brother, and we are called to bear their burdens, making their joys and sorrows our own. If only we had the courage truly to be transcripts of the Trinity, we could turn the world upside down.

Every form of community has as its vocation to become a living icon of the Trinity. This is true above all of the church, which is par excellence an image of the Trinity. The *perichōrēsis* of Father, Son and Holy Spirit is to be reflected in the mutual coinherence of the members of the church: as in heaven, so on earth. God the Trinity is a mystery of unity-in-diversity; so also, more fully than any other form of community, is the church. In the Trinity the three persons constitute one God, yet each remains personally distinct; so likewise within the church a multitude of human persons is united in one, yet we each preserve unimpaired our personal diversity.

The analogy between the Trinity and the church illuminates more particularly the proper understanding of authority and primacy within the ecclesial community. In a celebrated text, the Thirty-fourth Apostolic Canon (late fourth century?), the relationship between the chief bishop in each district and his fellow bishops is compared to the *perichōrēsis* subsisting between the three divine persons:

> The bishops of each nation must recognize him who is first among them and must regard him as head, and they must do nothing exceptional without his consent; each bishop is to do only such things as concern his own diocese and the areas dependent upon it. But neither is the first bishop to do anything without the consent of all. For in this way there will be concord, and God will be glorified through the Lord in the Holy Spirit: the Father, the Son and the Holy Spirit.[54]

The concord and coresponsibility prevailing between the chief bishop and his colleagues is seen as a reflection of trinitarian life and a means whereby the three divine persons are glorified: as above, so below. Although the canon refers to local primacy, surely the principle it expresses may be applied also to the universal primacy of the pope (and likewise to that of the ecumenical patriarch).

In this connection the doctrine of the monarchy of the Father is directly relevant to a proper exercise of primacy within the church. In the Trinity the Father is recognized as enjoying priority as the unique source and fountainhead of the Deity; and yet at the same time the Son and the Spirit are acknowledged as enjoying full equality with him, for both of them are true and perfect God in the same sense that he is true and perfect God. A parallel relationship exists on the ecclesiological level. The pope is endowed with universal primacy over the whole of the earthly church, and yet all the other bishops are essentially equal to him in their sacramental status. When the pope is honored as the first, he is regarded as *primus inter pares,* first among equals.

The trinitarian understanding of primacy is a theme that deserves to be further explored in the current Catholic-Orthodox dialogue.

Praying the Trinity

There remains our third and final question: How can we make our personal prayer more trinitarian? The Trinity is indeed central to the liturgical worship of all traditional Christians. There is no phrase more frequent in our service books than the trinitarian doxology, "Glory be to the Father, and to the Son, and to the Holy Spirit." A high proportion of our formal prayers is explicitly directed to the Father, through the Son, in the Holy Spirit. But how far is this trinitarian structure reflected in your and my personal prayer when we are alone, whether we speak with God in our own words or rest quietly in him without using any words at all? Does the Trinity live in our prayer? Do we pray the Trinity?

All too often we tend to envisage prayer as "God and me" facing one another, two persons looking each at the other: me speaking to God or God speaking to me. On this model there are just two subjects, the one human and the other divine, engaged in mutual dialogue. But if our prayer is to be genuinely trinitarian, it needs to have a greater depth than this. It should be not just two-dimensional but multidimensional. More exactly, true prayer is not simply a dialogue between me and God. It is the dialogue within the Trinity—the three-personed *perichōrēsis* of mutual love—into which I as the human subject am caught and taken up. In true prayer at its highest I do not merely talk to God, but I become part of the interpersonal exchange that passes among the divine three.

When we try to practice inner prayer, what tends to happen? At first we commonly experience distraction, dimness, obscurity. We want to concentrate, but our mind is filled with a relentless sequence of irrelevant images and wandering thoughts—like buzzing flies on a summer evening, to use the phrase of the nineteenth-century spiritual master St. Theophan the Recluse. We seem powerless to switch off the inner television set by a simple act of will.

Then, if we persevere, there may come to us a faint awareness of something else. It is not unlike what sometimes happens when we lift the telephone receiver to make a call: the lines are crossed, and instead of hearing the dial tone we find ourselves listening unintentionally to a conversation between two other people. Our reaction is (I hope) at once to stop listening and to put the receiver down. In prayer we may have a similar experience. Within the initial dimness and obscurity we begin to hear fragments of a conversation—a conversation beyond words, silent yet filled with meaning. The spiritual telephone lines seem to have become crossed, and we hear (as it were) other people talking to one another. But this time it is not an accident, and so far from putting down the spiritual telephone we should listen with deep attentiveness. For we are not intruders, but are meant to hear this conversation; and it is the conversation of the Holy Trinity. What we come to realize at this point, however faintly and incompletely, is that the activity of prayer, which at first we take to be of our own making, is in fact the activity of Another, or rather of three Others. We have the sense of being "prayed in." We realize that at the deepest level it is not I who am praying, but God the Holy Trinity who is praying in me.

This experience of entering into the dialogue of the Trinity is described by St. Paul in Romans 8:9-27 and in 1 Corinthians 2:9-16, among other passages. "We do not know how to pray as we should," he writes (Rom 8:26): here he refers to our sense of helplessness as we struggle to pray. The one who assists us in our difficulty, St. Paul continues, is the Holy Spirit: "The Spirit also helps our weakness . . . the Spirit Himself intercedes for us" (Rom 8:26). It is the Paraclete Spirit who initiates us into the trinitarian dialogue. He reveals to us "the deep things of God" (1 Cor 2:10), enabling us to share the "mind of Christ" (1 Cor 2:16) and so to participate in Christ's response to the Father. In the Spirit we begin to cry out with Christ, "Abba, Father!" (Rom 8:15), becoming "sons in the Son": "The Spirit Himself bears witness with our spirit that we are children of God" (Rom 8:16). So, in and through the Spirit, we become part of the dialogue between the Father and the Son. We each hear the Father say to us personally, "Thou art My beloved [s]on" (Mk 1:11), and with the Son we respond, "Abba, Father!" In this way St. Paul can truly affirm, "It is no longer I who live, but Christ lives in me" (Gal 2:20).

It may be that this sense of being caught up into the trinitarian *perichōrēsis* happens to us only once or twice in our life. But these short and sudden glimpses are by God's mercy a genuine foreshadowing of the heavenly kingdom that is our true home.

My Trinity

After seeking to express as best we can the meaning of the Trinity for our personhood and our prayer, we need always to return beyond all images and analogies to the point from which we started. The Trinity is a mystery surpassing our comprehension. As living mystery, the Trinity cannot be proved or explained by human reason but can only be approached in adoration.

Yet at the same time, as we draw near to the trinitarian mystery, it is not only with awe in our hearts but with a wonder full of joy. What is most striking about St. Gregory of Nazianzus, who is par excellence the theologian of the Trinity, is not so much his reverence for the Trinity, profound though this is, as his sense of intimacy with the triune God, the warmth of his affection, the personal quality of his love. "Beloved Trinity," he says, and yet more vividly, "my Trinity."[55] Let us each make his words our own.

A Catholic Response to Kallistos Ware

Robert Fastiggi

I must confess a profound sense of awe at the task set before me. I am in awe first because of the subject matter under discussion. After all, the Holy Trinity is not simply *a* mystery of the faith; the Holy Trinity is *the* mystery of the Christian faith. It is the mystery of God himself in his own inner life and his own self-communication. I am also in awe before the person to whom I am responding. For many of us, Bishop Kallistos Ware is not only an authority on Eastern Orthodoxy but in many respects *the* authority on Eastern Orthodoxy for the English-speaking world.

Faced with this double challenge of addressing the most sublime mystery of the Christian faith as well as responding to such an eminent authority, I thought help was needed, and so in my prayers I have been invoking the aid of that human person who knows the Trinity most intimately. I speak of the Theotokos, the Panagia, Mary, ever-virgin. To her I call for assistance so that

I may understand the Trinity more deeply, so, as Francisco Suárez says, *ut dignitas intercessoris suppleat inopiam nostram* (that the dignity of the intercessor may make up for our deficiency).

My basic reaction to Bishop Kallistos's paper is one of deep gratitude and affirmation. In a conference on traditional Christianity, the question should not be whether a paper on the Trinity would be appropriate but whether the conference would be appropriate without such a paper. I would like to mention three major contributions of the bishop's paper: his stress on prayer, liturgy and Scripture as the true starting points for penetrating the mystery of the Trinity; his delicate and insightful discussion of the strengths and limitations of various analogies of the Trinity; and his creative and moving explanation of how the Trinity, as a *perichōrēsis* of mutual love, should inspire us toward a praxis of mutual assistance, compassion and social action.

In my response I will concentrate on the first two and simply affirm the third. In regard to prayer as the starting point for understanding the Trinity, I would like to build upon Bishop Kallistos's discussion with a historical example from the Latin Catholic tradition. In the early part of this century a French Carmelite nun dedicated her life of prayer to "the indwelling of the Triune God of love" who rests in the hearts of all the baptized. She died in 1906 at the age of twenty-six and since 1984 has been honored as Blessed Elizabeth of the Trinity. Elizabeth saw her religious life as being twofold: that of being a virgin spouse of Christ and that of being a spiritual mother "multiplying the adopted children of the Father, co-heirs with Christ."[1] Taking the Virgin Mary as her model for spiritual motherhood, Blessed Elizabeth, like Bishop Kallistos, understands the Annunciation as a central trinitarian moment in salvation history. As she writes:

> I should like to respond by spending my earthly life as Our Lady did. . . . I unite myself to the soul of the Virgin at the moment in which the Father was covering her with His shadow, while the Word was taking flesh within her and the Holy Spirit came upon her to accomplish this great mystery. It is the entire Trinity in action, yielding itself; and is it not in these divine embraces that the Carmelite's life has to unfold?[2]

We see here how Blessed Elizabeth places herself spiritually in the event of the Annunciation and this luminous moment assumes a trinitarian structure. Such a spiritual union with a specific moment in salvation history is characteristic of both Ignatian spirituality and the French school of spirituality associated with

Cardinal Pierre de Bérulle.[3] Following this method and inspired by Bishop Kallistos's recognition of the Trinity as "the heart of our life," we can discern a means by which we can unite with all the trinitarian moments of the gospel—not only with Mary at the annunciation but also with Jesus at his baptism, transfiguration and crucifixion. In addition we can place ourselves with the disciples at Pentecost. These moments can be reexperienced in a process of meditative *anamnesis* or mystical remembrance so that the Trinity can really become the heart of our life.

While the sacred liturgy provides the richest context for the experience of the Trinity, Bishop Kallistos reminds us that our personal prayer life must also be trinitarian. But how is this to be done? I have suggested meditation on the central trinitarian moments of the New Testament as a good starting point. However, I think that Bishop Kallistos is correct to point us toward the actual experience of the trinitarian *perichōrēsis* in which we not only pray the Trinity but the Trinity prays in us. The bishop writes that this sense of being caught up in the actual interpersonal communication of the Godhead might happen to us "only once or twice in our life." Nevertheless, as he notes, "these short and sudden glimpses are, by God's mercy, a genuine foreshadowing of the heavenly kingdom that is our true home."

What then is the proper context for understanding the Trinity? I believe Bishop Kallistos is correct to point to the life of prayer and worship. As he writes, "Any theology of the Trinity that does not interpret the mystery in terms of praise, blessing and the giving of glory has gone gravely astray." Here the bishop is within the heart of the Eastern Christian tradition, which understands prayer as the true source of theology. As the patristic saying goes: "the one who prays is a theologian and a theologian is the one who prays."

I think that Bishop Kallistos would agree that, of the three questions he asks in his paper, the third question, which concerns our prayer life, really should come first. For only a person who prays in the Trinity would be prepared to deal with the other questions concerning trinitarian analogies and images and the influence of trinitarian faith on our understanding of the human person. Blessed Elizabeth of the Trinity was not a scholar, but by means of her intense prayer life she knew that "to belong to God's household . . . is to live in the bosom of the Trinity,"[4] and she could address God as "my Three, my All, my Beatitude, infinite Solitude, immensity, wherein I lose myself!"[5]

It is clear that both Blessed Elizabeth and Bishop Kallistos understand the

Trinity as the heart of our life, and I think that the bishop's emphasis on prayer and spirituality is not only important but essential. However, I probably would fail in my duties as a respondent if all I can offer is praise instead of a critique. I therefore would like to raise a number of questions and issues for consideration that perhaps could use further elaboration.

The first relates to the status of natural theology. Bishop Kallistos is correct to note that the God of the Christian faith is not an Ultimate Ground of Being or an Uncaused Cause. However, does this mean that what has traditionally been called "natural theology" is held in suspicion? Is it improper to call the Trinity the ultimate ground of being or the uncaused cause?

My second concern is with interreligious dialogue. How can we present the Trinity to monotheists like Jews and Muslims in a manner that appears to them truly respectful of the unity of God? I realize that this is a far-reaching question, but it is important. Perhaps only a Christian, immersed in the trinitarian life, can begin to understand this mystery. Nevertheless, we still must be able to communicate with those who reject the concept of the Trinity and yet believe in God.

The third issue is over the images and analogies of the Trinity. I believe that Bishop Kallistos's discussion of the difference between unipersonal and interpersonal analogies of the Trinity is extraordinarily rich and subtle. However, I think he is a bit too negative about the analogy of light. Thus he notes that "analogies from the realm of sight fail to convey the personal character of the trinitarian God. They turn God into an object rather than a subject, into an It rather than a Thou."

While light does tend to be a physical and spatial metaphor, light can also be personalized. Scripture does tell us that "God is light, and in him is no darkness at all" (1 Jn 1:5 KJV). Since God is always personal, the light that is God is the light of a person. Thus, in canto 33:67-72 of the *Paradiso,* Dante addresses the divine light in the second person singular:

O somma luce, che tanto ti levi
Dai concetti mortali, a la mia mente
Ripresta un poco di quel che parevi,
E fa la lingua mia tanto possente
Che una favilla sol de la tua gloria
Possa lasciare a la futura gente.[6]

Another example of speaking to the divine light as "Thou" comes from the

1833 poem of the great English writer and theologian John Henry Newman:
Lead Kindly Light, amid the encircling gloom
    Lead Thou me on!
The night is dark and I am far from home—
    Lead Thou me on!⁷

Here we see from both Dante and Newman that the divine light can also be addressed as a personal Thou.

The fourth and final issue I wish to address is by far the most delicate—the monarchy of the Father and the procession of the Holy Spirit. If, as Bishop Kallistos notes, we walk along a ridgeway between modalism (due to uniper-sonal models of the Trinity) and tritheism (due to interpersonal models), it would also seem that, in regard to the monarchy of the Father and the procession of the Spirit, we also walk along a ridgeway between the dangers of subordinationism (when monopatrism is emphasized) and dual origination-ism (when the double procession of the Spirit in the *filioque* is emphasized). The issue is quite subtle and, as is well known, a cause for some tension between the Catholic and Eastern Orthodox churches. While Bishop Kallistos makes only one reference to this issue in his paper, he develops the question a bit more in his footnote 42.

Without pretending to offer a definitive solution to this delicate matter, I wish to present ten points for consideration.

1. As Father Aidan Nichols, O.P., and others have noted, the introduction of the *filioque* into the theology of parts of the West (most notably in Spain and Gaul) as well as parts of the East (e.g., Alexandria) was originally motivated by a desire to highlight the divinity of the Son in reaction to the heresies of Arianism and Sabellianism.⁸

2. After the time of Augustine (354-430), the West by and large accepted the *filioque,* though there was a reluctance by the popes to insert it into the creed.

3. It was well known in the East that belief in the *filioque* was widespread in the West. This, however, was not regarded as a reason for breaking communion with the West until the Photian crisis of 867. The Photian schism, however, was healed, and Photius died in communion with Rome. Pope John VIII, it is alleged, promised Photius that he would attempt to remove the *filioque* from the creed in those parts of the West where it had been introduced. The letter that makes this promise, however, is of questionable authenticity.⁹

4. While a number of Eastern fathers can be understood as supporting the *filioque,* most notably Epiphanius (c. 315-403) and Cyril of Alexandria (c. 380-444), the East tended to prefer the expression *per filium* or *dia tou hyiou* rather than *filioque* or *ek kai tou hyiou.* The ultimate question is whether these formulas are complementary or mutually exclusive. The other question is whether the *filioque* threatens the monarchy of the Father.

5. A possible resolution to this question may be found in the letter of Maximus the Confessor (580-662) to Marinus. As the great saint observes:

> On this basis they [the Latins] showed that they themselves have not made the Son the cause (*aitia*) of the Spirit. They know, indeed, that the Father is the sole cause of the Son and of the Spirit, of one by generation and of the other by *ekporeusis* (original procession)—but they explained that the latter comes (*proienai*) through the Son, and they showed in this way the unity and the immutability of the essence. (*Letter to Marinus of Cyprus* PG 90:972)[10]

Thus for Maximus the *filioque* and the *per filium* appear to be complementary formulas.

6. If Maximus's understanding is correct, it is quite significant. This is particularly so in light of the creed composed by Patriarch Tarasios (730-806) and approved by the fathers of the Seventh Ecumenical Council (Nicaea 11, 787). This creed confesses that the Holy Spirit proceeds from the Father through the Son (*to Pneuma to agion . . . to ek tou Patros dia tou Uiou ekporeuomenon*).[11]

If the *filioque* is a Latin way of expressing the same truth as the Eastern *per filium,* then the conflict over the double procession of the Spirit is less theological then ecclesiological. In other words, the real issue is whether or not the pope could authorize an addition to the creed without the consent of his brother bishops of the East. This is why Father Nichols has stated that "*au fond* only the papacy divides the Orthodox and the Catholic Churches."[12]

7. The theological issue is whether the *filioque* by necessity challenges the monarchy of the Father. A possible resolution to this question is provided by Bishop Kallistos in footnote 42 of his paper. He points out: "It should be noted that St. Augustine, while upholding the double procession of the Holy Spirit from both the Father and the Son, is at the same time careful to insist that the Holy Spirit proceeds principally (*principaliter*) from the Father and that he proceeds from the Son only through the Father's gift (*per donum patris*). Thus

although using a different terminology, Augustine agrees basically with the Cappadocians concerning the Father's monarchy."

8. The monarchy of the Father, understood in the Augustinian sense, has been respected in Western church councils. Thus Council XI of Toledo (675) states that "the Father is not generated nor created, but is unbegotten. He does not derive His origin from anyone, and from Him, the Son receives His birth and the Holy Spirit His procession." The Father, therefore, is "the origin and fountain of the entire divinity" *(fons ergo ipse et origo est totius divintatis)*.[13]

At Lyons II (1274) it is stated: "We confess faithfully and devoutedly that the Holy Spirit proceeds eternally from the Father and the Son, "not as by two origins but by one origin" *(non tanquem ex duobis principiis, sed tanquam ex uno principio)*.[14]

At Florence (1439) the monarchy of the Father was likewise affirmed: "The Holy Spirit is eternally from the Father and the Son; He has His nature and His subsistence at once from the Father and Son. He proceeds eternally from both as from one origin and through one spiration" *(ab uno principio et unica spiratione procedit)*.[15] In other words, there is only one origin of the one spiration—the Father. However, the Son likewise shares in this spirating of the Spirit, proceeding from the one origin or *principium* of the Father.

9. Some of the confusion over the *filioque* may be linguistic. Various scholars have noted a distinction between the Greek verb *ekporeuestai* and the Latin verb *procedere*. As Jean-Marie Garriques has noted,

> The Greek verb suggests a principle from which a distinction arises; the Latin suggests the starting point of a continuous process. The *ekporeusis* of the Spirit is then His arising in His hypostatic particularity from the Father; the *processio* of the Spirit from the Father and the Son is the last moment in the communication of the consubstantial divinity which proceeds according to the order of the divine persons, Father to Son, Father and Son to Spirit.[16]

In a similar vein Giuseppe Ferraro, S.J., observes: "The Greek *ekporeuomenai*, which literally means 'to exit' or 'to leave from an original source,' refers, above all, to the origin from which the reality comes forth; while the Latin *procedere*, which literally means 'to advance' refers, above all, to the reality which advances without considering directly whether the origin from which it comes is or is not the original source."[17] This linguistic difference is crucial for understanding why the *filioque* can be acceptable in the Latin but not in the

Greek. Indeed, the recent statement by the Vatican's Pontifical Council for Promoting Christian Unity states that the *filioque* should not be included in the Greek symbol because of the difference in meaning.

10. The New Testament can be understood in several senses. The Spirit is referred to as "the Spirit of the Son" (see Gal 4:6; Rom 8:15). Likewise, the Spirit is sent by the Son (see Jn 15:26). The question, though, is whether this refers to a temporal sending forth of the Spirit or an eternal one. Clearly Jesus receives all that he has from the Father, including the Spirit (see Jn 17:15), and he does breathe the Spirit onto his apostles (Jn 20:22). Is there a way of reading these Scriptures in a manner that preserves both the monarchy of the Father and the double procession of the Spirit from the Father and the Son? Many in the West have done just that, but perhaps this is an issue that cannot be settled by Scripture alone. The present climate for reconciliation between Catholics and the Orthodox, however, appears to be more promising than before, especially in light of recent theological discussions.

Conclusion

In the mystery of the Trinity we find the perfect communication of mutual love and interpersonal sharing *(koinōnia)*. God is love (1 Jn 4:17) and the Trinity is the heart of our lives by which and through which we are capable of loving. The sad truth is that the perfect *koinōnia* of the divine persons of the Trinity is not realized among Christians here on earth. This is due to human sin.

The present Roman pontiff, John Paul II, has committed himself to the "dialogue of love" between the Catholic and Orthodox churches. His status as the first Slavic pope places him in a unique position to be a "Slav among the Latins and a Latin among the Slavs." He has been self-consciously trinitarian in his writings, especially in preparation for the third millennium. The pontiff has often invoked the metaphor of the East and the West as the two lungs by which the church must breathe, and in his apostolic letter *Orientale lumen*[18] he points to the "great values" of the Christian East that are especially expressed in monasticism, liturgy and spirituality. The pope clearly hopes for reunion between Catholic and Orthodox, and his prayer is: "May Christ, the *Orientale Lumen*, soon, very soon, grant us to discover that in fact, despite so many centuries of distance, we were very close, because together, perhaps without knowing it, we were walking towards the one Lord and towards one another."[19]

If Christians go to the heart of reality—the one God who is Father, Son and Holy Spirit—they cannot help but draw closer to each other, and if reunion is not achieved during this early sojourn, we know we will celebrate it with joy in the heavenly kingdom that, as Bishop Kallistos has said, is our true home.

6

ON FROM ORR
Cultural Crisis, Rational Realism & Incarnational Ontology

J. I. Packer

*O*ur announced aim is to "test whether an 'ecumenical orthodoxy,' solidly based upon the classic Christian faith, can become the foundation for a unified and transformative witness to the age we live in."[1] The first thing I want to do is to state firmly that I believe it can, and to explain where I come from in saying that.

As an Anglican, a Protestant, an evangelical and in C. S. Lewis's sense a "mere Christian,"[2] that is, as it is sometimes put, a small-*c* catholic, I theologize out of what I see as the authentic biblical and creedal mainstream of Christian identity, the confessional and liturgical great tradition that the church on earth has characteristically maintained from the start. History tells me how reactions against abuses, syncretisms with secular culture, lack of theological competence, individual idiosyncrasies and corporate deadness of heart have on occasion led sections of the church to deviate from the great tradition. History also tells me, however, how the Holy Spirit, operating through the biblical Word of God, has again and again reformed and renewed lapsed sections and faulty facets of the church. My present hope is that the Holy Spirit is preparing to do this, indeed is beginning to do it, again in the English-speaking West and in those European countries that were once called Christendom, just as he is currently causing the gospel to advance by breathtaking leaps and bounds in Asia, Africa and Latin America. *Pace* Nietzsche and some already outmoded moderns, I affirm that God is most certainly not dead, and the great tradition will most surely survive.

At the Reformation skewed Western understandings of the church, the sacraments, justification, faith, prayer and ministry were, as I believe, corrected; but the corrections took place within the frame of the great tradition and did not break it. (Such is my theological judgment, as it was the judgment of the magisterial Reformers against the Anabaptists. The visible church, of course, fragmented, but that is another story.) The great tradition of Christian faith and life includes the following:

☐ recognizing the canonical Scriptures as the repository and channel of Christ-centered divine revelation.

☐ acknowledging the triune God as sovereign in creation, providence and grace.

☐ focusing faith, in the sense both of belief and of trust, on Jesus Christ as God incarnate; as our crucified and living Savior, Lord, master, friend, life and hope; and as the one mediator of, and thus the only way to, a filial relationship with God his Father.

☐ seeing Christians as a family of forgiven sinners, now supernaturally regenerated in Christ and empowered for godliness by the Holy Spirit.

☐ seeing the church as a single supernatural society, and the two dominical sacraments as necessities of obedience, gestures of worship and means of communion with God in Christ.

☐ practicing prayer, obedience, purity, love and service, and sanctifying all relationships in the home, the church and the wider world, as the Christian's proper individual lifestyle.

☐ reckoning with the personal reality of evil and maintaining purposeful hostility to sin and the devil.

☐ expecting death and final judgment to lead into the endless joy of heaven, where the glorified saints will live with Christ and each other forever.

The great tradition has from time to time embraced different ways of explicating these things, but the things themselves are the nonnegotiables of

Christianity according to Christ, and the reconceiving specifically of theological method, of salvation and of the church in Reformation theology should be seen as an attempt—essentially, in my view, a successful attempt—to spell out all these themes in the most accurate way. The great tradition has witnessed many misconceptions (about the Trinity, and grace and justification, for instance) that, if consistently held, would make true saving knowledge of Jesus Christ inaccessible. Responsible theology is motivated in part by the desire to prevent such a thing from ever happening. Theological watchfulness for the sake of the gospel, such as Paul models in Romans, 1 Corinthians, Galatians, Colossians and the Pastorals, and John and Jude in their letters also, is itself part of the great tradition, and there is nothing unspiritual about theological controversy and debate when gospel truth and evangelical life are at stake.

The Reformation split the Western church, and nationalism, combined later with differences about church order and more recently with ventures in personal leadership, has given us a Protestant world now divided into a four- or five-figure number of separate ecclesiastical organizations. About this state of affairs I would say only that convergence in faith and fellowship ought to be desired and sought wherever the worldwide visible church has come apart. However much historic splits may have been justified as the only way to preserve faith, wisdom and spiritual life intact at a particular time, continuing them in complacency and without unease is unwarrantable. To regard emergency arrangements as the normal order of things is defective thinking. So we are right to be seeking convergence now, for reasons of theology (God's one family, scattered worldwide, ought to look and act like one family, as Jesus prayed it might), and also for reasons of strategy relating to our mission of witness and influence (divided we can only expect to fall, united we might hope with God's help to stand). In face of our own divisions, which are sad, and the resurgent paganism of our culture, which is sadder, let us, without forfeiting or fudging any specific truth as we see it, but in a fellowship that is shaped by our common anchorage within the great tradition, continue to seek substantive convergence together. As C. S. Lewis wrote to his onetime pupil Dom Bede Griffiths: "When all is said (and truly said) about the divisions of Christendom, there remains, by God's mercy, an enormous common ground."[3] We should labor to occupy that common ground properly, as a priority task.

The Current Cultural Crisis

We are seeking to envision effective witness to the age we live in. Though no sociologist, and thus no expert on cultural shifts, and therefore very dependent at this point on others' insights, my argument requires me to state here how I see the overall trend and trajectory of Western intellectual life today. We are told that a major transition is in process: that modernism is giving way to postmodernism and secular hopefulness to cynicism, narcissism and despair. On this I have two remarks to make.

First, if a major cultural transition is indeed taking place in the West it will not be the first time the church has been involved in such a thing. Cultural transition is in fact a major part of the historic Christian story. The early church itself was a force for cultural change. When Christianity hit the Gentile world in the second half of the first century it faced Gnostic dualism, superstitious fatalism and philosophical pessimism in myriad forms, and had to engineer its own cultural transition from paganism to Christendom—which it did, most brilliantly and successfully, with Augustine's *City of God* standing out as a monument to the process. Christendom, once established, then lasted for more than a millennium. But in the seventeenth century the West began to shake loose from its Christian moorings, and the secular rationalism of the Enlightenment, which we now call modernism, increasingly took control of the Western mind and milieu. Enlightenment modernism elbowed the churches of the West out of cultural leadership in the eighteenth and nine-teenth centuries, and this trauma produced different responses. Protestants divided; some maintained the great tradition against modernism by rear-guard action, others recast the tradition in modernist terms, which really meant abandoning it, and many mediating attempts to square the circle by marrying the two points of view were made. Thus confusion grew. Meantime, modernist hostility to the tradition reinforced the Roman Catholic siege mentality that the conflict with Protestantism had already induced. Rome put up the shutters and until Vatican II resisted modernist pressure far better than Protestantism did. The irony now, however, is that great-tradition Protestantism is making a spectacular comeback in these latter years of the twentieth century, while Rome is having to struggle to survive the modernist inroads to which Vatican II wittingly or unwittingly opened the door. The present pope has labored mightily to counter this modernism by reasserting the Catholic version of the great tradition, and it is clear that his lead is being widely followed, though the long-term outcome remains uncertain. The Eastern Orthodox story has been different, but in the one-time Soviet world, despite two generations of enormous pressure from atheistic statist secularism, itself a product of the modernist mentality, the great tradition has not been stamped out, and today Orthodoxy is being set forth with new energy.

Surely I say again we may be confident that whatever happens to current Western culture the tradition will continue to survive. After all, if we are right, God is in it and with it. Christ has promised that the gates of hell will not prevail against his church, and they certainly have not done so in their modernist form. So we have no reason to panic as we look to the future.

Second, I grant that a genuine cultural transition from modernism to postmodernism is occurring in some places, if not everywhere, but I note that it is very differently analyzed by different people, which is why I must lay before you my own understanding of it before I go further.[4] What I think we have to face up to is this:

In cultural modernism and in the humanism that is its child, truth and value are thought to be determined by reason working empirically on the basis of observation and experiment. Reason, thus used, is called scientific, and the conclusions of scientific reason are made the lodestar for organizing education and all forms of community life. Optimistically assuming that everything can be improved by planning and technology and will in any case sooner or later evolve into something better, modernism has for two centuries sought to shape society through industrial development, social engineering, urban triumphalism and materialistic enrichment. This process has been expected to bring health, harmony and happiness to all the world; but the unmistakable witness of our barbaric twentieth century is that it has totally failed to do so and moreover is totally lacking in resources for doing so in the future. So among intellectuals and particularly in the universities, which are of course the first units of society that intellectuals impact, there is understandably in progress a reaction of disillusionment against the modernist habit of mind.

What form does the reaction take? In place of the quasi-behaviorist ideal of rational objectivity creating a collectivist community of like-thinking, well-socialized human ants in smoothly functioning anthills, a new ideal of freedom and fulfillment for the individual has emerged. This ideal assumes the technological conveniences of the anthill as a given, but rejects the notion of universal public truth on questions involving values; muffles and scrambles all communication, oral or documentary, by a process of deconstruction; debunks other people's absolutes and values by playful or cynical negation; and reduces public disagreements to power plays and power struggles between competing subcultures and manipulators. In postmodernism individualistic subjectivity is set in a critical relation to all forms of supposedly scientific and consensual objectivity, and the personal story of each human being is allowed to stand in judgment over the corporate stories of all human groups, both secular and churchly. Spirituality without truth, individuality without constraints, pluralistic pragmatism, whimsy claiming to be wisdom, desire masquerading as morality, and benevolent tolerance of any and every view that does not tell you that you yourself are wrong thus constitute the essence of postmodern culture. Relativistic randomness replaces rationalistic purpose; to think, say and do your own thing in conscious detachment from and sometimes opposition to conventional public humanism now becomes the true heart of humanness. Such is the new view of reality that is sprouting all over the Western world today.

That the shadows of French existentialism, Marxist atheism and American hippiedom hang heavy over postmodernism, that reductionism rules its head while cynicism eats at its heart, and that its idea of political correctness makes it tyrannical toward dissentients much sooner than was ever the case with modernism itself are surely evident facts, and very disturbing facts too. Claiming to be a bracing disinfectant for the mind, postmodernism appears as a mode of intellectual anarchy and in cultural terms as very much a dead-end street. Some Christians, seeking ways of effective witness, have welcomed postmodernism as enhancing the significance of personal testimony and dissolving cultural prejudice against the supernatural, but by and large the shift from modernism to postmodernism seems to be a move from the frying pan into the fire so far as Christian existence and outreach are concerned, for it makes the necessary affirmation of absolutes twice as hard as it was before. Words from G. K. Chesterton's "Ballad of the White Horse" may well round off our glance at the postmodernist mindset:

I bring you naught for your comfort,
    Yea, naught for your desire,
But that the sky grows darker yet
    And the sea rises higher.

Our present agenda is not, however, to develop jeremiads, but to seek the most effective way of united Christian witness in a world where modernism and postmodernism divide the control between them, and to this task I now turn. What has been said puts us in a position to sketch out a strategy, and at this point I want to introduce someone who should be better known than he is, namely, James Orr, who I believe can help us in a major way.

About James Orr

Orr (1844-1913) was a Scottish theologian and apologist of real distinction who contended tirelessly for great-tradition Christianity in days before the First World War, when Ritschlian liberalism, Wellhausenite higher criticism and philosophical idealism of a kind that would today be called panentheistic were riding high in the Protestant world, and the redemptive supernaturalism of mainstream Christian faith was being steadily dissolved away in the older evangelical churches. As a man of his time Orr did not interact with Roman Catholics, who in those days had no place in Scottish theological life, nor with Orthodox, about whom he had no specific knowledge as far as one can tell; his battles were with the liberal and modernist academic leadership in German and British Protestantism, and here he fought most effectively. He was a polymath with a remarkable range of exact learning in philosophy, history, theology and biblical studies; he was thoroughly abreast of German theological literature, more so it would seem than any of his peers; and he established himself as something of a one-man band in traditionalist polemics. Because he was swimming against the stream in the British churches, on intellectual lines similar to those of his contemporaries at old Princeton but without the solid ecclesiastical support that the Princetonians could command; because most of his academic peers viewed him as an extremely able, but ultimately tiresome, dinosaur; and because his ability in high-level debate so far outstripped that of his conservative supporters that while approving him they were unable properly to appreciate him; he was not valued at his true worth in his own day. Since his death he has been largely neglected, as expositors of massive argument in a monochrome literary style all too often are.[5] But something of his quality can be seen from the following paragraphs, which I take out of Alan Sell's brilliant survey of eight turn-of-the-century Scottish Presbyterian teachers:

> Orr's was no unthinking, narrow traditionalism. If he ended, more or less, with the faith of his fathers, it was because, having departed thence for

argument's sake, he had returned to base, after slaying numerous foes *en route*. He was in no sense one who needed the security of the blinkered. On the contrary, he was at his best when judiciously dissecting the views of those who were far removed from him in spirit . . . of all our divines, Orr's interests were the most catholic . . . in detailed knowledge of the Christian thought of the ages he outclassed them all.[6]

[Orr's] conviction [was] that doctrinal theology cannot be expunged from Christianity. The fact is that "there is a truth, or sum of truths, involved in the Biblical revelation, for [sic] which it is the duty of the Church to bear witness; that Christianity . . . has an ascertainable, statable content, which it is the business of the Church to find out, to declare, and to defend, and ever more perfectly to seek to unfold in the connection of its parts, and in relation to advancing knowledge; that this content of truth is not something that can be manipulated into any shape man's fancies please, but something in regard to which we should not despair of being able to arrive at a large measure of agreement . . ."[7] When he adds the comment, "I venture to say that what the church suffers from today is not, as so many think, too much theology, but too little theology, of an earnest [i.e., serious] kind",[8] it is difficult not to apply his words directly to our own time.

Orr defines doctrine as "the direct, often naive, expression by Christian faith of the knowledge it possesses, or the convictions it holds, regarding God and divine things." Theology is the "reflective exercise of mind upon the doctrines of faith." "Dogma" stands for "those formulations of Christian doctrine which have obtained authoritative recognition in wide sections of the Church, and are embodied in historical creeds."[9] Although the ultimate test of dogma is Scripture, Orr would have us remember that "we are more dependent on the past than we think even in our interpretation of Scripture . . ."[10] Other tests include the inner coherence of the dogmatic system, and its correlation with the vital experience, not of the individual, but of the Church as a whole; there is the appeal to the practical results which have followed the upholding of dogma; and—what particularly concerns Orr—there is the "practically unerring verdict of *history* . . . the history of dogma is the judgment of dogma."[11]

Orr's "fundamental presupposition," writes Sell, was that "Christian truth forms an *organism*—has a unity and coherence which cannot be arbitrarily disturbed in any of its parts without the whole undergoing injury. Conversely, the proof that any doctrine fits in essentially to that organism—is an integral part of it—is one of the strongest evidences we have of its correctness."[12] The point of Orr's appeal to the history of doctrine was that ongoing review and restatement in relation to intellectual life in both the church and the world will show up inadequacies and intrinsic incoherences as surely as ongoing use shows up the design faults of commercially manufactured objects. Continues Sell, "While every part of the organism is sensitive to change in any other, the pivotal truth is that concerning God: 'As a man thinks God to be, so will his theology be.' "[13] Orr worked with the classic Christian notion of God, that of the great tradition, precisely grasped and lucidly set forth, and his contribution to apologetics and systematics was in consequence a vindicating and elaborating of old paths.

Orr was in one sense a conservative; but it is important to see that he was not a confessional theologian in the manner of those Lutheran and Reformed writers, ancient and modern, who treat their own church's creedal statement as their sole lookout point for surveying the church and the world. Orr, who actually helped to detach his original denomination, the United Presbyterian Church, from line-by-line adherence to the Westminster Confession,[14] should rather be thought of as a heritage theologian, whose pervasive sense that the times were out of joint philosophically and theologically led him to polemics that at every point constituted (to borrow the perceptive title of Glen Scorgie's book on Orr) *A Call for Continuity*. Orr's lifelong defense of continuity with the mainstream Christian past required him to argue, first, for holding to ontological and epistemological realism and rejecting both Kantian agnosticism and Hegelian idealism; second, for rating canonical Scripture as inspired revelation from God and rejecting lower estimates of it;[15] third, for viewing humanity as basically noble but actually sinful and without Christ lost and for rejecting all forms of evolutionary optimism;[16] and, fourth, for affirming a generically Chalcedonian Christology and a generically Augustinian soteriology against all nonincarnational and nonmediatorial accounts of Jesus our Lord.[17] Orr wrote books criticizing Hume's reductionist epistemology, Ritschl's Kantian skewing of the gospel, Harnack's Ritschlian history of dogma, and the J-E-D-P pentateuchal criticism of Wellhausen, Graf and Kuenen,[18] and in each of these clashes he showed himself to be a rational polemicist with a masterful line of counterargument that made demonstrably better sense in biblical, logical and human terms than did the theories he was opposing.

Orr's stature as an apologist for the historic faith is comparable to that of his much better known contemporaries B. B. Warfield and Charles Gore; but his literary style was less weighty than Warfield's and lower-voltage than Gore's, and his peers took less notice of him than was the case with the other two. Scandalously, as I hinted earlier, by the end of his life he had won so many battles and become so formidable in debate that British theologians who could not answer him formed the habit of ignoring him or treating him as an instance of academic bad taste. I urge now that it is time he is rediscovered, for Orr's stances in face of what he saw as the aberrant *Zeitgeist* of his day can, I believe, help us considerably as we face the incoherence of postmodern relativism and clever anti-intellectualism (I here call it by the name that fits) in our own day. Let me try to show how.

"Unified and Transformative Witness"

As I hope I have made clear, I do not maintain that Orr was the greatest turn-of-the-century Christian theologian, nor that he was the most influential apologist of his time. It seems that in the flesh he was a lively debater, genial and commanding, with shafts of satirical humor and massive appeals to common sense adorning lucid and compelling argumentation; but on paper his admirable clarity hovers on the edge of dullness. He was not the equal of Warfield or Bavinck for expository weight, nor of Gore for pastoral passion, nor of Forsyth for evangelical eloquence, nor of Kuyper for intellectual vision, nor of Denney for rapierlike rhetoric. He was not so impressive in building up structures of truth as he was in showing up the irrationalities of error. Yet he had a wider range, a deeper philosophical involvement and a more formidable array of learning than anyone else at least on the British scene in his time, and I am venturing the claim that his work of a century ago models for us the kind of apologetic stance and strategy that can best serve us today. The rest of this presentation will be devoted to trying to make that claim good.

What would an Orr-type program for persuasive Christian discourse look like? How would it give substance to our desire for a convergent conservative testimony to "mere Christianity," unified and transformative, according to the announced terms of our quest together? As I try to answer these questions, I shall bear in mind the difference between the modernity of Orr's milieu and the postmodernity of ours, and I shall feel free to amplify and develop Orr's principles of procedure as I deploy and apply them. But here are four basic guidelines for us that spring directly from Orr's own work.

1. Display the rational coherence of historic mainstream Christian beliefs, both as a crystallizing of the doctrinal content of the Bible and also as a full-scale, comprehensive and satisfying philosophy of life: one that embraces all the facts of human experience, good and bad; that ennobles human existence; and that makes better sense than any known alternative.

Orr's first and arguably greatest book, *The Christian View of God and the World as Centring in the Incarnation* (1893), hews to this line for nearly five hundred pages and does so with notable success. Of it Scorgie wrote: "Charles Gore once claimed to be a philosopher in the sense that he felt compelled to try to make sense of existence and to discern his place within a framework of meaning. By such a definition, Orr also would have claimed to be a philosopher. And insofar as philosophy is understood to be a quest for a unified account of reality, it is accurate to describe *The Christian View* as a work of philosophical apologetics."[19] It was in fact the first attempt in Britain to articulate a full-scale Christian world and life view against modernist variants. Orr saw with prophetic clarity that

> the opposition which Christianity has to encounter is no longer confined to special doctrines or to points of supposed conflict with the natural sciences,—for example, the relations of Genesis and geology,—but extends to the whole manner of conceiving of the world, and of man's place in it. . . . It is the Christian view of things in general which is attacked, and it is by an exposition and vindication of the Christian view of things as a whole that the attack can most successfully be met.[20]

So he set himself to show

> that there is a definite Christian view of things, which has a character, coherence, and unity of its own, and stands in sharp contrast with counter theories and speculations, and that this world-view has the stamp of reason and reality upon itself, and can amply justify itself at the bar both of history and of experience.[21]

The strength of *The Christian View* and of Orr's subsequent apologetic writings, which are best seen as so many detailed studies subordinate to *The Christian View,* lies in the precision and skill with which he follows his self-imposed agenda, taking Jesus Christ—the Christ of the Scriptures and of the church's historic faith—as his central point of reference. "He who with his whole heart believes in Jesus as the Son of God," writes Orr, "is thereby committed to much else besides . . . to a view of God . . . of man . . . of sin . . . of Redemption . . . of the purpose of God in creation and history . . . of human destiny, found only in Christianity."[22] The detailed interactions involved in Orr's masterful treatment of these themes are inevitably dated and somewhat dull, but his identifying of the connections between one theme and another is as compelling today as ever it was.

Works of this kind, doing this job, are needed in every age if Christian testimony is to have credibility, and certainly such works are needed today. Despite the irrational and antirational posturings of many around us, the human mind as such, today as always, craves wisdom and understanding, so that no serious person can ever settle for living without a philosophy in the Gore and Orr sense, or with a philosophy that seems to them self-contradictory. One reason why historic Christianity has been put on the shelf in today's Western world is that secular thinkers believe (often without looking) that it lacks internal coherence, and cannot assimilate today's knowledge about the nature and history of the world, and is unable to account for the actual quality of human experience, with its tensions, tribalisms, hypocrisies, barbarisms, brutalities, traumas, disillusionments, madnesses and miseries. But when, with Pascal and Orr (to look no further), we insist that the basic dynamics of human existence are, first, sin—original sin, as Augustinians call it—corrupting all natural instincts and desires more or less, and then, second, God's grace in Jesus our Lord redeeming and restoring, the realities of our disordered human lives become intelligible, while theism, correctly, that is, biblically, formulated proves able to accommodate all the knowledge of historical events and physical processes in this world that modern study yields or can yield. By explaining these things the rationality and viability of the Christian faith can be made clear. And because of the widespread anti-Christianity in the worlds of education and opinion-making, this is currently a major task.

Orr's arguments are a century old; have there been model apologists of his type more recently? Perhaps the most effective exponents of the rationality of the Christian faith in this century have been G. K. Chesterton and C. S. Lewis: both laymen, we may note. Francis Schaeffer addressed himself to this task, but his communicative style was comparable to that of the cartoonist, and his vivid popular presentations of biblical Christianity, with accompanying critiques of alternative views, though cogent for their own pastoral purpose, had academic limitations.[23] It is arguable that the present pope comes close to qualifying as Orr's successor. But, however that may be, it is certain that without a flow of wide-ranging, well-focused and magisterially combative declarations of the total Christian view of things as being supremely realistic and rational, apologetic renewal among us will not get very far. Gratefully to encourage, therefore, those who engage in authentically Christian philosophy, at both technical and broad-brush level, is a present-day priority for the people of God.

2. Highlight the content and coherence of the Christian view of God in particular as the focal and structural center of the Christian understanding of everything else. Spell out trinitarian theocentricity as the foundational frame for Christian thought.

"As a man thinks God to be, so will his theology be." Sell, as we saw, described this as the pivotal point for Orr; so indeed it was, and so it must be for every apologist and theologian worthy of the name. Theocentricity as a habit of mind and life is basic to Christianity. It is not enough to bring God in as predicative to something else that is the real focus of our concern. Cosmocentricity and anthropocentricity in any form are distorting perspectives, no matter how precisely Christian specifics are fitted into these frames. As God is the object of Christian worship, so he must be the controlling center of Christian thought about everything; and he himself must be thought about in a rigorously biblical way. Orr discerned that an immanentist unitarian view of God underlay the liberal Protestant distortions against which he constantly battled, and firmly pointed out the greater intellectual adequacy, as well as the more solid biblical basis, of trinitarian theism. Some of his sentences, written over a hundred years ago, are worth quoting here: the wisdom they express does not date with age.

The doctrine of the Trinity is not a result of mere speculation . . . still less, as some eminent writers would maintain,[24] the result of the importation of Greek metaphysics into Christian theology. It is, in the first instance, the result of a simple process of induction from the facts of the Christian Revelation . . . Our faith in the Trinity does not rest even on the proof-texts which are adduced from the Scriptures in support of the Trinitarian distinction. These have their value as summaries of the truth we gain from the complex of facts of the New Testament Revelation, and serve to assure us that we are on the right lines in our interpretation of these facts, but the fundamental ground on which we rest is the facts themselves. The triune conception of God is justified when it is shown to be the conception which underlies the triune Revelation God has given of himself, and the triune activity of the work of redemption.[25]

From this Orr moves on to make the now familiar point that unless one posits the eternity of the world it is impossible on unitarian principles to give substance to the thought of love as an eternal divine characteristic.

> What can love in God mean on the supposition of His absolute solitariness? What can be the object of God's love throughout eternity, if there is no triune distinction in God? . . . Either, therefore, we must . . . seek an object for God's love in the finite, created world, or recognize that God has an infinitely blessed life of love within himself, and this brings us to the doctrine of an immanent Trinity.[26]

A most significant development in contemporary theology is the emphasis increasingly being laid on the fact that God the Creator is essentially relational in his own being; in other words, that "he" is "they" within the unity of the Godhead, and that as these internal divine relationships are the vital clue to apprehending God so they are the vital clue to understanding in an existential way what it means for us humans to be made in God's image and then remade in it by saving grace after sin has marred and disfigured us. Prominent names in this recovery include such as Leonard Hodgson,[27] Robert Jenson,[28] Thomas Torrance and James Torrance,[29] Colin Gunton,[30] Millard Erickson,[31] Jürgen Moltmann[32] and Wolfhart Pannenberg.[33]

Three factors at least have prompted the recovery. The first is a growing recognition that unitarian thought-forms and New Testament data are out of sync with each other and can never be fitted together. The second is the insistence of modern psychology that personal relationships constitute the essence of personal lives, which forces us to ask whether the same is not true of the God whose image we bear. The third is the emergence of the isolation of the individual as an increasingly agonizing problem in our increasingly unstable and fragmented Western society, which obliges the church to muster its resources for ministering to this condition. The bottom line is a renewed awareness that a consistent and thoroughgoing trinitarianism is basic both to authentic Christian theology and to authentic Christian discipling—that is, to evangelism, nurture and pastoral care, all leading into the life of prayer, purity and praise, which is our true spiritual health.

So I am bold to believe that the subliminal unitarianism that has been at the heart of liberal theology ever since Schleiermacher is finally on its way out.[34] Process theology, which is a finite-God mutation of the unitarian view and the most recent form of it to generate anything like a school of thought, is losing ground,[35] and while there are currently on offer many personal theologies of a radical kind, no "politically correct" alternative to classical theism can claim establishment status in the way that evolutionary panentheism could and did within the older Protestant churches in Orr's day. This gives heritage Christians a great opportunity to highlight the "social Trinity" of the Cappadocians, of Augustine (who if I read him right stood on Cappadocian shoulders), of Calvin and John Owen, and of the present-day theologians just mentioned, as our resource for discipling, for personal spiritual growth, for rebuilding human and humane community in the family and the church, and for the rescue of Christian worship from the swamps of subjectivity in which it is today so frequently bogged down.

Orr, were he alive now, would I think tell us emphatically that this is an opportunity that all heritage Christians—conservative, if you wish to call us that—should take, not only for the restoring of spiritual health to individuals and communities, but also for the purging and re-forming of our respective theological traditions and thereby the furthering of their convergence: the convergence out of which alone, as I see it, contemporary witness to God that is sufficiently strong and significant can emerge. To continue at this point on the trajectory of Orr's thought thus seems to me a priority task at present.

3. Stress that the incarnation, atonement, bodily resurrection and ascension, present heavenly reign and future public return of Jesus Christ are central to the Christian story, and by projecting this biblical christocentricity establish the fact that the Christian gospel is first and foremost news of redemption for lost sinners.

For Orr, belief in the reality and centrality of the Christ of the New Testament was crucial. His first book, as we saw, presented the Christian view of God and the world as "centering in the Incarnation." He there categorized the truth of the Trinity as "the first of the corollaries of the doctrine of the incarnation,"[36] thus displaying his awareness that Christian trinitarianism is essentially affirmation about Jesus Christ. In a published speech delivered in 1904 he declared war on all forms of naturalistic Christology,[37] and he followed this up with two substantial volumes, *The Virgin Birth of Christ* (1907) and *The Resurrection of Jesus* (1908). His last major piece of writing, in fact his main contribution to the five-volume *International Standard Bible Encyclo-paedia*, which he organized and edited and which was published shortly after his death,[38] was the book-length article "Jesus Christ," which was in effect a full-scale life of Christ based on a harmony of the Gospels with a minimum of polemical interactions.

Always Orr argued Christianity's credentials on the basis that as the apostolic witness to Jesus' divine saviorhood grew out of the historical impact that the historical Jesus had made on his first followers, so the evidence for the truth of the gospel was and is space-time phenomena, to be assessed by the historical type of argument that looks for causes adequate to produce the events under study. The antimiraculous a prioris that operated as blinders on the minds of so many of Orr's theological contemporaries, keeping them from discerning the weight and the force of the historical evidence for Jesus, could, he believed, be shown to be unreasonable and inappropriate, while the Gospel accounts of Jesus had a certain self-authenticating quality that would surely be recognized once they were viewed as a coherent whole. What had to be explained was the fact that Christianity began and spread as the worship of a Creator-God truly manifested in a risen, living, miracle-working divine Savior who forgives sins and bestows the divine Holy Spirit, thereby transforming believers into loving, rejoicing, praying, worshiping persons who live in an unquenchable hope of sharing Christ's heavenly glory forever.

This characteristic new life, Orr argued, requires the supernatural Christ of the Gospels and Epistles to explain it; no other hypothesis is adequate. His argument seems unanswerable, and perhaps against our twentieth-century background of resurgent barbarism worldwide it is easier for us to see that than it was for the children of the evolution-besotted, perfectionist culture with whom Orr had to deal. The liberal fancy that Christianity is in essence humankind's natural religion, coming naturally to all who live in relatively civilized communities, is clearly a nonsense. As in yesterday's Roman Empire, so today in both East and West the Christian life involves a wholesale reversal of what comes naturally out of the egocentric human heart and cannot be accounted for in terms merely of education and social conditioning. Living in pre-narrative theology days, Orr did not use the phrase "the Christian story" as theological shorthand in the way that we do; but his thought is fully in line with our use of it. Redemption through the Christ of the Gospels and Epistles for sinful human beings, flawed and foolish, guilty, vile and helpless, with our shameworthy and blameworthy track records and our pathetic inadequacies for the business of living, is for Orr the authentic Christian story, and any affirmation of it and apologetic for it must be historical and redemptive throughout. That is as true today as it was when Orr wrote a century ago, and as it was in the first century when this affirmation and apologetic first broke through the lips of Paul and his apostolic peers on a culturally dying world.

Orr's witness to Jesus Christ did not stop here, however, and neither must ours. In *The Christian View,* having shown most effectively that the New Testament is unanimous in viewing Jesus as a person to be worshiped and thereby acknowledged as divine, and having drawn out of this a basic trinitarianism, Orr then spends half a chapter exploring the cosmic role of the Son of God, linking the creating and upholding of things with redemption "as parts of one grand whole."[39] Introducing this section by posing the old question, whether there would have been an incarnation of the Son had there been no sin, he frankly acknowledges that Scripture always relates the incarnation to our need of salvation and to the Father's purpose that the Son should ultimately head up a redeemed and remade universe. But then he affirms:

> God's plan is in reality one, and it is but an abstract way of thinking that leads us to suppose otherwise . . . we speak as if God had first one plan of creation—complete and rounded off in itself—in which sin was to have no place; then, when it was foreseen that sin would enter, another plan was introduced, which vitally altered and enlarged the former. But . . . the plan of the universe is one, and . . . however harsh the expression may sound, the foresight and permission of sin were from the first included in it . . . God has chosen to create a universe into which it was foreseen that sin would enter; and the Incarnation is part of the plan of such a creation. This being so, it may well be conceived that the Incarnation was the pivot on which everything else in this plan of creation was made to turn . . . Christ's relation to the universe cannot be thought of as something adventitious and contingent; it is vital and organic. This means that His Incarnation had a relation to the whole plan of the world, and not simply to sin.[40]

Facing as he did nonsupernatural hypotheses about the life and identity of Jesus on the one hand, and nontrinitarian conceptions of the divine on the other hand, Orr was skillfully hitting his way out of trouble by insisting that the historical and cosmic dimensions of New Testament faith in Jesus Christ are inseparable parts of a single whole, so that neither can be fairly and adequately assessed save in the light of the other, and the final assessment must be of both together. And in doing this Orr was doing more than pursuing a tactic for evading trouble; he was showing what is involved in this or any age in facing the full reality of the New Testament witness to Jesus.

Here is a guideline for our testimony today. In explaining and commending Christ to positivistic modernists and relativistic postmodernists alike there is need to bring together both the Evangelists' account of the Son of God's life in this world—his words, works, ways and wars—and the apostolic conviction of his cocreatorship with the Father; of his activity as the upholding source of our existence and life every moment; of his identity as "the truth" in the sense of being the final source and goal of the cosmos, the ultimate answer to all ultimate questions; and of his destiny as the person through and in whom the whole universe is to find its perfection when he reappears in glory. The christocentricity of the world in this sense is an integral part of the Christian understanding of Jesus and must ever be set forth as an integral element in the Christian witness to Jesus. Both the coherence of our own faith and its correspondence with the faith of Christianity's founders depend on the clarity and firmness with which we grasp that this is so and practice the principle accordingly.

So here is a further pointer to the way our current witness must go.

4. Celebrate the life-changing impact of the gospel of Jesus Christ as an integral part of our testimony.

Let Orr himself introduce this section with his account of the gospel's original triumph in the Roman Empire.

Christianity won the day because . . . it met the deepest necessity of the age into which it had come . . . it met the deep craving of the age for spiritual peace and rest, its need of certainty, its longing for redemption, and for direct communion with God. To these wants it brought a satisfaction which no other religion of the time could pretend to offer. It did not meet them by teaching merely—as if Christ were a new Socrates—but it met them by the positive exhibition of the redeeming love of God in Christ, by the setting forth of the personal Jesus in His life, death and resurrection, by the proclamation of the forgiveness of sins through Him, by the bestowal of the power of the Holy Spirit. It was not a doctrinal religion merely, but a religion of *dynamic*—of power. It did not only tell men what to do, but gave them power to do it.[41]

Today a quest for spirituality—that is, as the word is used, for some transforming contact with the transcendent, whatever that may be—has once again become a feature of Western culture: which means that the door for declaring the nature and quality of Christian spiritual life is once more wide open. Deep craving for inner peace and rest, for certainty and hope, for rescue from oneself and for fellowship with God is widespread, and within the churches, Protestant, Catholic and Orthodox, serious study of life in the Spirit has again begun to take hold. Maximize this, Orr would urge; the life-changing power of the gospel, or rather of the Christ and the Holy Spirit of whom the gospel speaks, is something to make much of; the transcultural unity of the Christian experience of prayer over two millennia, and the proven capacity of Christian conviction to sustain itself through cultural change and persecuting pressure constitute weighty prima facie arguments for the claim that Christianity is true.

Here surely is a project that can both express and further convergence of our traditions in Christian testimony. Nothing is nearer the heart of the great tradition, and therefore more purely and gloriously ecumenical, than loving the Lord who in love died for us and now lives in us, and with that hating sin, and practicing repentance, and testifying that we live by being forgiven, and proving God's power to enable us to resist sin's down-drag. Protestant liberalism, with its enfeebled notions of God and sin and redemption, lost this supernaturalizing of daily life, substituting for it a culture of moralism and bonhomie, and the various liberation theologies of our time are in process even now of undergoing a similar loss. For the exponents of classical Christian orthodoxy to recover and display these inner aspects of classical Christian orthopraxy is a clear and urgent call from God at this time. The world needs to know of the supernatural action whereby God transfigures personal life in Christ and imparts resilience for righteousness and liberty for love in a way that makes believers a mystery to those who do not share their faith.

When Jesus told Nicodemus that with those born of the Spirit it was like the wind—"you hear its sound, but you cannot tell where it comes from or where it is going" (Jn 3:8)—he was referring to bewilderment on the part of unbelievers as to what makes Christians tick; true life in Christ will always have a supernatural quality that generates such bewilderment. Part of our calling is to unite to tell the world of this supernaturalizing of the natural and of the Christ who brings it to pass—and with that to demonstrate through the devotion of our own lives the supernaturalizing of which we speak. "Make your light shine," says Jesus, "so that others will see the good that you do and will praise your Father in heaven" (Mt 5:16 CEV).

Conclusion

Can conservative Protestants, Eastern Orthodox and Roman Catholics of mainstream type join together in bearing witness to all that I have spoken of? I urge that we can, despite our known and continuing differences about the specifics of the salvation process and the place of the church in that process. From the great tradition, or rather from the Scriptures as they have always been read within that tradition, we receive a shared understanding of ruin, redemption, regeneration and the reality of fellowship with our risen Savior that suffices for the purpose, and if we can agree as a rule of procedure to base our testimony directly on what we can find in Scripture as we exegete and expound it together we shall be home and dry. To be sure, fundamentalists within our three traditions are unlikely to join us in this, for it is the way of fundamentalists to follow the path of contentious orthodoxism, as if the mercy of God in Christ automatically rests on persons who are notionally correct and is just as automatically withheld from those who fall short of notional correct-ness on any point of substance. But this concept of, in effect, justification, not by works but by words—words, that is, of notional soundness and precision—is near to being a cultic heresy in its own right and need not detain us further, however much we may regret the fact that some in all our traditions are bogged down in it.

I would have liked at this point to be able to draw from Orr a fifth guiding principle for our present-day witness, which would have read as follows:

5. Highlight the international supracultural phenomenon of the church, the new human race that is committed here and now to worship, to brother-hood, to loving and serving and to spreading the gospel, while anticipating the future joy of endless loving fellowship with the Father and the Son through the Spirit, and in and through God with one another.

This principle is needed to complete the program that Orr has so far suggested to us: for despite the church's many shortcomings, past and present, this new society that God is constantly building embodies in itself impressive evidence of divine power at work on the grand scale. The evangelizing and nurturing church has had a uniquely unifying, humanizing and civilizing impact on world history. It seems to me that the transcultural solidarity of the church's corporate demonstration in experience of worship, prayer, suffering, resolute hope, faithfulness even to martyrdom and divine enabling for right-eousness and ministry give prima facie credibility to the claim that the institutional church is home to a supernatural life in Christ and is thus powerful evidence for the truth of the gospel.

But I cannot draw this principle from Orr, because to my knowledge he never voiced it. Like most other Protestants, Orr is robustly aware that God is building the believing community for his glory and that we all need the church for our nurture; yet, like many other Protestants, he does not appear as a man whose imagination has been caught by the church, so that he sees the church as integral to his evidential scheme. Perhaps in Orr's Scotland, heavily imbued as it was with Presbyterian formalism, it was harder to sense the unique quality of true church fellowship than it is for us today; but certainly the full strength of Orr's cerebral argument for the truth of the faith is likely to be felt only where it is backed up by the watching world's perception in the first Christian centuries—"see how these Christians love one another!"

As myself, like Orr, a Protestant—that is, a catholic Christian protesting against what appear as uncatholic specifics—I urge that we need this fifth principle as a guideline if we are to achieve in our day the coherent cogency of classical Christian understanding that Orr was contending for throughout. Unified and transformative witness to a world in which the deep-level loneli-ness of the individual has become an epidemic disease requires celebration of the new community in which through new creation "there is neither Jew nor Greek, slave nor free, male nor female, for you are all one in Christ Jesus" (Gal 3:28)—with transcendent new togetherness resulting both within and across denominational lines. May such witness be forthcoming from now on; we need it, desperately.

What success can we expect from such a united witness here in the West, where the departure from us of the glory of God seems such an obvious fact? Perhaps not much, at any rate in the short term. But the call at present is surely to resolve to do our best, in collaboration as close as we can make it, and commit the outcome to God—and then to emulate Orr, who never doubted that he was on the victory side, but who knew that anyone maintaining the faith in its classic biblical form was in for the long haul.

In an article titled "Prevailing Tendencies in Modern Theology," published in 1906, Orr declared that in face of the current flowing of the Western intellectual stream against the faith "what was needed in the way of a proper response was 'above all, a cool head, strong faith, a little patience, action like that of the mariners with Paul, who when they feared lest they should have fallen among rocks, and when for many days neither sea nor star appeared, sensibly dropped four anchors, and waited for the day.' "[42] Wise advice! Let us, like Orr, resolve to work and wait together, and see what God will do.

An Eastern Orthodox Response to J. I. Packer

Bradley Nassif

I would like to begin by acknowledging the invaluable role Dr. Packer has played in advancing unity among conservative Christians. A scholar of his stature appears all too rarely in the course of church history. When such a person speaks, he deserves a most thoughtful reply. I shall respond as an Eastern Orthodox theologian who is committed to the belief that the Orthodox Church embodies the fullness of that "great tradition" of which Dr. Packer has spoken. In what follows I want to respond to the particular points that Dr. Packer has made through his "Orr-type program for convergent orthodox witness." I will do so by evaluating how each point fits into the theological history of the Orthodox Church and developing some of the most important features of Eastern Orthodoxy which are vital and attractive to this conference.

Evaluation

The short answer to Dr. Packer's paper is, Yes, but! Yes, the Eastern Orthodox Church must agree to join together and bear testimony to all that he has said; but we must also challenge Dr. Packer to adopt a *fuller vision* of that great tradition which he himself has proposed as grounds for a "convergent orthodox witness." I will give the details of this general assessment through three specific evaluations of his proposals.

1. Packer's *hermeneutical* grounds for convergence require Orthodox support because they are theoretically identical to Orthodox hermeneutics.

In order to effect a "unified and transformative witness," Dr. Packer begins by theologizing out of "the authentic biblical and creedal mainstream, the 'great tradition' that the church on earth has characteristically maintained from the start." From that premise he calls us to "display the coherence of historic mainstream Christian beliefs, both as a crystallizing of the doctrinal content of the Bible and as a comprehensive philosophy of life."

From an Orthodox perspective no starting point could be more acceptable. The unique contribution of Orthodoxy to discussions on unity has been its claim to be the one visible and complete body of Christ. My revered teacher, the late Father John Meyendorff of blessed memory, summarized the church's stance on this crucial issue:

> The Orthodox witness must be *traditional* in the sense of authenticity. There is no Orthodoxy without Holy Tradition, which implies communion in Spirit and in truth with the witness of the apostles and the fathers, based upon the belief that, by the power of God and in spite of all historical human weaknesses, there was and there is an uninterrupted, consistent and continuous Holy Tradition of faith held by the Church throughout the centuries. This belief in Tradition is not identical with simple conservatism. Holy Tradition is a living tradition. It is a witness to the unchanging Truth in a changing world.[1]

This Orthodox witness to an uninterrupted tradition of ecclesial unity, worship and dogma should be viewed as a *paradosis* of the *kērygma*. It is nothing more and nothing less than the apostolic faith of the New Testament handed down and received by the faithful through the ages. In Eastern Orthodoxy, Scripture serves as both an internal *norm* to tradition and a *witness* to tradition, while tradition serves as the interpretative context of Scripture.[2]

Dr. Packer accepts this. He also restates the majority position of the Protestant Reformers who in principle held the early church in high regard and generally guided themselves by patristic and conciliar interpretations of the faith. Dr. Packer's hermeneutics of dogma contrasts with the approach taken by many modern-day children of the Reformation who naively imagine that they can leap directly from the Scriptures to the present without showing much awareness that the Bible is the book of the church. He proceeds on the conviction that the Christian faith substantially stands or falls with the creeds, councils and fathers of the great church. Consequently I enthusiastically support Packer's position as essentially identical with that of the Orthodox Church.[3] The consensual hermeneutics of the great church provide common ground for a common faith. Hence the criteriological question for discerning and expressing Christian truth is substantially in place.

Misunderstandings of Orthodox descriptions of ourselves as the "one true church" regularly occur in ecumenical dialogue, so clarification is needed on this point. The claim should not be understood exclusively in institutional terms. Eastern Christianity does not strictly follow St. Cyprian's identification of the church in purely institutional terms as if it were a closed box, the ark of Noah, in which one is clearly inside or outside the ship. The church's practice over the centuries more closely follows the theology of St. Basil the Great, who recognized that even in schisms people can still remain "of the Church" (to use Basil's expression). Heresy, not schism, is what separates from the body of Christ. In Basil's perspective there is no clear-cut identification of the church's charismatic boundaries with its canonical, institutional boundaries.[4] This places an imperative on the Orthodox to affirm that other Christians belong to the church even though they exist outside our own organizational boundaries. If a person is "in Christ" he or she cannot be anywhere else but "in the Church." If one reduces the church simply to an institution, as is often done even by well-intentioned Orthodox, then one has simply misdefined the Orthodox Church's self-understanding as the "one true Church."

This does not mean that Christians may have unity without structures, for spiritual unity alone implies a Docetic ecclesiology altogether. But neither does the claim to being the "one true Church" mean that we ascribe to the institution a finished perfection in every last structure. We cannot say, as so many triumphalists do today, that "we know where the church is, but not where it is not." The most self-consistent way to interpret this claim is to affirm that within the various structures of the Orthodox Church, and above all in its sacramental life, God's saving revelation of himself is present without distortion or deviation.

From the standpoint of Ephesians the church is "one" (Eph 4:4-6), yet "already" and "not yet" (Eph 4:13). There is one single confession of Christian truth (however diverse its expressions may be among the New Testament authors, all their individual theologies are compatible or complementary to the faith once given); but that unity in faith is a gift to be visibly preserved, enjoyed and displayed. The unity that the Spirit generates is not an object to be sought after but a gift to be preserved and manifested. When this principle is applied to an Orthodox self-understanding, we maintain that the fullness of the faith is "already" present within the sacramental life of the Orthodox Church, but it is still "not yet" effectively understood, proclaimed and manifested in every last detail. In particular, it should be noted that the theological problems raised by the modern study of liturgical history are only beginning to be taken seriously by Orthodox theologians and church leaders. To claim that God's saving revelation of himself is present without distortion or deviation in the Orthodox Church obligates us to qualify that claim in the light of modern liturgical scholarship (e.g., translational problems, the meaning of the rites themselves, the hermeneutics of liturgical exegesis, etc.).

Therefore the first criterion of an authentic Orthodox witness to being the "one true Church" is to test the spirits to see if our own local parishes reflect an Orthodoxy that is rightly proclaimed and understood. When that is done it becomes apparent to most biblically minded people that a healthy understanding of the faith is terribly lacking in some if not most Orthodox churches today. It is a contradictory church that is often inconsistent with its own convictions about the teachings of the apostles and fathers. It is essential, therefore, for the Orthodox to be what we say we are: the church "catholic" (full, complete, lacking in nothing).[5]

As a historical theologian I am painfully aware that at no time has the empirical reality of the church fully lived up to its nature, especially in our own day. To define the church in this way is to challenge the present realities of Orthodoxy in America. To take a recent example, a growing number of evangelical and Anglican Christians have decided to become Orthodox. Oftentimes they join the church out of theologically sound ideals but soon sadly discover the realities of ethnicism, ritualism, theological illiteracy and "fundamentalism" (for lack of a better term). A "hermeneutics of discovery" settles in to provoke the deepest kind of soul-searching.[6] They encounter a profound crisis in world Orthodoxy that seems able to be remedied only by repentance and a renewed emphasis on the Bible.

Despite these conditions, however, I believe that the norms of Orthodox doctrine, ecclesiology and canonical order are clear in the sources and provide us with criteria for establishing a common faith for checking deviations and abuses. Although visibly deficient in the apprehension of its own religion, the Orthodox Church has most faithfully preserved the apostolic faith in its theological history and liturgical and mystical life.

2. The four points of Packer's "Orr-type program for convergent orthodox witness" demand our enthusiastic support because they are *theologically* consistent with a great amount of conciliar tradition in the Orthodox Church.

Once again I see his four principles as solid grounds for raising a unified voice with evangelicals that is "not of this world." The ecumenical councils (A.D. 325-787) arose out of doctrinal challenges that directly threatened the unity of the faith. Reflecting an approach to theology that is similar to Packer's "Orr-type program," the councils were simultaneously conservative and contemporary. They were conservative because the fathers were deeply concerned to maintain consistency and continuity with the past by making sure that their formulations were following Scripture and the holy fathers. But they were also contemporary by couching their affirmations in the terms and idioms of the Hellenistic world. The controversies were much more than spirited debates over how to correctly formulate the faith. The ultimate issue at stake behind the councils' concern for orthodoxy was the need to clarify the meaning of salvation. Over the course of the fourth to eighth centuries, the fathers endeavored to clarify and protect the salvation accomplished by the Son who was coeternal *(homoousios)* with the Father (trinitarian controversy), lived on earth as both God and human (christological controversy) and made it possible to portray himself and others in iconographic form (iconoclasm). These are not abstract doctrines but dynamic pastoral, liturgical and mystical realities.

Dr. Packer's stress on the Trinity as the foundation of all life (point two) and centrality of the Incarnation as the good news of redemption (point three) accords well with St. Athanasius and the Cappadocian fathers. Here lies a strong christocentrism within a firmly trinitarian framework. It maximizes the ontological grounding of the soteriological truth espoused by St. Athanasius that only God can reveal God. It also harmonizes with the Cappadocian vision of communion with God. Communion among the three Persons of the Trinity was viewed as the source, model and goal for the saving communion of humans with God and each other in the church.[7]

Dr. Packer's invitation for us to "celebrate the life-changing impact of the gospel as an integral part of our testimony" (point four) mirrors the whole mystical experience of the Eastern Church. It advances the convergence of our traditions by maximizing our Christian witness to those who are not yet in Christ. If Eastern Orthodoxy has anything at all to say to the world surely it is this: "Christ is risen!" The paschal proclamation of the empty tomb is a baptismal call to repentance and faith in Jesus Christ as Lord and Savior. For Athanasius and the whole Greek patristic tradition this involves both a moment of conversion and a lifelong process of growth *(theōsis):* "He was made man that we might be made divine" (*De incarnatione* 54). This is where the evangelical core of the monastic tradition intersects with Dr. Packer's proposal. The monastic fathers emphasized the centrality of Scripture, evangelistic and social outreach and a prophetic and eschatological ministry of renewal.[8] From the Abbas and Ammas (fathers and mothers) of the Egyptian desert through great mystics such as Sts. John Climacus, Symeon the New Theologian and Gregory Palamas, all displayed through their ascetical efforts the life-changing impact of the good news on the totality of human existence, both body and soul. The voice of monasticism speaks through the megaphone of the Packer program to call our fallen world to the transfigured life of Mount Tabor.

3. Because Eastern Orthodoxy should endorse Packer's proposals on *hermeneutical* and *theological* grounds, it is for those very reasons that we must also challenge the *consistency* of those views with the great tradition on which they are based.

A vital question must be raised at this juncture. If the great tradition sets the boundaries within which a common witness must occur, how consistent is Orr's and Packer's theology with that tradition? It is here that I must challenge the comprehensiveness of their proposal. In my humble opinion Dr. Packer has indeed formulated the right hermeneutics for convergence, but has not been consistent in their application. Since the great tradition serves as a reference point from which to evaluate issues of convergence, that reference point embraces a more holistic vision of Christian orthodoxy than the Packer/Orr program allows. I will explain by making recourse to the ecclesiology and conciliar history of the great tradition itself.

Ecclesiologically, as I stated earlier, the Orthodox Church claims to have maintained an unbroken succession of truth from the apostolic age to the present. Nevertheless, New Testament scholarship has demonstrated that there were a variety of patterns of church polity in the apostolic age and that there was no uniform pattern of government that all churches everywhere followed. The Ignatian model of the monarchical episcopate in the late first and early second centuries appears to represent a dramatic change in ecclesiology.

How then may unity and continuity of the faith be seen and traced from the New Testament to the second-century church and beyond? And, more important for Christian convergence, what does the answer to this question have to say about the consensual theology that Dr. Packer is advocating? No Orthodox consensus exists that can definitively address the transition from the New Testament to Ignatius.[9] An informed judgment *(theologoumenon)* must be rendered to link the apostolic with the postapostolic church and account for the ecclesiology that operated during the age of the ecumenical councils and continues in the Orthodox Church to this day.

Three doctrinal themes seem to unite the church in the New Testament with the mainstream history of the second century and following: pneumatology, Christology and the sacraments. The pneumatological link views all those who believe and have been baptized in Jesus Christ as the Spirit-filled, eschatological people of God in fulfillment of the Old Testament prophecies concerning the last times (Acts 10:44; Gal 3:2-5; 1 Pet 2:9; Is 43:20). Christologically, this Spirit-filled people of God assemble for communion with the Father on the basis of right belief in Jesus Christ as both God and human, Lord and Savior of the world (Rom 1:3-4; 1 Cor 6:5-6; Gal 3:11-14; 1 Jn 5:1, 5). Sacramentally, through Christ and the Spirit, this same people of God are called together to participate in the Father through the Eucharist. In the church and its sacramental life believers participate here and now in the kingdom of God to come (1 Cor 10:16; 11:17-34 with Lk 22:7-23 and Mt 26:17-30). The eschatalogical structure of the sacraments assures that the church in Jerusalem, Antioch and elsewhere share the same faith and common participation in the heavenly banquet. It is the most dramatic element of continuity between the apostolic and postapostolic age and assures the unity of the church throughout the world. For these reasons the Eucharist has played a central role in defining the content of the Orthodox faith.

These sacramental dynamics can be seen during the age of the great ecumenical councils. Even there the Eucharist helped ensure the correctness of Orthodox belief. St. Cyril of Alexandria and other church fathers believed that a faulty Christology led to a faulty eucharistic theology. One reason Nestorian Christology, for example, was so opposed by the Orthodox was that in Nestorianism (as perceived by its adversaries) there is no real unity between the divine and human natures of Christ. If there is only a juxtaposition between God and man in Christ, there can be no real union between the divine and human in the Eucharist.

Conversely, during the Byzantine iconoclastic controversy (A.D. 726-843) a correct definition of an icon had direct implications for properly describing the meaning of Eucharist. The iconoclasts insisted that the only true icon of Christ was the Eucharist, since by their definition an icon was identical in essence *(homoousios)* with Christ, its prototype. The Orthodox defined the term *icon* in a way that would not allow images to be equated with the Eucharist. The Eucharist could not be considered an icon because images were only symbols of reality, not reality itself.[10] Behind the liturgical arguments for and against images, however, lay a Chalcedonian Christology upon which the whole controversy rested. Since Christ exists as "two natures in one Person" the Incarnation stood as the ultimate justification for icons. The Chalcedonian definition (A.D. 451) became the source and reference point for the church's eucharistic and iconic theology.

Moreover, an ecumenical council was guaranteed ecclesiologically by the "reception" of the church, which was mystically authoritative and normative. The decisions of an ecumenical council had to be received by the whole church. The ecclesiology of the councils implies that the church is both hierarchical and conciliar. It is hierarchical because the bishops personify their eucharistic communities in the assembly; it is conciliar because it expresses the mind of the whole church.[11]

The point of it all is this: these issues exemplify the mode of theological decision-making in the Byzantine Orthodox Church. It is extremely important for the whole question of truth in theology, because if an ecumenical council is in fact a council of the great tradition, then its authenticity presupposes an already existing unity of faith in eucharistic communion. This we do not have. Dr. Packer's program therefore lacks a theological maximalism in sacramental and ecclesial realities that the Orthodox have always insisted on as a precondition for authentic Christian unity.

Conclusion
Of all the Christian traditions, evangelicalism is by far the closest to the *spirit* of Eastern Orthodoxy. As I have attempted to demonstrate, we agree on most major hermeneutical and theological grounds. However, our known and

continuing differences in sacramental theology and ecclesiology should not be minimized; the "Orr program" for convergence has, as it were, only one oar in the water. This means that we should further seek to remove the false barriers that have divided us while identifying legitimate differences without proselytizing each other in the process. Nevertheless, even now, precisely because there is so much theological truth between us, the Orthodox can and do unite with evangelicals.

The "Orr program" offered by Dr. Packer models a strategy and apologetic stance that is largely consistent with the great tradition of the creeds, councils and fathers of the Orthodox Church. It is now time for us to recognize that the cup is just as much half full as it is half empty. We must harness the energy we have previously used against each other and combine it to work toward a common agenda at the dawn of the third millennium. It is with eager anticipation that we now join evangelicals with one determined voice to defend and proclaim a common faith that is "not of this world"!

EPILOGUE
Theology Pro Ecclesia—Evangelical, Catholic & Orthodox

Carl E. Braaten

*I*t was my privilege to participate in the Rose Hill ecumenical conference for traditional Christians under the theme "Not of This World." Those who attended were united in the belief that they and their communities were called to be stewards of God's mysteries, servants of Christ and his kingdom in but not of this world (1 Cor 4:1; Jn 17:14). We came from evangelical, Catholic and Orthodox churches to learn from each other how we might do theology more faithfully for the church in our time of cultural crisis. In his paper J. I. Packer spoke for many when he said, "I theologize out of what I see as the authentic biblical and creedal mainstream of Christian identity, the confessional and liturgical 'great tradition' that the church on earth has characteristically maintained from the start." We came prepared to "test whether an 'ecumenical orthodoxy,' solidly based upon the classic Christian faith, can become the foundation for a unified and transformative witness to the age we live in."[1] I believe we all sensed that on behalf of our churches we were exploring the conditions of the possibility of doing theology ecumenically, which is bound to be different from a mere repristination of our respective confessional traditions. There would hardly be any point in coming together if we were looking merely for a platform and an audience to explain our private or denominational party lines.

Of course we were not starting from scratch. All the participants have made significant contributions to various bilateral or multilateral ecumenical dialogues. The major ecumenical dialogues and documents of the twentieth century show that there is broad and deep agreement on the gospel of Jesus Christ as the focal point of Christian unity. Richard John Neuhaus reminded us of the great new ecumenical fact—after the millennium-long breach between East and West and the almost five hundred years of separation between Rome and the Reformation—that evangelicals, Catholics and Orthodox now accept each other as brothers and sisters in Christ. This "represents a great change, a great achievement and most importantly a great gift." The most notable examples of ecumenical theology *pro ecclesia* are the two Faith and Order texts, *Baptism, Eucharist and Ministry* and, more recently, *Confessing the One Faith: An Ecumenical Explication of the Apostolic Faith As It Is Confessed in the Nicene-Constantinopolitan Creed (381)*. These texts do not merely reflect dialogue between theologians of different traditions but exemplify a collaborative model where theologians from across the ecumenical spectrum inquire into what the church is to believe, teach and confess on the basis of the Holy Scriptures and the ecumenical creeds, confronting and challenging the ideologies of contemporary culture and the heresies that circulate within the churches wearing the masks of currents trends and values.

The Starting Point: God's Revelation in Jesus Christ

As confessional theologians we all serve particular communities, yet each particular community would make the claim that what it is teaching is the true faith of the one Christian church and not merely the doctrines of a sect. Each of our traditions may stress a particular aspect; for example, Lutherans are prone to emphasize the doctrine of justification by faith alone, yet we always make the claim that we are thereby being faithful to God's revelation in Jesus Christ. The ecumenical encounter forces us to ask and to answer the question, But is it really so? It provides the opportunity to give reasons for the hope that is in us (1 Pet 3:15). Whatever adjective we use in the dogmatics we teach, whether evangelical, Catholic or Orthodox, we all intend to be faithful to what believers in Christ and members of his church believe on the basis of God's special revelation in Jesus Christ.

Vincent, the fifth-century monk of Lerins, is famous for at least one saying. In his *Commonitorium* he wrote, "In the Catholic Church all possible care should be taken that we hold that faith which has been believed everywhere, always and by all" *(quod ubique, quod semper, quod ab omnibus)*. Do we have at least a starting point for ecumenical theology *pro ecclesia* that passes Vincent's test? I believe we do. The one thing that all Christians and all churches in all times and places claim to share is the gospel of Jesus Christ according to the Scriptures. This brief statement calls for some explanation.

One of the earliest summaries of this gospel comes from Paul the apostle in 1 Corinthians 15:3-5: "For I handed on to you as of first importance what I in turn had received: that Christ died for our sins in accordance with the scriptures, and that he was buried, and that he was raised on the third day in accordance with the scriptures, and he appeared to Cephas, then to the twelve." In a day when theologies calling themselves Christian begin and end without handing on what we have received from the apostolic tradition as the core of the faith, it seems necessary for us to start with what is of "first importance" and not with something else, no matter how existentially poignant, apologetically persuasive, universally relevant or philosophically sophisticated that something or other attached to the Christian tradition might happen to be. By "starting point" we mean the place to concentrate in explicating the essential faith of the Christian church.

The revelation in Jesus Christ is the gospel of the triune God. Today theologians from different schools are clamoring for theocentricity (Hick, Knitter, S. C. Smith, Samartha, Panikkar, Gustafson, Ruether, Driver, Gilkey, to name a mere handful), but they do this at the expense of Christology. This is a false move. The gospel that Jesus preached (Mk 1:14) and the gospel preached about Jesus by Paul and the apostles (Rom 1:1) are nothing else than the one gospel of God that was a long time in preparation, going back to the dawn of history (Gen 3:15) and the election of Israel. When we consider the phrase "the gospel of Jesus Christ," we are not affirming a Christomonism that separates Jesus from God's covenant people through whom he gave the law and the promise as a *praeparatio evangelica*. The God who speaks in his Son Jesus in these last days is the same God who spoke of old through the prophets (Heb 1:1). Jesus as the Messiah turned out to be the content of the prophetic message that God delivered to Israel before Jesus was born, as the apostles tell the story.

What is exclusive and unique about God's revelation in Jesus Christ is the person himself, for he is "true God from true God." In Christ God himself comes in the power and glory of his kingdom; the new age dawns in the personal life, death and resurrection of Jesus as God's Messiah promised beforehand to Israel's prophets. There is nothing like this in any of the religions, no matter how much they might otherwise witness to truth, beauty and goodness.

Ecclesial Versus Private Theology

The first sentence of the introduction of Paul Tillich's *Systematic Theology* states: "Theology is a function of the church." There is much suspicion of churchly theology in the academy. Hospitality is granted every other form of advocacy—religious, moral, political—except that which emanates from the church as the subject of faith standing on the revelation of God in Christ. Ecclesial theology cuts against the grain. Theology as someone's reflection on one kind or another of religious experience is acceptable.

In the "Letters to the Editor" section of the *Religious Studies News* (November 1993) Paul J. Griffiths writes in response to letters by Gary Lease and Donald Wiebe, both of whom had argued for the separation of churchly theology from the scientific study of religion and the religions. Their point was: Keep theology out of the American Academy of Religion. Theology is bound to a confession, that of a church, and is therefore totalitarian. Theology approaches the study of religion with presuppositions, a set of prior commitments. Griffiths argues back that the only alternative to coming at religion with acknowledged presuppositions is to conceal them. He writes: "All intellectual work implies some set of metaphysical commitments . . . , and so no reasonable distinction between neutral, objective, value-free, and secular intellectual work, on the one hand, and committed, engaged, value-laden, and theological intellectual work, on the other, can finally be made." Griffiths continues:

> What could be more "totalitarian" than the desire to exclude from the academy all those with interesting and complex intellectual commitments that differ from one's own? . . . My commitments include, *inter alia,* that I accept as true what I take the propositional content of the Nicene Creed to be; Mr. Lease's and Mr. Wiebe's include accepting as true claims every

bit as controversial as these. . . . Doesn't it seem a bit odd that they should want to rule themselves into the American Academy of Religion and me out of it as a matter of principle?

S. M. Hutchens was also referring to the hostile environment of the academy in writing, "As the academic world grows ever more hostile to Christianity, anything resembling Christian orthodoxy is now called fundamentalism. . . . More than ever before capitulation to the *Zeitgeist* is the price of the doctor's degree, and more than ever this capitulation is the dark secret of the doctors of philosophy at the evangelical schools."

Today we encounter in most of the schools of theology the triumph of the category of experience. Tillich described experience as the "medium" and not the "source" of theology, and he certainly did not allow that it should become the "object" and "norm" of theology. "Experience receives and does not produce," said Tillich. Such cautious distinctions are hard to find among the current trends in theology. Tillich intended to define precisely the place of experience in theological method without capitulating to the legacies of Friedrich Schleiermacher and William James.

Tillich was perhaps not so clear about the identity of the church of which theology was to be its function. Which church? In volume three of his *Systematic Theology* he writes his ecclesiology. There he defines the church as the "spiritual community." But is this the "one, holy, catholic and apostolic church" of the Nicene-Constantinopolitan Creed? The "spiritual community" spills over into everything, not only the churches in their ambiguous and fragmentary character but also in all cultural creations, in the "latent church," in which there is no explicit confession to Christ, as well as in political, artistic and non-Christian religious groups and movements, some of which are explicitly anti-Christian and antichurch. Being a theologian of the church in the sense of such a transcendental community accounts for the fact that Tillich has been received mostly as a theologian of culture, in line with nineteenth-century *Kulturprotestantismus,* and rarely as a good example of churchly theology. George Lindbeck uses Tillich as a prime example of the type of theology he calls "experiential expressivism," the type that characterizes almost all of modern American academic theology.

Karl Barth was critical of the *Erfahrungstheologie* in the line from Schleiermacher through the Erlangen theology of J. C. K. Hofmann and his teacher Wilhelm Herrmann. We have come full circle in theology; modern academic theology has drifted back into the slough of experiential subjectivism. Barth's critique is more applicable than ever. The distinctive element of experientialism in theology is the idea that faith or religious experience is productive of the data available for theological reflection. Von Hofmann said: "I as a Christian am the object of knowledge for myself as a theologian." For the word *Christian* substitute whatever other badge of personal identity one may choose, and there we have the going model of method in theology. It leads away from churchly theology centered in God's revelation in Jesus Christ into a multiplicity of private theologies centered in the self.

The reduction of theology to experience, both as its primary source and norm, corresponds to the collapse of traditional authority, the authority of Scripture and church dogma. Nor has the vigorous use of the historical critical method in biblical interpretation provided a deterrent to the subjective arbitrariness of experience as source and norm of theology. For example, biblical theologian Elisabeth Schüssler Fiorenza writes, "The personally and politically reflected experience of oppression and liberation must become the criterion of appropriateness for biblical interpretation and evaluation of biblical authority claims."[2] Only those texts and traditions that can support women in their struggle for liberation can have the theological authority of revelation. The interpretation of the experience of women given by feminist ideology subverts the authority of the gospel given by Scripture. In this way the biblical theologian can fiddle with the texts until some reconstruction thereof rhymes with her own experience of liberation.

Scripture and Tradition

An inescapable issue in ecumenical theology is the hermeneutical problem of the authority of Scripture and its relation to the church. Harold O. J. Brown, speaking as an evangelical, stated that "there can be no question that the Bible, the Word of God, is of the utmost importance for Christians and for the church." Protestants and Roman Catholics have traditionally held different views on the relation between Scripture and church. Roman Catholics have emphasized that the Bible is the book of the church and that church authority authenticates it, whereas Protestants stress that the Bible is the Word of God that creates the church. Brown formulates the matter this way: "It is certainly true that it is the Word that creates the church, which is built on the foundation of the prophets and apostles, that is, on their word, but it would be a historical anachronism to say that the Bible created the church. . . . There is no way to make the New Testament older than the church."

The bilateral conversations between Catholics and Lutherans among others have shed new light on the relation between Scripture and church tradition. Today we can see that both sides were right in what they affirmed, but given the polemical situation, both tended to view the relationship between Scripture and the church in a static, undialectical way. The results of the dialogues acknowledge that there are two dialectically related truths that form the necessary conditions for affirming the authority of the Bible. The first condition of biblical authority is that the Bible can be used by the church to define its identity and mission in the world, its being and doing, as the community calling itself Christian. Where there is no church, there is no canon of Scripture and no need for it. The Bible will always be studied as sacred Scripture only within the context of the church. Brown admits that "contemporary Protestantism tends to have a defective view of the fundamental significance of the church."

The Bible is acknowledged as authority only where the gospel of Jesus Christ is proclaimed within a worshiping community of believers. The Bible provides the point of reference by which the church understands its identity and mission in the world. Without the Bible the church is blind and without the church the Bible is dumb. The church finds itself in the Bible as God's missionary people on the way to the nations with the gospel of Jesus Christ until the end of time. The biblical message is the norm for its ongoing life and faith. The church binds itself to the revelation of God in Jesus Christ according to the Scriptures and does not look for a new revelation above and beyond this one.

The second condition of the Bible's authority lies in its function as a medium of the authority of Jesus Christ himself. Christ is the Lord of Scripture. If we examine various theological accounts of biblical authority, they all witness to the promise, presence and power of the gospel of Jesus Christ. For Karl Barth Christ is God's revelation witnessed to by the Bible; for Oscar Cullmann Christ is the midpoint of salvation history; for Rudolf Bultmann Christ is the heart of the *kērygma;* for Paul Tillich the new being has appeared in Jesus as the Christ; for Wolfhart Pannenberg Jesus' resurrection is the proleptic event anticipating the unifying end of universal history. For the Christian church and for all believers the ultimate authority of the Bible depends on its witness to

Jesus Christ, who lived, died and rose again for the world's salvation.

So it is on account of Christ that the church confesses the authority of the Bible. The Scriptures are Christ-centered. Luther's dictum *Was Christum treibt* is still a useful way to speak of the Bible's authority, provided we do not apply it in a reductionistic way.

By stressing these two conditions, the ecclesial context and the gospel content, we have perhaps begun to unify what came apart in the conflict between the Reformation and Roman Catholic theology. Roman Catholic doctrine has emphasized that Scripture is a book of the church. In the post-Reformation era Protestant polemics tended to set Scripture against tradition. Now we know that this is not possible, because the New Testament itself is a piece of the tradition of the early church.

Reformation doctrine emphasized that the living witness of the church points beyond its own tradition to what is ultimately the eschatological revelation of God in Jesus Christ. The teaching office of the church does not place itself above the authority of the living tradition of apostolic Christianity set forth in Scripture. But Scripture is not a norm outside the church. It functions as the norm, conveying the Word, communicating the Spirit, awakening faith, only within the context of the worshiping and proclaiming community of believers.

Orthodox theologians offered a different perspective on the relation between Scripture and tradition. Bradley Nassif and Father Andrew Melton were not happy with the terms of the debate between Catholics and Protestants. Nassif expressed profound appreciation for J. I. Packer's paper but pressed him "to adopt a *fuller vision* of that great tradition which he himself has proposed as grounds for a 'convergent orthodox witness.' " Father Andrew observed that even Vatican II "perpetuated the dichotomy between them." He said, "This split between Scripture and tradition is not found in the writings of the fathers, Eastern or Western, nor, as we shall see, in the Holy Scriptures themselves." In his response to Dr. Brown's paper, Father Andrew stated that "he continues to view Scripture and Tradition as totally distinct categories." Strikingly, he states: "The Orthodox Church regards all aspects of holy Tradition as Spirit-inspired." And again: "In the Orthodox view, Tradition does not add to the message—Tradition is the message."

Obviously the Western dialogue between Catholics and Protestants needs to be expanded into a trialogue to include the Orthodox perspective. There is a hint of the difference in that the Orthodox typically spell Tradition with a capital *T,* whereas in the West the smaller case will usually do just fine.

The Communion of the Triune God

In Reformation theology the church has been defined as the creature of the Word *(creatura verbi divini)* or of the gospel (Luther: *Ecclesia creatura est evangelii*). This implies a strong bent toward a christological approach to ecclesiology. Yves Congar has pointed out that this is more or less characteristic of the Western Latin tradition in general and uses the term *Christomonism* to describe the prevailing view of the church in Catholic theology prior to Vatican II. Thanks to the influence of Eastern Orthodox theologians, our attention is increasingly directed to the patristic tradition, where we find a trinitarian perspective on ecclesiology, one in which the doctrine of the Spirit is coequal with the Word. The church is the communion of the triune God, and the Trinity is the source (Father), image (Son) and goal (Spirit) of the church.

Bishop Kallistos Ware's paper on "The Trinity: Heart of Our Life" showed that a strong christocentric emphasis does not compete with trinitarian faith but provides it revelatory locus and foundation in biblical theology. He asks: "Where then do we find the mystery of the Trinity revealed?" He answers: "We find it revealed in Christ Jesus. More specifically it is disclosed in the five central moments of New Testament salvation history, within each of which there is evident a basic trinitarian structure."

Father Patrick Henry Reardon's paper, "Father, Glorify Thy Name!" issued a stern warning against attempts to speak of the mystery of God *remoto Christo.* He said,

> There persists among Christians today a disposition to talk of God apart from Christ. . . . I am referring . . . to a tendency to describe even the true God . . . in very general, abstract terms not rooted in the living experience of God in Christ. It seems that some Christians, having found God in Christ, feel free to separate him from this unique font of revelation and to discuss and describe him in terms that are hardly related at all to the vision of his glory manifest in the face of Christ.

The tight linkage between Trinity and Christology is especially crucial on two fronts. One is the radical feminist deconstruction of the biblical-Christian naming of God as Father, Son and Holy Spirit and its freewheeling substitution of other symbols and metaphors that allegedly are more user-friendly. This approach falls under the indictment of what Father Reardon's paper calls "vulgar apophaticism." The other is the pluralistic theology of religions that deconstructs traditional Christology for the sake of interreligious dialogue. The pluralistic theologians are basically unitarian in their doctrine of God and Ebionitic or at least Arian in their view of Christ. For the sake of dialogue with people of other religions, their strategy is to find common ground in the doctrine of God at the highest level of abstraction ("the really Real"), and since Christology introduces the chief point of difference, especially the high Christology of the ecumenical creeds so deeply embedded in the Trinity, Christology has got to go.

The hallmark of neoliberal theology is to drive a wedge between God and Christ, with the result that Christology becomes so reductionistically negligible that only the lowest possible Christology in the history of the tradition is considered worthy of modern belief. This in essence is what is going on in the notorious Jesus Seminar, which brackets out the faith of the Christian church, especially the resurrection and Pentecost, in its reconstruction of the historical Jesus. The outcome of the surgery is the death of the patient, not a new reformation of Christianity, as Robert Funk, head of the Jesus Seminar, claims, but an unimaginative construction of a new religion dead on arrival.

William Abraham comments on what is currently happening with the resurgence of neoliberal theology in its various renderings: "What is at stake is not just an attack on the doctrine of the Trinity. . . . What is really at issue is the creation of new canonical materials. . . . What we are witnessing is the emergence of a new creed, a new moral code and a new cult, that is, the invention of post-Christian religion."

We have to say, if Christ does not reveal what Christian believers mean by God in a definitive way, then something else must provide the key to the mystery of God. But why should Christians want to opt for something or someone other than Jesus Christ as the subject who gives to the word *God* a new and definitive content and meaning? And if the Christian doctrine of the Trinity no longer provides the frame of reference for negotiating what Christians mean by God, then some other set of presuppositions must take its place. For we cannot proceed in religion and theology with a neutral frame of reference or with no presuppositions. If one doesn't think like a trinitarian, one will most likely think like a unitarian. Bishop Ware cites Karl Rahner's statement that "in practice all too many Christians are just 'monotheists'; all references to the Trinity could be omitted from most Christian books, and yet the author's argument would be virtually unaffected."[3] If being "just a monotheist" implies that one has no need for Christ, one will have then opted for a different gospel from that of the apostolic church.

What kind of God are we talking about when Christ is omitted from the definition? At best we have the God of general revelation, the God of natural theology, or the God of that "vulgar apophaticism" who fades "into the night in which all cows are black." We have the *deus absconditus*, the hidden God without a name that Luther contrasted with the *deus revelatus*, the human face of the loving God in the person of Jesus.

The specific truth-claim inherent in Christian self-understanding and that is nonnegotiable in interreligious dialogue focuses on the move made by the first Christians from the confession of the one God of Israel, which Christians share with Jews, to the confession that Jesus is Lord, whom the God of Israel exalted by raising him from the dead. Abraham reminded the group that

> God was indeed known in Israel before he was known as the triune Mystery revealed in Christ. . . . It was at the right and proper time that the fullness of revelation was given to us, and acknowledging that fullness is not exalted by disparaging the crucial revelation vouchsafed to Israel and made available in the Old Testament. . . . The same applies *mutatis mutandis* to what has been made known of God in creation, that is, in nature and in conscience. To do justice to the subtleties of such revelation we cannot revert to the Christomonism of the early Barth.

The seeds of trinitarian doctrine were sown when at the beginning of the Christian movement some Jews began to call on the name of Jesus in worship in a way that seemed astonishing for Jews, for monotheists who were determined to worship no other God than YHWH. The first Christians worshiped the one God of Israel, whom they newly qualified as the Father of Jesus Christ. Now they prayed prayers of petition and praise that inescapably and obtrusively associated Jesus with the holy name of YHWH. Within the communal context of worship the apostolic gospel proclaimed this one human being, Jesus of Nazareth, not merely as a good and righteous man, not merely as one whose moral teachings are to be followed, but as the crucified and risen Lord with whom the God of Israel had identified himself in a singularly unique way. He sits at God's right hand and rules with God's own authority.

And so Jesus of Nazareth, whom the God of Israel exalted by raising him from the dead, has been given "the name that is above every name," the supername that can be nothing less than the majestic name of God. We get to trinitarian faith at its highest development by following the trajectory from the God of Israel to the history of Jesus through the *kērygma* of the apostles to the dogmas of the ecumenical councils of the ancient undivided church. Any deviation from this path forward has always led to heresies of one kind or another.

Christianity and Culture

The Christian belief that God's act of salvation is uniquely mediated through Christ and that there is salvation in "no other name" does not mean that there is no knowledge of God apart from biblical revelation. In the book of Acts Paul and Barnabas tell the temple worshipers: "Friends, . . . we bring you good news, that you should turn from these worthless things to the living God, who made the heaven and the earth and the sea and all that is in them. In past generations he allowed all the nations to follow their own ways; yet he has not left himself without a witness in doing good" (Acts 14:15-17). Paul does concede something about morality, that these pagans knew something about doing good. In front of the Areopagus Paul acknowledged to the Athenians that apart from God's revelation in Christ people do "search for God and perhaps grope for him and find him—though indeed he is not far from each one of us. For 'In him we live and move and have our being'; as even some of your own poets have said" (Acts 17:27-28).

There have been debates in the Christian tradition on how to speak of the knowledge of God and his activity in general apart from the Bible and the church. In Romans 1 Paul writes, "For what can be known about God is plain to them, because God has shown it to them. Ever since the creation of the world his eternal power and divine nature, invisible though they are, have been understood and seen through the things he has made" (vv. 19-20). This passage, together with the one in Genesis 1:27 that affirms that God created man and woman in his own image, place the great weight of the Christian tradition on the side of teaching a general revelation in the religions and a universal natural law in culture and morality.

A number of the papers at the conference rang the apocalyptic bell in the midst of the contemporary cultural crisis. With such a strong emphasis on the particularity of christocentric trinitarian faith, have we neglected the bridge to the wider culture? Robert Fastiggi notes that Bishop Ware speaks of the God of Christian faith in the concrete language of the Bible and then asks, "Does this mean that what has traditionally been called 'natural theology' is held in suspicion?" Peter Kreeft depicts the cultural crisis in what he calls the "age of the antichrist," piling up statistics on crime, violence, illegitimacy, divorce, adultery and homosexual acts, and then points to the recovery of natural law as an essential part of the solution. He laments, "Not one nonreligious law school in America teaches or even tolerates the theory of a real, moral natural law. . . . But objective morality, or the natural law, is not one among many moral options; it is the very definition of morality."

The problem is that morality as the foundation of social order is not self-generating but is founded on religion. But we live in a pluralistic society in which all religions are granted equality before the law, and the state is prohibited from establishing a particular one. Kreeft identifies the trilemma for the state: "Either it must support a specific religion, which is not going to happen in a religiously plural society, and is probably unjust as well; or it supports generic religion, which is weak; or it supports no religion, which is fatal."

Kreeft opts for the least of the three evils, the support of generic religion. The response to this by the Orthodox theologian Theodore Pulcini was not favorable. He sees Kreeft's solution as part of the problem, "the bland mixture of mainstream culture and religion that has so effectively blunted the effectiveness of the latter." The opposite strategy is to be preferred. Rather than calling for a "generic mainstream form of religion," Father Pulcini proposes that "our energies be devoted to building up a religious subculture, or a whole set of religious subcultures, in our society." On this point he would seem to be agreeing more with Stanley Hauerwas's concept of Christians as "resident aliens."

The fact that the two theologians respond to the current moral crisis in such opposite ways reflects the diversity of ways of relating Christianity and culture in the Christian tradition. By going more deeply into the sources of the Christian faith we do not find a unifying common ground on how to relate Christ and culture; rather we find a multiplicity of models that H. Richard Niebuhr typologized in *Christ and Culture*. Tertullian is not like Clement, Aquinas is not like Francis, Luther not like Calvin or Müntzer in answering the question, What does Jerusalem have to do with Athens? Similarly we could expect that this gathering of traditional Christians would reflect major differences of outlook on the issue of Christ and culture, not only among the major confessional bodies, evangelicals, Catholics and Orthodox, but also within each of the major blocs. The Christian tradition does not provide a single answer to the question of how the church is to live simultaneously within the City of God and the City of the World.

Christians within the same church notoriously disagree on matters of social ethics. Bishop Ware quotes Fyodorov: "Our social programme is the dogma of the Trinity," and then goes on to comment, "Every form of community has as its vocation to become a living icon of the Trinity." These statements are similar to Stanley Hauerwas's bon mot: "The church does not have a social ethic; the church is a social ethic."

But when it comes to translating these faith statements into concrete positions, the churches are internally divided on all the hot ethical issues—human rights, world peace, economic justice, ecological survival, equality for women. The churches have been dealt no trump cards in these areas of common human concern; they have been given no special divine wisdom on how to deal with the global crisis. Some ecumenical leaders, Konrad Raiser included,[4] are attempting to put new life into the ecumenical movement by moving away from the traditional agenda of faith and order, centered in Christ, to a social secular agenda dealing with the struggles going on in the world for liberty, solidarity, justice and peace. This is a move fatal to ecumenism. To reconstruct the agenda around such highly divisive social ethical issues will threaten to tear the delicate fabric of the ecumenical movement so carefully woven in the past.

The ecumenical movement at its best has not ignored social, economic and political dimensions of human existence and global life, but these have always been taken up within a frame of reference clearly committed to the priority of Christ, the authority of Scripture and the faith of the church. The only path to unity is by way of Christ and his gospel, not by letting the world set the agenda.

Notes

Introduction/Cutsinger
[1]C. S. Lewis, *Mere Christianity* (New York: Macmillan, 1943), p. viii.
[2]"Today's Ecumenism and the 'Still, Small Voice,' " *Orthodox America,* May-June 1994, p. 12.

Reasserting Boundaries: Response to Kreeft/Pulcini
[1]James Davison Hunter, *Culture Wars: The Struggle to Define America* (New York: BasicBooks, 1991), pp. 96-106.
[2]R. Robertson and J. Chirico, "Humanity, Globalization and Worldwide Religious Resurgence: A Theoretical Exploration," *Sociological Analysis* 46 (1995): 234.
[3]W. Garrett, "Thinking Religion in the Global Circumstance: A Critique of Roland Robertson's Globalization Theory," *Journal for the Scientific Study of Religion* 31 (1992): 302.
[4]Robertson and Chirico, "Humanity, Globalization, and Worldwide Religious Resurgence," p. 238.

2: A New Thing/Neuhaus
[1]For something on the background and significance of these developments, see *Baptism and Eucharist: Ecumenical Convergence in Celebration,* ed. Max Thurian and Geoffrey Wainwright (Geneva: World Council of Churches; Grand Rapids, Mich.: Eerdmans, 1984).
[2]*Evangelicals and Catholics Together: Toward a Common Mission,* ed. Charles W. Colson and Richard John Neuhaus (Dallas: Word, 1995).
[3]George Lindbeck, *The Nature of Doctrine: Religion and Theology in a Postliberal Age* (Philadelphia: Westminster Press, 1984), p. 15.
[4]Joseph Cardinal Ratzinger, *Church, Ecumenism and Politics: New Essays in Ecclesiology*

(New York: Crossroad, 1988), p. 138.

[5]Ibid., p. 98.

[6]See "Justification by Faith," in *Origins,* October 6, 1983, p. 300, n. 51.

3: Proclamation and Preservation/Brown

[1]Properly speaking the term *liberal* applies only to an older type of Protestantism represented by people such as Harry Emerson Fosdick and Adolf von Harnack, for contemporary nonevangelical Protestants prefer to be called by other names; here we are using it, as evangelicals generally do, as a convenient term to cover all those trends that deprecate biblical authority and reliability.

[2]Should anyone object that the church came into existence with Jesus, not with Adam, let it be noted that Adam and Eve were called to faith in the promise of eventual restoration in what is called the *protoevangelium* of Genesis 3:15.

[3]Despite a certain number of disputed texts—none of them of significance for doctrinal differences between the great Christian confessions—the sixty-six books of the Bible, excluding the Apocrypha of the Old Testament, are universally acknowledged and readily available to the whole church as well as to peripheral groups and cults and the secular world.

[4]Although Roman Catholics and Eastern Orthodox place far more emphasis on the role of the church in authenticating the Scripture that it hands over to us, they too rely on the work of the Holy Spirit in the life of the believer to give full persuasion of the authority of the Book as well as of the reliability of the body, the church, that preserved it and gave it to us. The question that this insight leaves unresolved is whether the Holy Spirit also guides the church in the development of traditions to flesh out the life of faith and worship, and if so, to what extent.

[5]The conduct of services in "a language not understanded [sic] of the people" is repudiated by the Thirty-nine Articles of the Church of England as "repugnant to the Word of God." Yet it was done for centuries by people thinking themselves faithful to the Bible. Eastern Orthodox services by contrast have been in the vernacular, but often in a vernacular that is so archaic that it does qualify as a "language not understood of the people." In the English-speaking Protestant world, the Authorized or King James Version of the Bible, published in 1611, dominated the field until the Revised Standard Version came out in the 1950s . The language of the Authorized Version is now archaic and difficult to understand, although not necessarily more difficult than that of Shakespeare, who wrote just a bit earlier. The Revised Standard Version itself has supposedly become outdated, and we now have a New Revised Standard Version. Thirty-odd years between versions: hardly a human generation. The suggestion is that one generation cannot understand the language of its fathers and mothers, and this in turn suggests that there will be great difficulties in handing down "the faith which was once delivered unto the saints" (Jude 3).

[6]See Pitirim A. Sorokin, *The Crisis of Our Age,* 3d ed. (Oxford: Oneworld, 1992),

and *The Reconstruction of Humanity* (Boston: Beacon, 1948), p. 157. According to his son, Professor Sergei P. Sorokin, Sorokin did not join an Orthodox congregation because he did not want to get involved in the conflict between those loyal to the Moscow patriarchate, which was regarded as subservient to the communists, and the American-based Russian Orthodox congregations.

Response to Brown/Fr. Andrew

[1]What impressed me most about the article, since that is what I remember, was his observation that much modern ecumenism represents not so much a desire for truth as not caring about Christian doctrine. I agreed with him then and still do. Given the ecumenical track record in the intervening years, little seems to have changed. What has changed, however, or at least has become obvious to many of us, including, I suspect, Dr. Brown, is that these same men and women are in fact radically concerned about doctrine; to be more precise, they are extremely concerned about dogma. But the dogmas they passionately care about are not those of the fathers but rather those of what is often identified as political correctness. Pope Pius X in his encyclical *Pascendi* (1907) called that mindset "Modernism." Many of us refer to it as secular humanism. Call it what you will, this politically correct worldview is the most fundamentalist of fundamentalisms, the hard-shell religion of some very religious people who stridently decry the intrusion of religion into national affairs.

[2]The scriptural use of the term *tradition* has nothing to do with oldness or with a practice or belief's being time-honored. A tradition, in the strict sense of the word, becomes tradition the instant it is handed over. For instance, both the parable of the good Samaritan and the Eucharist became established parts of the Christian Tradition nearly two thousand years ago at the very moment they were delivered to us by Christ. The Tradition is timeless and ever timely.

[3]Orthodox Christians find it rather discomfiting to be pigeonholed with their "separated brethren" of the Roman obedience. Orthodoxy is not, as is often thought, "Roman Catholicism independent from the pope" but a quite different faith. We pray for reunion, and there are many warm friendships between members of the two confessions. We share many similarities in faith and practice, and of course common origins, but there also exist a number of fundamental, dynamic and often subtle yet radical differences in approach, attitudes and ethos, as well as in some important teachings, such as the doctrine of the church.

[4]In a multitude of Christian groups the Scriptures are divorced from their traditional setting. Reinserting into and reinterpreting the Bible in such nontraditional settings gives rise to ideas and practices, as well as interpretations of the Bible, that would baffle the fathers.

[5]The Bible may even be used in ways which contradict the faith, and today we are witnessing the use of the Bible against the faith. (The Jesus Seminar, for example, does precisely that.) One notes, reviewing history, that liturgy also can be used in the same negative ways. But none of this is by design meant to be.

[6]I am reminded of an occasion in my Anglican days when two thuribles were used in a service. Afterward one member of the congregation grumbled, "I don't know why we had to have *two* incense pots." To which an Anglican wit replied with the very Orthodox answer, "Because we didn't have any more!"

[7]In Constantinople we might have found the patriarch serving with a dozen bishops, many concelebrating presbyters, a host of deacons and subdeacons, a huge choir and a congregation of thousands.

[8]The rules of fasting are similarly maximalistic. Those rules, which by modern Western standards are severe in the extreme, are the ideal attainable by the strictest monk or nun in the strictest monastery. Everyone else is expected to keep them as best one can, given one's state in life and spiritual development. But the rules themselves are not to be reduced, for such a lowering of the standards would breed complacency and inspire minimalistic legalism. The Orthodox Church is not given to dumbing down standards for its members but rather maintains the ideal as the goal to strive for.

[9]One motivating factor leading toward such subjectivism is Western scholastic (both Roman Catholic and Calvinist) hyperobjectivism that eschews the subjective and emotional. This continues very strong in certain Bible-belt denominations. Many people raised in this atmosphere are in full rebellion against it. In the Christianity of the fathers there is a place for both objectivism and subjectivism, the latter always being dependent on the former, since that which is objective gives reality to subjective experience.

4: Father, Glorify Thy Name!/Reardon

[1]See P. H. Reardon, "Imaging God," *Touchstone* 3, no. 4 (1990): 13-17.

[2]See P. H. Reardon, "Classroom Chaos," *Touchstone* 8, no. 1 (1995): 12.

[3]See P. H. Reardon, "Christology and the Psalter," *Touchstone* 7, no. 2 (1994): 9-10.

[4]Cf. Vladimir Lossky, *The Mystical Theology of the Eastern Church* (Crestwood, N.Y.: St. Vladimir's Seminary Press), pp. 29-31.

[5]*Maitri* 6.3, 7, in *The Thirteen Principal Upanishads* (London: Oxford University Press, 1934), p. 425. See also *Brihadaranyaka* 3.7.1-23 (pp. 115-17); *Chandogya* 6.8.6 and 12 (pp. 246-47).

[6]When I ventured this mild and nearly self-evident assertion in print a few years ago (see n. 1), Donald G. Bloesch judged it an "astounding statement"; see his "Beyond Patriarchalism and Feminism," *Touchstone* 4, no. 1 (1990): 9. When he went on to claim, however, that to "teach the monarchy of the Father almost invariably ends in subordinationism," I confess to a reaction quite beyond astonishment. Among those who have somehow managed this allegedly improbable task—that is, to teach the monarchy of the Father without ending in subordinationism—mention may be made of Sts. Athanasius (*Contra Arianos* 4.1), Basil (*Homiliae* 24), Gregory Nazianzen (*Orationes theologicae* 20.7; 31.14; 42.15), Maximus the Confessor (*Scholia* 2.3) and John of Damascus (*De fide orthodoxa* 1.8). Identical, nonsubordinationist testimo-

nies in the West include Toledo VI (in Heinrich Denzinger and Adolf Schonmetzer, eds., *Enchiridion Symbolorum* [Freiburg: Herder, 1973], p. 168), Toledo XI (p. 175), Toledo XVI (p. 192) and the 1897 encyclical of Pope Leo XIII, *Spiritus Sanctus* (p. 652). For the position of the Orthodox Catholic Church on this point, one may consult its standard dogmatic textbooks, such as Panagiotos Trempela, Δογματικη της Ορθοδοξου Καθολικης Εκκλησιας (Athens: Brotherhood of Theologians, 1978), 1:272-73.

[7]"But through the prayer which grants us the right to address God as 'Father' we learn of our genuine adoption through the grace of the Holy Spirit" (St. Maximus the Confessor *Mystagogia* 24).

[8]Bloesch, "Beyond Patriarchalism and Feminism."

[9]See, for example, St. Hilary of Poitiers *De synodis* 20; St. Ambrose *De fide* 2.1.18. On the "reality" and necessity of the trinitarian names in the Cappadocian fathers, see the magisterial study of Deborah Belonick, "Revelation in Metaphors," *The Union Theological Seminary Quarterly,* 1984, pp. 31-41.

[10]*Summa theologica* 1.33.2, corp. art., ad 3um and ad 4um. Following the thought of the Cappadocians, Jaroslav Pelikan reasons that "father" is a metaphor when applied to anyone but God; see Pelikan's *Christianity and Classical Culture: The Metamorphosis of Natural Theology in the Christian Encounter with Hellenism* (New Haven, Conn.: Yale University Press, 1993), p. 88.

[11]In Denzinger and Schonmetzer, *Enchiridion Symbolorum,* p. 176.

[12]For example, Janet Martin Soskice, "Can a Feminist Call God 'Father'?" in *Speaking the Christian God: The Holy Trinity and the Challenge of Feminism,* ed. Alvin F. Kimel Jr. (Grand Rapids, Mich.: Eerdmans, 1992), pp. 92-93.

[13]Jürgen Moltmann, "The Motherly Father," *Concilium* 143 (1981): 51-52.

[14]Cf. Belonick, "Revelation in Metaphors."

[15]This juxtaposition is found as early as the Council of Caesarea in 325 (Denzinger and Schonmetzer, *Enchiridion Symbolorum,* p. 30). Other witnesses prior to Toledo XI include St. Epiphanius (*Enchiridion Symbolorum,* p. 31), late fourth-century councils in Armenia (p. 33) and Antioch (p. 35), Theodore of Mopsuestia (p. 35), the ecumenical council of Constantinople in 381 (pp. 66-67), Toledo I in 400 (p. 75) and Pope St. Sixtus III (p. 98).

[16]Josef A. Jungmann, *The Early Liturgy, to the Time of Gregory the Great* (South Bend, Ind.: Notre Dame University Press, 1959), p. 107.

[17]Toledo's appeal to the Latin Bible here was evidently lost even on a historian otherwise so perceptive as Sister Verna Harrison, although she recognizes that same line of the Psalter when she finds it in Greek liturgical texts. This failure causes her to put what I think is an unwarranted spin on Toledo XI. See "The Fatherhood of God in Orthodox Theology," *St. Vladimir's Theological Quarterly* 37, no. 2-3 (1993): 206-7.

[18]For example, Eucher of Lyons: "The womb of the Lord is the secret place whence he brings forth the Son" (*Liber formularum spiritalis intelligentiae* 2; PL 50.737D);

and Rabanus Maurus: "The womb is the Father's substance" (*Allegoriae in sacram scripturam;* PL 112. 1086B).

[19]St. Ignatius of Antioch *Romans* 7.2.

[20]St. Isaac the Syrian *Homiliae* 60.

Trinitarian Theology and the Quest for Ecumenical Orthodoxy: Response to Reardon/Abraham

[1]Janet Martin Soskice, *Metaphor and Religious Language* (Oxford: Clarendon, 1986).

[2]The Confessing Movement, a movement committed to doctrinal renewal and reform within the United Methodist Church, was formed in 1994.

[3]"C. S. Lewis and the Conversion of the West," *Perspectives,* January 1995, pp. 12-17.

[4]Ellen T. Charry, "Literature as Scripture, Privileged Reading in Current Religious Reflection," *Soundings* 74 (1991): 65-99.

5: The Trinity/Ware

[1]St. Gregory of Nazianzus *Oration* 45, 4.

[2]Karl Rahner, *Theological Investigations* (London: Darton, Longman and Todd, 1966), 4:79.

[3]*The Forgotten Trinity: The Report of the British Council of Churches Study Commission on Trinitarian Doctrine Today,* ed. Alistair I. C. Heron (London: British Council of Churches, 1989). To their credit the members of this commission firmly upheld the central significance and the practical implications of faith in the Trinity.

[4]G. L. Prestige, *Fathers and Heretics,* Bampton Lectures for 1940 (London: S.P.C.K., 1968), p. 76.

[5]C. C. Richardson, *The Doctrine of the Trinity* (New York: Abingdon, 1958), pp. 148-49.

[6]St. Basil the Great *On the Holy Spirit* 18 (44).

[7]Vladimir Lossky, *The Mystical Theology of the Eastern Church* (London: James Clarke, 1957), p. 66.

[8]Gregory of Nazianzus *Oration* 23.11-12.

[9]Georges Florovsky, in the periodical *One Church* 13, no. 1-2 (1959): 24.

[10]St. Irenaeus of Lyons *Against Heresies* 4.18.5.

[11]St. Gregory of Nazianzus *Poems* 2.1.11, vv. 1947-49.

[12]Justin Martyr *Dialogue with Trypho* 61.

[13]Tatian *Address to the Greeks* 5. Justin and Tatian speak of only two torches (representing the Father and Son), but obviously the analogy can be extended to include the Holy Spirit.

[14]Justin Martyr *Dialogue with Trypho* 128. The sun-radiance analogy is frequent in later writers: see, for example, Athanasius *Against the Arians* 3.12 and 24; *On the Decrees* 20.

[15]Tertullian *Against Praxeas* 8. Tertullian's other analogies—root, branch, fruit; spring, river, irrigation canal—are less satisfactory, possessing as they do too materialistic and

spatial a character.

[16]St. Gregory of Nyssa *On the Difference Between Essence and Hypostasis* 5 (= Basil *Letter* 38).

[17]In the Western Middle Ages a popular trinitarian analogy from the sense of sight is three concentric or interlocking circles: examples of this can be found in Joachim of Fiore and in Dante (*Paradiso,* canto 33). Are there patristic parallels to this?

[18]Gregory of Nazianzus *Oration* 31.31-33 (*Theological Oration* 5).

[19]St. Ignatius of Antioch *To the Romans* 8.2; *To the Magnesians* 8.2.

[20]See J. N. D. Kelly, *Early Christian Doctrines,* 5th ed. (London: A. and C. Black, 1977), p. 270.

[21]St. Hildegard of Bingen, *Symphonia,* ed. Barbara Newman (Ithaca, N.Y.: Cornell University Press, 1988), pp. 142-43. The Latin says *sonus,* not *musica,* but the context favors a musical interpretation.

[22]St. Augustine *On the Trinity* 9.4 (4); 10.17 (11).

[23]Gregory of Nazianzus *Oration* 23.11. For the *nous-logos* relationship as an analogy for Father and Son, see Irenaeus *Against Heresies* 2.28.5; Clement of Alexandria *Stromateis* 4.25 (320, 18-19); Origen *Commentary on John* 1.38 (49, 5-6).

[24]For instance, in St. Maximus the Confessor (d. 662), Nicetas Stethatos (eleventh century), Theoleptos of Philadelphia (fourteenth century) and St. Gregory of Sinai (d. 1346). How many of these (if any) were influenced by St. Augustine?

[25]*The One Hundred and Fifty Chapters* 35-37, ed. Robert E. Sinkewicz, Studies and Texts 83 (Toronto: Pontifical Institute of Mediaeval Studies, 1988), pp. 118-25.

[26]C. G. Jung, "A Psychological Approach to the Dogma of the Trinity," in *Psychology and Religion: West and East,* vol. 11 of *The Collected Works of C. G. Jung,* 2d ed. (London: Routledge and Kegan Paul, 1981), pp. 156-59, 181-84. Jung goes on to suggest that the Christian Trinity needs to be expanded into a quaternity by including the feminine (the blessed Virgin Mary) and even evil (the devil). While it is possible to appreciate Jung's motives, the connection between this and any traditional understanding of the Trinity becomes exceedingly tenuous. In any case Jung seems to overlook the distinction between the Uncreated (God) and the created (the blessed Virgin). The bodily assumption of the Virgin does not mean that she became a goddess.

[27]Dorothy L. Sayers, *The Zeal of Thy House* (London: Gollancz, 1937), pp. 110-11; taken up and developed in *The Mind of the Maker* (London: Methuen, 1942), pp. 26-34. There is a useful discussion of Sayers in John Thurmer, *A Detection of the Trinity* (Exeter, U.K.: Paternoster, 1984), especially pp. 59-63, 77-79.

[28]Augustine *On the Trinity* 8.14 (10).

[29]Ibid., 15.10 (6); cf. 15.27 (17).

[30]Augustine *On the Trinity* 3.19; 3.15. For further discussion of Richard of St. Victor, see Kallistos (Ware), "The Human Person as an Icon of the Trinity," *Sobornost Incorporating Eastern Churches Review* 8, no. 2 (1986): 9-11.

[31]Basil *On the Holy Spirit* 18 (45).

[32]John Zizioulas, *Being as Communion: Studies in Personhood and the Church* (London: Darton, Longman and Todd, 1985), p. 17.

[33]St. Ignatius of Antioch *To the Magnesians* 7.1.

[34]Augustine *On the Trinity* 8.9 (6) (at the end).

[35]Walter de la Mare, *Collected Poems* (London: Faber & Faber, 1942), p. 57.

[36]St. John of Damascus *Exposition of the Orthodox Faith* 1.8 (ed. B. Kotter, §8, line 25).

[37]Quoted by Anne Ridler in her introduction to Charles Williams, *The Image of the City and Other Essays* (London: Oxford University Press, 1958), p. xlv. Ridler comments, "This aphoristic misquotation from Genesis is one I heard from Williams's own lips: I think he ascribed it to Belloc, but my memory may be at fault."

[38]From a hymn used by the Orthodox Church at vespers on the feast of Pentecost. Compare St. John of Damascus *Exposition of the Orthodox Faith* 1.7 (ed. B. Kotter, §7, lines 19-20).

[39]For further discussion of this see Ware, "The Human Person as an Icon of the Trinity," pp. 12-15, n. 30.

[40]For example, St. Gregory the Theologian more than once compares Father, Son and Spirit to the human triad of Adam, Eve and Seth: *Oration* 31.11 (*Theological Oration* 5); 39.12, etc. The context makes it clear that the comparison is not to be pressed to extremes.

[41]Gregory of Nazianzus *Oration* 42.15.

[42]On Orthodox objections to the *filioque,* see the classic discussion by Vladimir Lossky, "The Procession of the Holy Spirit in Orthodox Trinitarian Doctrine," in *In the Image and Likeness of God,* ed. John H. Erickson and Thomas E. Bird (Crestwood, N.Y.: St. Vladimir's Seminary Press, 1974), pp. 71-96; here Lossky draws attention not only to the question of the Father's monarchy but also to the Sabellianism to be found in some of the Western formulations of the *filioque.* For a more recent discussion see Father Boris Bobrinskoy, *Le mystère de la Trinité* (Paris: Cerf, 1986), pp. 283-305. Compare Timothy (Kallistos) Ware, *The Orthodox Church,* rev. ed. (Harmondsworth, U.K.: Penguin, 1993), pp. 211-18. It should be noted that St. Augustine, while upholding the double procession of the Holy Spirit from both the Father and the Son, is at the same time careful to insist that the Spirit proceeds principally *(principaliter)* from the Father and that he proceeds from the Son only through the Father's gift *(per donum patris);* thus, although using a different manner of expression, Augustine agrees basically with the Cappadocians concerning the Father's monarchy. See *On the Trinity* 15.29 (17); 47 (26); 48 (27); also Gerald Bonner, "St. Augustine's Doctrine of the Holy Spirit," *Sobornost* 4, no. 2 (1960): 51-65.

[43]Gregory of Nyssa *On the Difference Between Essence and Hypostasis* 8 (= Basil *Letter* 38).

[44]St. Maximus the Confessor *Second Century on Theology* 1, in *The Philokalia: The Complete Text,* ed. and trans. G. E. H. Palmer, Philip Sherrard and Kallistos Ware

(London: Faber & Faber, 1981), 2:137-38.

[45]*Perichōrēsis* is derived from *chōra,* meaning "room," "space," "place," and not from choros, meaning "dance." But dubious etymology can sometimes lead us to good theology.

[46]St. Basil the Great *Letter* 189.7.

[47]St. Gregory of Nyssa, *To Ablabius: That There Are Not Three Gods,* ed. W. Jaeger and F. Mueller (Leiden: Brill, 1958), pp. 47-48.

[48]Jung, "A Psychological Approach to the Dogma of the Trinity," p. 161 (quoting Georg Koepgen).

[49]William Blake, *Jerusalem,* §96, line 26, in *Poetry and Prose of William Blake,* ed. Geoffrey Keynes (London: Nonesuch, 1948), p. 564.

[50]Williams, *The Image of the City,* p. xlv.

[51]From *The Region of the Summer Stars,* in *Arthurian Poets: Charles Williams,* ed. David Llewellyn Dodds (Woodbridge, U.K.: Boydell, 1991), pp. 125-26.

[52]Lossky, *Mystical Theology of the Eastern Church,* p. 66.

[53]Nicholas Fyodorov, quoted in Olivier Clément, *L'Eglise orthodoxe* (Paris: Presses Universitaires de France, 1961), p. 63.

[54]In P.-P. Joannou, *Discipline générale antique (IVe-IXes),* vol. 1, 2 (Grottaferrata [Rome]: Tiopografia Italo-Orientale [S. Nilo], 1962), p. 24.

[55]Gregory of Nazianzus *Poems* 2.1.87, v. 19; 2.1.11, v. 1948; 2.1.34, v. 78.

Response to Ware/Fastiggi

[1]Blessed Elizabeth of the Trinity, *Reflections from Her Writings* (Darlington Carmel, n.d.), p. 16. See also Hans Urs von Balthasar, *Elizabeth of Dijon: An Interpretation of Her Spiritual Mission,* trans. A. V. Littledale (New York: Pantheon, 1956), p. 115. More background about Blessed Elizabeth can be found in M. M. Philipon, *La doctrine spirituelle de Soeur Élisabeth de la Trinité* (Montréal: Granger Freres, 1938), and M. M. Philipon, ed., *Sister Elizabeth of the Trinity, Spiritual Writings,* trans. G. Chapman (New York: P. J. Kenedy & Sons, 1962). The translation of her complete writings into English is currently in progress.

[2]Elizabeth of the Trinity, *Reflections,* p. 16. See also von Balthasar, *Elizabeth of Dijon,* pp. 125-26.

[3]See William Thompson, ed., *Bérulle and the French School: Selected Writings* (New York: Paulist, 1989), pp. 109-71.

[4]Elizabeth of the Trinity, *Reflections,* p. 30.

[5]Ibid., p. 35.

[6]"O supreme Light, thou who elevates thyself so much above human thoughts, return to my mind a little of that which thou seemed, and make my tongue so powerful that I may leave to future generations only a spark of thy glory" (my translation).

[7]J. H. Newman, "The Pillar and the Cloud," in *The Essential Newman,* ed. Vincent F. Biehl (New York: New American Library, 1933), p. 42.

[8]See Aidan Nichols, *Rome and the Eastern Churches: A Study in Schism* (Collegeville,

Minn.: Liturgical, 1992), pp. 188-218. More recently this point has been made in a document prepared by the Pontifical Council for Promoting Christian Unity entitled "The Greek and Latin Traditions Regarding the Procession of the Holy Spirit." This document can be found in *L'Osservatore Romano* (English ed.), no. 28 (September 20, 1995).

[9]See Nichols, *Rome and the Eastern Churches,* pp. 205-6.

[10]Maximus the Confessor PG 91, 136 A-B. The translation used is from the text in *L'Osservatore Romano,* cited above.

[11]J. D. Mansi, ed., *Sacrorum Conciliorum Nova et Amplissima Collectio* (Florence, 1759-1827), 12, 1122D.

[12]Ibid., p. 274.

[13]Heinrich Denzinger and Adolf Schonmetzer, eds., *Enchiridion Symbolorum* (Barcelona: Herder, 1962), no. 275-525.

[14]Ibid., no. 460-850.

[15]Ibid., no. 691-1300.

[16]As summarized in Nichols, *Rome and the Eastern Churches,* p. 225. The same point is made in the document prepared by the Pontifical Council for Promoting Christian Unity.

[17]Giuseppe Ferraro, "L'Origine dello Spirito Santo Nella Trinitita Secondo le Tradizioni Greca e Latina," *La Civiltà Cattolica* (Roma), February 3, 1996, pp. 222-31 (my translation).

[18]The full text of *Orientale lumen* can be found in *Origins* 25, no. 1 (May 18, 1995): 1-13.

[19]John Paul II, *Orientale lumen,* 28; *Origins,* p. 13.

6: On from Orr/Packer

[1]From the brochure advertising the conference.

[2]The phrase means a generic Christian who does not see denominational distinctions as a matter of prime importance. Lewis took the phrase from the ecumenically minded Puritan Richard Baxter, who was happy to describe himself as a "meer Catholick."

[3]C. S. Lewis, *Christian Reflections,* ed. Walter Hooper (London: Geoffrey Bles, 1967), p. vii.

[4]I have been helped here by essays in *The Challenge of Postmodernism: An Evangelical Engagement,* ed. David Dockery (Wheaton, Ill.: Victor, 1995), and by Gene E. Veith Jr., *Postmodern Times: A Christian Guide to Contemporary Thought and Culture* (Wheaton, Ill.: Crossway, 1994).

[5]The most significant studies of Orr have been Alan P. F. Sell, *Defending and Declaring the Faith: Some Scottish Examples, 1860-1920* (Colorado Springs, Colo.: Helmers & Howard, 1987), pp. 137-71; and Glen G. Scorgie, *A Call for Continuity: The Theological Contribution of James Orr* (Macon, Ga.: Mercer University Press, 1988). See also Scorgie on Orr in *Handbook of Evangelical Theologians,* ed. Walter A. Elwell (Grand Rapids, Mich.: Baker Book House, 1993), pp. 12-25.

[6]Sell, *Defending and Declaring the Faith*, p. 141.

[7]Ibid., pp. 144-45, citing James Orr, *The Progress of Dogma* (London: James Clarke, 1901), pp. 8-9.

[8]Ibid., p. 9n.

[9]Ibid., pp. 12-13.

[10]Ibid., p. 15.

[11]Ibid, p. 17. The whole extract is from Sell, *Defending and Declaring the Faith*, pp. 144-45. The final sentence from Orr is an adaptation of Schelling's dictum "The history of the world is the judgment of the world."

[12]Orr, *God's Image in Man and Its Defacement in the Light of Modern Denials* (London: Hodder & Stoughton, 1907), pp. 260-61, quoted from Sell, *Defending and Declaring the Faith*, p. 150. This sentiment belonged to Orr's larger vision, in which both the Common Sense and idealist philosophies that nurtured him academically would support him, of the coherence of all knowledge. "The mind for him was just the instrument for the unification of all truth within our reach" (James Denney, "The Late Professor Orr," *British Weekly*, September 11, 1913, p. 567).

[13]Sell, *Defending and Declaring the Faith*, pp. 150-51, quoting Orr, *God's Image in Man*, p. 7.

[14]See Scorgie, *A Call for Continuity*, pp. 39-46.

[15]James Orr, *Revelation and Inspiration* (London: Duckworth, 1910).

[16]James Orr, *God's Image in Man* and *Sin as a Problem of Today* (London: Hodder & Stoughton, 1910).

[17]James Orr, *The Faith of a Modern Christian* (London: Hodder & Stoughton, 1910).

[18]James Orr, *David Hume and His Influence on Philosophy and Theology* (Edinburgh: T & T Clark, 1903); *The Ritschlian Theology and the Evangelical Faith* (London: Hodder & Stoughton, 1897); *Ritschlianism: Expository and Critical Essays* (London: Hodder & Stoughton, 1903); *The Problem of the Old Testament* (London: James Nisbet, 1906).

[19]Scorgie, *Call for Continuity*, pp. 48-49, referring to James Orr, *The Christian View of God and the World As Centring in the Incarnation* (Edinburgh: Andrew Elliot, 1893).

[20]Orr, *Christian View of God*, p. 4.

[21]Ibid., p. 16.

[22]Ibid., p. 4.

[23]See *Reflections on Francis Schaeffer*, ed. Ronald Ruegsegger (Grand Rapids, Mich.: Zondervan, 1986).

[24]Orr had Edwin Hatch and Adolf von Harnack in his mind. We today might add Rudolf Bultmann.

[25]Orr, *Christian View of God*, pp. 263-64.

[26]Ibid., 274.

[27]Leonard Hodgson, *The Doctrine of the Trinity* (Welwyn, U.K.: James Nisbet, 1943).

[28]Robert Jenson, *The Triune Identity: God According to the Gospel* (Philadelphia:

Fortress, 1982).

[29]Thomas F. Torrance, *The Trinitarian Faith: The Evangelical Theology of the Ancient Catholic Church* (Edinburgh: T & T Clark, 1988); *Trinitarian Perspectives: Toward Doctrinal Agreement* (Edinburgh: T & T Clark, 1994). See also James B. Torrance, "Contemplating the Trinitarian Mystery of Christ," in *Alive to God,* ed. J. I. Packer and Loren Wilkinson (Downers Grove, Ill.: InterVarsity Press, 1992), pp. 140-51, and *The Forgotten Trinity,* ed. Alistair I. C. Heron (London: British Council of Churches, 1991).

[30]Colin Gunton, *The Promise of Trinitarian Theology* (Edinburgh: T & T Clark, 1991); *The One, the Three and the Many: God, Creation and the Culture of Modernity* (Cambridge: Cambridge University Press, 1993).

[31]Millard Erickson, *God in Three Persons: A Contemporary Interpretation of the Trinity* (Grand Rapids, Mich.: Baker Book House, 1995).

[32]Jürgen Moltmann, *The Trinity and the Kingdom: The Doctrine of God* (San Francisco: Harper & Row, 1981).

[33]Wolfhart Pannenberg, *Systematic Theology,* trans. Geoffrey W. Bromiley (Grand Rapids, Mich.: Eerdmans, 1991-1994).

[34]Cf. Alister McGrath, *The Renewal of Anglicanism* (Harrisburg, Penn.: Morehouse, 1993), pp. 33-47, 71-75, 95-113, 121-24.

[35]See Royce Gordon Gruenler, *The Inexhaustible God: Biblical Theology and the Challenge of Process Theism* (Grand Rapids, Mich.: Baker Book House, 1987); *Process Theology,* ed. Ronald Nash (Grand Rapids, Mich.: Baker Book House, 1987).

[36]Orr, *Christian View of God,* p. 262.

[37]See Scorgie, *Call for Continuity,* pp. 124-27.

[38]*International Standard Bible Encyclopaedia,* ed. James Orr, 5 vols. (Chicago: Howard-Severance, 1915).

[39]Orr, *Christian View of God,* p. 176.

[40]Ibid., pp. 279-81.

[41]James Orr, "The Factors in the Expansion of the Christian Church," in *Christ and Civilization,* ed. J. B. Paton et al. (London: National Council of Evangelical Free Churches, 1910), pp. 218-19; quoted in Sell, *Defending and Declaring the Faith,* p. 144.

[42]Scorgie, *Call for Continuity,* p. 166, quoting Orr in *Review and Expositor* 3 (1906): 571.

Response to Packer/Nassif

[1]John Meyendorff, "From Byzantium to the New World," in *The Legacy of St. Vladimir: Byzantium, Russia, America,* ed. J. Breck, J. Meyendorff and E. Silk (Crestwood, N.Y.: St. Vladimir's Press, 1990), p. 15. For a fresh examination of key issues in classical and contemporary theology see Bradley Nassif, ed., *New Perspectives on Historical Theology: Essays in Memory of John Meyendorff,* foreword by Henry Chadwick (Grand Rapids, Mich.: Eerdmans, 1996).

[2]As I have noted elsewhere, the use of the Bible by modern Orthodox theologians has often been shallow and exegetically unpersuasive. More than anything else, what is most urgently needed today is a balanced recovery of Orthodox dogmatic values through a revival in biblical studies. Many working in the fields of dogmatic theology, canon law, patristics and liturgics have tended to define Orthodoxy chiefly in terms of its historical development in Byzantium and Russia more than in terms of its biblical and apostolic foundations. The most valuable dialogue partner for the Orthodox to pursue in coming to terms with modern biblical criticism appears to be the work of evangelical biblical scholars. See Nassif, ed., *New Perspectives on Historical Theology*, p. xiv.

[3]A constructive evaluation of my position and others has been undertaken by an evangelical New Testament scholar. See Grant Osborne, "The Many and the One: The Interface Between Orthodox and Evangelical Protestant Hermeneutics," *St. Vladimir's Seminary Quarterly* 39 (1995): 281-304. The article is an outgrowth of his presentation to the Society for the Study of Eastern Orthodoxy and Evangelicalism at Wheaton College, September 25, 1993.

[4]See George Florovsky's "charismatic" view of church authority in *Bible, Church, Tradition: An Eastern Orthodox View* (Belmont, Mass.: Nordland, 1972), especially chap. 6, "The Authority of the Ancient Councils and the Tradition of the Fathers," pp. 93-104, and chap. 2, "Revelation and Interpretation," pp. 17-36. Also Christoph Kunkel, "The True Church Is Not Yet the Perfect Church," in *Tausend Jahre Christentum in Russland*, ed. K. C. Felmy et al. (Göttingen: Vandenhoeck und Ruprecht, 1988), pp. 583-90. This work dispels ultra-Orthodox caricatures and offers a balanced appraisal of Florovsky's ecumenism in light of his claim that Orthodoxy represents the "one true Church."

[5]Much of modern writing on Orthodox ecclesiology has emphasized the theme that "the Church becomes truly itself, truly the 'locus of communion' of people with each other and with God" when it assembles for the eucharistic assembly. See Alexander Schmemann, *The Eucharist* (New York: St. Vladimir's Seminary Press, 1988), and *For the Life of the World* (New York: St. Vladimir's Seminary Press, 1973). While it is true so far as it goes, this theme is often imbalanced in its presentation. It has tended to create a dangerous kind of liturgical legalism in many Orthodox parishes, reducing church life to taking Communion. Certainly it is not exclusively in assembling together for the Eucharist that the church becomes itself as the locus of communion. As the liturgy itself reminds us, there are other important means of grace by which God effects communion with his people, not the least of which is the preaching of the Word of God.

[6]The conversion of Franky Schaeffer to the Greek Orthodox Church and his subsequent railings against it illustrate the point. For the historical background of recent evangelical conversions to Orthodoxy by an American historian see Timothy Weber, "Looking for Home: Evangelical Orthodoxy and the Search for the Original Church," in *New Perspectives on Historical Theology*, ed. Nassif, pp. 95-121.

[7]For the Orthodox doctrine of the church as communion see John Zizioulos, *Being as Communion: Studies in Personhood and the Church* (Crestwood, N.Y.: St. Vladimir's Seminary Press, 1985). For an evangelical response to some of the key issues raised by Zizioulos, see Miroslav Volf, "The Catholicity of Two or Three: Free Church Reflections on the Catholicity of the Local Church," *The Jurist* 52 (1992): 525-46. For the doctrine of the Trinity as a central issue for contemporary life see Geoffrey Wainwright, "The Doctrine of the Trinity: Where the Church Stands or Falls," *Interpretation* 45 (1991): 117-32.

[8]See Douglas Burton-Christie, *The Word in the Desert: Scripture and the Quest for Holiness in Early Christian Monasticism* (Oxford: Oxford University Press, 1993).

[9]Two notable essays on this subject are by John Zizioulos, "Apostolic Continuity and Succession," in *Being as Communion*, chap. 5; Veselin Kesich, "Unity and Diversity in New Testament Ecclesiology," *St. Vladimir's Seminary Quarterly* 19, no. 2 (1975). Zizioulos is essential reading on these matters. However, neither the New Testament nor Ignatius is probably as developed with regard to the episcopate as Zizioulos suggests. Other Orthodox writers have been less careful to distinguish their own personal views *(theologoumenon)* from official church dogma. See, for example, the popular but often critically uninformed works of Thomas Hopko.

[10]Bradley Nassif, "The Semantics of 'Image' and 'Idolatry' in the Byzantine Iconoclastic Controversy," *Phronema* 6 (1991): 21-26.

[11]Alexander Schmemann, "Toward a Theology of Councils," in *Church, World, Mission: Reflections on Orthodoxy in the West* (Crestwood, N.Y.: St. Vladimir's Seminary Press, 1979), pp. 159-78; John Meyendorff, "Light from the East? 'Doing Theology' in an Eastern Orthodox Perspective," in *Doing Theology in Today's World: Essays in Honor of Kenneth S. Kantzer,* ed. John Woodbridge and Thomas McComiskey (Grand Rapids, Mich.: Zondervan, 1991).

Epilogue/Braaten
[1]From the brochure announcing the conference.

[2]Elisabeth Schüssler Fiorenza, *In Memory of Her: A Feminist Theological Reconstruction of Christian Origins* (New York: Crossroad, 1985), p. 32.

[3]Karl Rahner, *Theological Investigations* (London: Darton, Longman and Todd, 1966), 4:79.

[4]Konrad Raiser, *Ecumenism in Transition: A Paradigm Shift in the Ecumenical Movement?* trans. Tony Coates (Geneva: World Council of Churches, 1991).

Contributors

William J. Abraham is professor of theology at Perkins School of Theology, Southern Methodist University. His books include *The Divine Inspiration of Holy Scripture, The Logic of Evangelism* and *Waking from Doctrinal Amnesia: The Healing of Doctrine in the United Methodist Church.*

Carl E. Braaten is professor of systematic theology at the Lutheran School of Theology at Chicago, executive director of the Center for Catholic and Evangelical Theology, and coeditor of *Pro Ecclesia.* His edited volumes include *Our Naming of God: Problems and Prospects of God-Talk Today,* and he is the author of numerous works, including *No Other Gospel* and *Justification: The Article by Which the Church Stands or Falls.*

Harold O. J. Brown is professor of theology at Trinity Evangelical Divinity School, cofounder of the Christian Action Council and director of the Rockford Institute Center on Religion and Society. His works include *The Protest of a Troubled Protestant, Evangelium und Gewalt* and *Heresies: The Image of Christ in the Mirror of Heresy and Orthodoxy.*

James S. Cutsinger is associate professor of theology and religious thought at the University of South Carolina. He is the author of *The Form of Transformed Vision: Coleridge and the Knowledge of God* and a volume of meditations on the spiritual life, *Advice to the Serious Seeker.*

Robert L. Fastiggi is associate professor of theology at St. Edward's University in Austin, Texas. He is the author of *The Natural Theology of Yves de Paris* and has contributed articles to such volumes as *Modern Christian Spirituality, Faith Seeking Understanding: Learning and the Catholic Tradition* and *Modernism as a Social Construct.*

S. M. Hutchens is chairman of the Fellowship of St. James and an associate editor of *Touchstone: A Journal of Ecumenical Orthodoxy.* He lives with his wife and two daughters in Racine, Wisconsin, works as a librarian in nearby Kenosha and is a serious amateur French hornist.

Peter Kreeft is professor of philosophy at Boston College. His many books include *Socrates Meets Jesus, Between Heaven and Hell, The Best Things in Life, The Journey: A Spiritual Roadmap for Modern Pilgrims* (all IVP) and *Fundamentals of the Faith.*

Father Andrew (Isaac Melton) is an Orthodox monk of St. Michael's Skete of the Monastery of the Glorious Ascension in Canones, New Mexico, and the editor of the magazine *DOXA.*

Bradley Nassif is visiting instructor of Eastern Orthodoxy at Trinity Evangelical Divinity School. The founder and president of the Society for the Study of Eastern Orthodoxy and Evangelicalism and a representative to the National Council of Churches, he is the editor of *New Perspectives on Historical Theology: Essays in Memory of John Meyendorff.*

Richard John Neuhaus is president of the Institute on Religion and Public Life and editor-in-chief of *First Things: A Monthly Journal of Religion and Public Life.* Among his best-known books are *Freedom for Ministry, The Naked Public Square: Religion and Democracy in America* and *The Catholic Moment: The Paradox of the Church in the Postmodern World.*

J. I. Packer is Sangwoo Youtong Chee Professor of Theology at Regent College, Vancouver, Canada. Widely published, he is the author of such titles as *Knowing God* (IVP), *A Quest for Godliness, A Passion for Faithfulness* and *Knowing God's Will.*

Theodore Pulcini is professor of religion at Dickinson College. An Orthodox priest, he holds degrees from Harvard College, University of Notre Dame, Catholic University of America and the University of Pittsburgh, and has contributed articles to such periodicals as *St. Vladimir's Theological Quarterly* and *Commonweal.*

Patrick Henry Reardon is pastor of Saint Anthony Orthodox Church in Butler, Pennsylvania, and an associate editor of *Touchstone: A Journal of Ecumenical Orthodoxy.* His articles have appeared in several periodicals, including *The Scottish Journal of Theology, The Catholic Biblical Quarterly, The Anglican Theological Review, Church History* and *Monastic Studies.*

Kallistos Ware is bishop of Diokleia and assistant bishop in the Orthodox Archdiocese of Thyateira and Great Britain. A lecturer in Eastern Orthodox studies at the University of Oxford and a Fellow of Pembroke College, Oxford, he is the author of *The Orthodox Church* and *The Orthodox Way,* cotranslator of *The Philokalia* and coeditor of *Sobornost,* the journal of the Fellowship of St. Alban and St. Sergius.

The Fellowship of St. James

PUBLISHER OF
TOUCHSTONE
A JOURNAL OF
MERE CHRISTIANITY

P. O. BOX 18237
CHICAGO, ILLINOIS
60618

(773) 267-1440
FAX (773) 267-6754
E-MAIL: FSTJAMES@AOL.COM

January 3, 1998

Dear Member or Friend of the Association for Church Renewal:

Greetings to you, with my prayers for blessings on you in this new year of Our Lord!

Enclosed you will find a complimentary copy of *Reclaiming the Great Tradition*. You might be interested in reviewing it for your constituency, but certainly I hope you at least will have the time to read it yourself.

As an alternative to the usual kind of ecumenism we see today, this book grew out of an ecumenical gathering of traditional Christians in 1995, sponsored in part by *Touchstone* magazine, the journal of which I am editor. One participant described this conference as "an ecumenical meeting for those who hate ecumenism." Overstated, of course, but it gets at the central idea that we who are committed to upholding the *whole* faith as it was delivered to us by our Lord and his apostles have much more in common with one another than we do with the liberal members and leadership of our

That is part of what *Touchstone* is all about and I thought the book a good expression of this, as well as an expression of my personal appreciation and gratitude to those involved in the meetings of renewal executives over the years and the new Association for Church Renewal—for your faithfulness and example.

Church renewal, I believe, can only come by returning the very things that formed the Church in the first place, and that is why I am eager to share with you *Reclaiming the Great Tradition*, which I hope will help to inspire such a return in our day. I hope you enjoy it.

Yours in Christ,

James M. Kushiner
Editor, *Touchstone*